D0259802

The **Austin Healey** Story

First published in Great Britain in 2001
by Greenwater Publishing
A division of Crystalsight Limited

A CIP catalogue record for this book is available
from the British Library

ISBN 1 903267 02 1

Printed and bound in Great Britain by Mackays of Chatham PLC

Covers by: Graham Flack

To Mum, Dad, Ashley and Louise -
a family of which I am very proud.

Contents

Acknowledgements

I would like to thank my family and friends, whose support has carried me through bad times and made the good times all the more enjoyable. Likewise to anyone who has given me well intended advice throughout my career. From Joe Green to Mum and Dad, the list is endless. You may think I was not listening but in fact I was, and I thank you for your patience and your time with me.

To my wife Louise, for letting me be part of her life and for making me smile whenever I think about her, thanks Lou. My gratitude also goes to Alex Spink. He is a rare breed, a member of the rugby press who is respected and trusted by the players. That reputation can only have been enhanced through his ability to remain sane after spending countless hours talking to me.

Finally, my thanks to the game of rugby, from which I have borrowed so much that I cannot possibly repay.

Austin Healey
Leicester
September 2001

introduction

The Man Behind The Myth

It's not easy for me to admit this but when I was a kid I was known as Melon Head. It was a childish reference to the fact that I appeared to have a big forehead. Ironically, it had nothing to do with the fact I thought I was God's gift to the world.

When you fancy yourself as much as I fancied myself, nobody pays you any compliments. So I paid them to myself. I was good at sport and quite clever. I was also, as I think my under-nine's rugby coach first pointed out, a big head. Humility was a far off land many miles from Merseyside.

To this day I haven't quite located it but certain traumas in my life have brought me closer to the region. Almost going to prison for assault and being twice banned for foul play on the rugby field have made me a slightly more humble person. But at heart I am still the smart arse kid they called Melon Head. I have never lost that arrogance that if something goes wrong, I can put it right.

When Leicester were staring at defeat against Stade Francais in the final minute of the Heineken Cup final last season I knew I could win it for us. Likewise when the Lions trailed ACT after the hooter in Canberra last summer. As I see it, if you doubt yourself off the pitch, you're going to doubt yourself all the more when you're on it. So I put up this curtain of invincibility by way of non-stop banter.

If you want the truth, there lurks a vulnerable streak inside me; a legacy, I suspect, of my childhood days. When I was small, I was bullied and I was never paid any compliments to my face. Behind the bravado I doubted myself.

But in professional sport there is no place for self doubt. You can't afford to let it surface. You end up getting hurt. So I go out of my way to talk myself up, to bury any feelings of vulnerability. I put pressure on myself to perform by denying myself any get-out. I'm at my best when it's make or break. Win or bust.

The 1999 World Cup illustrates my point. I had just come back from a lengthy ban for stamping on Kevin Putt. I'd had abuse heaped on me and my self-esteem was low. I thought to myself 'this won't do. I've got to tell people how good I am but more importantly I've got to show them'.

The result was that I played some of my best ever rugby during the tournament and sustained it through until the start of last season, when I felt the doubts resurface after Leicester moved me back from fly-half to scrum-half and I lost my England shirt.

It's when I don't have the answers that I start to question myself. Leicester weren't picking me in the position I wanted to play and I couldn't fathom why. I couldn't find a rational explanation. So I turned up the heat on myself. I courted publicity and used it to pile the pressure onto my own shoulders.

All of a sudden I was back to being the Austin Healey that everyone knew. The gobby little so and so. And it suited me and my rugby. It's a high-risk strategy. Sometimes my mouth runs away with me. I come out with comments I later regret or I say things I don't even believe.

But it's all an act, a way of psyching myself up. And as I go further up the rugby ladder and the expectation on me to perform grows, so I have a tendency to become more outrageous. But see me away from the game, at home with my family, and that's not me at all. I'm a normal lad.

Just as well, mind, because my wife Louise is my biggest critic and she would change the locks if I started playing up. She tells me if I've had a bad game and she tells me if I've let myself down.

I remember immediately after the Kevin Putt episode, when I was cited by London Irish and eventually banned for eight weeks, I turned to her for comfort. What did I get? 'Why did you kick him in the face you idiot?'

Normally it is more constructive than that. When I didn't get picked by England against Australia in the summer of 1999 I went on holiday with Lou, Martin 'Cozza' Corry, Craig Joiner and their partners and for the first week I was unplayable. Snappy, irritable, the works.

She took me to one side and said "Look at yourself, look at the way you're going on. Now look at Cozza. He's had another awesome season yet he never gets picked. And do you ever hear him whinge like this?" That brought it home to me that I'd been a complete embarrassment. We all went out to dinner that night and I apologised for my bad attitude.

My biggest problem when I was younger was my reluctance to listen to people. Unless someone had achieved certain things in rugby I tended to dismiss their opinions. 'They've never played, they've never done this, they don't know what they're going on about'.

At school if I respected a teacher I would listen to him or her, but if I didn't I would switch off. I would go out of my way to piss them off. I thought I knew better. It stemmed from sport. As a six-year-old I started playing rugby - for the under-nines. I then moved onto football and I was captain of Wirral District by the time I was eleven.

It was only later that I started listening to others; to my schoolteachers Joe Green and Mike Briers, to Clive Woodward, Brian Ashton, Dean Richards, John Wells and Joel Stransky. Joel and I didn't always see eye to eye when we were playing together at Leicester, another case of me wanting the limelight that he was hogging. Yet when I moved to fly-half in 1999 I learned more from

Joel in three conversations than other coaches have taught me in my whole career.

Such experience has taught me that you are never too smart to learn. That's why I think I so resented Bob Dwyer, during his time at Leicester, and Graham Henry, on the Lions tour, for always thinking they knew best, for closing their ears to my, or anyone else's ideas.

I pretend to have all the answers but of course I do not. None of us do. Inside me there is a normal person, prone to the same failings as everyone else. It's just that I don't want to be normal. So I don't let him out.

Part one:

Life Before the Lions

chapter one

From a Scally to a Tiger

I blame Mark and Paul Stewart. There was I happily playing football for as many teams as I could fit into a weekend and those two went and switched sports. I can still recall the bombshell dropped on me by Mrs Stewart: 'Sorry Austin, they've gone to play rugby'.

I could have been a soccer legend, following in the footsteps of my Everton icons onto the hallowed turf at Goodison Park. I know I was good enough. Trevor Steven, Kevin Radcliffe and Neville Southall were my sporting heroes. I had never heard of Bill Beaumont, Fran Cotton, even Clive Woodward.

Where I was born, Wallasey on Merseyside, the sporting choice is a straight one. It is not soccer or rugby it is blue or red. Everton or Liverpool. For everyone in my family except my sister Ashley, who supported Liverpool just to annoy us, it was Everton. The last thing I would see before I turned my light off at night would be the faces of Trev, Kev and Nev on my bedroom wall.

Liverpool were league champions when I was born in October 1973 which was unfortunate, but Everton's time would come. Named Austin Healey, most people wrongly assume that my Mum and Dad, Denise and Allan, were car lovers - and some more literally than others. To this day Martin Johnson thinks I was given the name after the vehicle in which I was conceived. My parents don't take too kindly to that, Johnno, you sad individual.

Because of my name everyone thought I had an interest in cars and I was forever being given car annuals and posters of various vehicles on birthdays. Consequently, I knew everything about cars from an early age, though even now I'm not as much of a car nause as Neil Back. Backy has memorised the 0-60 times of every single car in the back of car mags.

The truth is that neither Mum nor Dad cared two hoots about cars, just so long as our motor got us from A to B in one piece. The love of a good chassis belonged to my Grandad, Sidney, an offshore powerboat racer who competed all over the world. It was he who put forward the name Austin. It was he, too, who fuelled my love of soccer in general and Everton Football Club in particular.

I used to go to all the home games with him, sitting in the Bullens Road stand. He was actually a nightmare to be with at football matches as he would shout at everyone and start fights. Not bad for an OAP. Even more frightening was the journey to Goodison in his tiny Fiat 126. He would point out where all the bombs had been dropped during the war and completely ignore the traffic lights. More than once I thought my number was up.

Anyway, I had these two friends, Mark and Paul, who lived at the top of Shamrock Road in Claughton Village. We spent all the time in the back alley kicking a football around. Soccer meant everything. It was a way of life...until one Sunday morning when I went to call for them and they weren't in. I asked their mum where they were and she said they had gone down to Birkenhead Park.

Now Wallasey was not exactly a hotbed for rugby union but Birkenhead Park were a pretty decent side at the time. So I was curious to learn how the two of them had got on. At school on the Monday I asked them and ended up following them down there the next weekend. I took to it straight away and have never really looked back.

Paul and Mark were big lads. By the age of six they must have been five feet tall. I was probably two foot two and so was immediately pigeon-holed as a scrum-half. I hate the way that happens. If you are tall you are put in the forwards, if you are small you must be a half-back. To my mind that is why we have seen so many forwards in England down the years with less than brilliant handling skills.

Rugby didn't really start seriously for me until I got to secondary school at St Anselm's College. Up until then I continued to play football, which was my passion, and to follow Everton who, at the time, were probably the best team in the world. My proudest moment had been appearing as a ballboy at Goodison. My proudest possession, a piece of the pitch I had nicked that day.

Mum and Dad thought I would become a footballer because I captained the district team and averaged a goal a game from defence. I was a sweeper for the county side and played right wing for Ashville. You know, versatile. But between the ages of eight and eleven rugby started competing for my time. I would play football on Saturday morning for Wirral District, then go to Birkenhead Park and operate the scoreboard in the afternoon. I'd then play for Birkenhead Park minis on Sunday morning before completing the weekend with an afternoon football match for Ashville.

My parents ferried me about to all these places and supported me in everything I did. Once a little bit too literally. While Dad was always quiet on the touchline Mum would shout to an embarrassing extent. She is from Zambia and has a fiery Zambian temperament. The first phrase she taught me was 'amunji munji capalla achiawanna' which she told me meant 'eat your food or I'm going to give you a slap'.

So there I was playing for Birkenhead Park Under-12s. I was only nine and we were up against this Rhyl team that were not only older but massively bigger. Still, I had scored a couple of tries and was going for my hat-trick when one of their monsters caught me and hammered me into touch. What followed next ranks as possibly the most embarrassing moment of my life. Mum and Dad say they are proud to have me as their son. And I'm even prouder to call them my parents...except when Mum came onto the pitch to see if I was alright. The last thing I remember was her swinging a handbag at the lad who floored me.

Mum ran our home and Dad was a self-employed tiler, who had good times and bad. I could tell the difference between the two because it was either a snooker table, a video game and water skis for Christmas, or an orange. They were easy-going parents and I owe them a huge amount for spending so much time driving me about. Only once did they fail me, and then it was the car rather than them. It refused to start one freezing morning and I had to run two miles to the pick-up, arriving just as the last car was leaving.

Luckily I was fast even in those days. I broke 11 seconds for the 100 metres whilst I was at secondary school, clocking 10.9sec at The Oval, where *Chariots of Fire* was filmed. Speed had other benefits too as I was small and gobby and so an obvious target for the bullies. Had I been bigger they might have left me alone. But I wasn't. In fact, I was on the front row of the school photo in my final year at primary middle school, at the age of 11. That's how small I was.

Rather than face confrontation my natural instinct was to run away (unless I was sticking up for my little sister). This continued until my very last day at primary when a lad called Marvin had a go at me. Normally I would have legged it but I finally snapped, thought 'sod it' and whacked him hard in the face. It felt surprisingly good.

It was a defining moment for me and from that point on I probably had a fight every day in school. If anyone said anything to me or about me it usually ended in violence of some sort. I would stand up and wait for them to swing and then nail them. The teachers told my parents but I think Dad was quite happy that I was starting to stick up for myself. He would say, "If they hit you first, whack them."

By the time I turned 16 I could look after myself and had

become something of a rugby mercenary. I would play for whoever asked me, as long as they sorted out the travel. I played for Hoylake before moving onto Birkenhead Park but I always returned to Hoylake on Friday nights as that was the venue for the weekly disco. My list of conquests is too long to detail, suffice to say that St Anselm's sister school was a convent and what they say about convent girls is completely true. I find it impossible to believe that any of the girls I knew at Upton Convent grew up to be nuns.

I have got a lot to thank religion for but none of it would make the church particularly proud. I went to a catholic school but was not catholic. I did think of switching codes but only because my convent girlfriend at the time had to go to Heswall Church every Sunday. We would stand at the back by the spare hymn books snogging through the service.

I was actually pretty clever as a boy but I didn't try at all. I was always going to be a sportsman. My rule at school was that those teachers I did not respect I annoyed. Maths and geography were the only subjects I didn't loathe. In both Latin and woodwind my teachers would walk into class and before opening their books would say 'Healey out!' My woodwind teacher wouldn't let me into his class for three years, so I had to swap the flute for the trumpet in the brass section next door. But I didn't waste the time I spent outside classroom doors. I met my good friend Simon McKee and we played pitch and toss - for three years. We became pretty useful.

As a rule of thumb if anything happened in primary school, junior school or senior school I got the blame for it. If there were no suspects Healey would do. It was that way with the exploding goldfish. I was only eight for Heaven's sake and it was my pal, not me, who fed them polystyrene. They ate it and 'bang'. That wasn't me but I took the rap. I had to stand outside the headmaster's office for two days and the school wrote a letter to my parents. Luckily my parents believed me because nobody else did.

Six years later I was the final person to get the strap at St

Anselm's before corporate punishment was banned. It was the last day of the summer term and spirits were typically high. But as usual I had to sit in the corner of my form room away from everyone else. The teachers called me a disruptive influence. All my classmates shared double desks except me. There was a six-foot exclusion zone around my place and it remained mine for five years.

On the day in question Mr Johnston, by coincidence the father of Saracens and England centre Ben, with whom I toured to South Africa in 2000, returned to the classroom just as I was in the process of moving my desk back to it's regular position. It was a tricky manoeuvre, sliding it backwards across the wooden floor from the door where I'd driven it. But I was doing pretty well. Anyway, Mr Johnston declined to acknowledge my skill. "What do you think you're doing, Healey?" he bellowed.

"Just testing it's wheels, sir," I replied quick as a flash, accompanied by the usual sniggers from the rest of the form. "Right, outside," he thundered.

"Hold on a sec, sir, I was only making a bit of a gag," I appealed. Did he see the funny side of it? No, he gave me the strap. And believe me that didn't have a funny side to it. It was a leather beast which must have been half an inch thick, two inches wide and eight inches long. When brought down with force across the palm of your hand it hurt like Hell. I got probably three swipes but infuriated Mr Johnston by smiling through the pain. I didn't make any noise until he'd left. Then "aaaaaaaaaagggggghhhhhh!"

Given my attitude I suppose it was something of a miracle that I emerged with 10 GCSEs at C grade or above and three A levels in theology, statistics and general studies. The one A level I failed was economics and my teacher was Tedd Rudd, who had played on the England wing in the mid 1960s. I was particularly immature in his class and shamefully made fun of his stutter. I am not at all proud of myself for that. He used to send me out all the time for finishing his sentences. He didn't have any interest in sport at all. He was pre-occupied with supply and demand.

The two teachers to escape my baiting were Joe Green and Martin Regan. Martin had played for England at fly-half between 1953-56, while Joe was a huge second row forward with a big loping stride. Yet Joe was the person who told me it was not good enough just spin-passing off my right hand. He also taught me to kick off both feet. He was an inspiration to me. I would have been suspended a number of times if it hadn't been for Joe suggesting that the school rugby team might have suffered.

Immaturity and me have always got on well, none more so than when, as a 17-year-old, I drove my mates - Simon McKee, Adrian Shannon and Andrew Murphy - back from my parent's caravan on Anglesea. There was always a huge traffic jam coming home so we stopped off at Conwy, got some fish and chips and a stick of rock each.

We then rejoined the traffic jam. Murph and I had both eaten our rock when Ade decided to open his. There was a car next to us with two rather tasty girls in it. We decided to engage in a bit of banter with them as we crawled along the motorway and they asked Ade if they could have some of his rock? At that moment the traffic moved in their lane and they pulled forward a few yards ahead of us. Ade grabbed the opportunity and proceeded to stick the rock where the sun don't shine before putting it back in the wrapper. We pulled up alongside them again. Ade told the girls he'd had enough and they could have it. One of them took the rock and gave him a grateful smile. She then undid the wrapper and licked the end of the stick before their car moved off. For five minutes our vehicle stood still in the now free-flowing fast lane as we were unable to breathe or speak for laughter.

I joke about being unable to breathe but for me it's really not a joking matter as I suffer badly from asthma and nearly died in Romania when I was eight years old. Don't ask me why we were holidaying in Romania but I had an attack on the very first day.

Normally the Ventolin inhaler I used would get rid of it but for some reason I was taking it and nothing was happening. It became quite a serious problem on that night. For 20 minutes I basically couldn't breathe. Just one breath here, one breath there. We had the doctors out and they gave me an injection of cortisone which saved me. For the remainder of the holiday we had to go a fair way to this clinic twice a day for more of the same. I had 13 jabs in all over there and by the time I got home I had a shadow on my lung. It was a pretty worrying time for my parents, a night they always look back on as the time they nearly lost me.

But it was not the first scare I'd given them with my asthma. Two years earlier I'd had another attack and been rushed to see our GP. He sent me straight to hospital where I was in an oxygen tent for a week. It was there that I developed my pathological fear of needles. Day after day I remember lying there and watching a nurse walk through the ward with a syringe in her hand. Not for me, but for the lad in the next-door bed who needed regular jabs in his leg. Every time she came near him he screamed the place down.

One day I saw her heading our way and assumed that she was coming with another injection for that poor boy. But she walked past his bed and stopped at the end of mine. Talk about terror. I've had a phobia for needles ever since.

In the early days asthma hindered my sport but the fitter I became the more it eased off. Through school I found it quite hard dealing with it but as I grew older and got myself into better shape so it became easier to control. Asthma is your inability to take air in because your bronchials contract so if you've got the ability to work with not much oxygen it helps to handle the condition when you're not playing.

Experience has taught me how to control my asthma better these days through breathing techniques and I also know what sets it off. Cats are particularly murderous for me. I don't mind dogs but I've got a deep hatred of our feline friends, who I believe were put on this earth to curse me. Sorry, cat owners but air is more important to me than your little pussies. A lot of people take it for granted nowadays that a little inhaler here and there can cure people, but you still have to be very careful.

Some forms are more serious than others, mind. I've met a fair few players down the years who have claimed to suffer from asthma, when in fact what they've got is exercise-induced asthma, which is slightly different. It's called being unfit.

chapter two

Living with Leicester

Leicester were the biggest and the best rugby club in the British Isles long before we finally won the Heineken Cup. I know that because Richard Cockerill told me the first time I met him. He also punched me in the face.

It was the summer of 1996 and Cocker, the small and imperfectly formed hooker for Tigers, thought I was a smart arse. I'd just joined the club from Orrell and was taking part in my first training session out of the gym with my new team mates. At least I thought they were team mates. My introduction to the lads was a game of touch rugby. My introduction to Cockerill was a knuckle sandwich. I made a half break and touched him and he swivelled round and caught me on the jaw. After I had stopped laughing I asked him what the hell he was doing? "There are no superstars here," he yelled, in that over-dramatic way of his. He obviously thought he had to show me the Leicester way. I laughed again.

I didn't want to be immersed in Cocker's idea of the Leicester way. I hadn't moved clubs to change the way I do things on the pitch. I had known from the outset that I was a different person to all the forwards - maybe with the exception of Neil Back, who shared my lateral thinking - but at no stage did I want to become a zombie. I wanted to have a spark, be a bit different, even if it meant being obnoxious and big-headed at times. I wanted to play for Leicester but I didn't want to become as insular as some were at that time; where they had become so obsessed with all things

Leicester that they couldn't see the wider picture of what was going on around the country.

That day at Oval Park was a testing ground for me. Cocker wanted to know how I'd react. I think the other lads expected me to bite back and go for him but when I just stood there laughing I had passed the initiation test. I didn't take it to heart because I soon discovered that he has a fight in training every single week, without fail. He's actually got a heart of gold. It's just that he thinks he's harder than he is. He whacked me, but it didn't really register.

He uses as an excuse for his actions the fact that he's doing it for the club (the lads now call him Captain Club Man because he will do anything for Leicester Tigers). In actual fact he's a nice lad, don't get me wrong. He and his wife Serge were the first to welcome me into their home when I joined.

For a long time myself and Will Greenwood, two northern lads who joined Leicester together, were seen as players who were using the club for our own devices, namely to get to play for England. This was a view held by the likes of Cockerill, Graham 'Wig' Rowntree and Darren Garforth, alias the ABC Club. They used to openly tell us. In their eyes we were regarded as parasites, at the club only for what we could get out of it. Because they saw us playing great for England they thought we weren't trying for Leicester. I bitterly resented that.

In fact I still do because the attitude persists in some. I find it so hypocritical. The forwards get injured themselves and they don't train. But if I pick up a knock they abuse me for not training. Yet nobody ever abuses them. The upshot of this is that now, when I'm injured, I feel obliged to train. I can't be arsed to have them have a go at me, to hear them say "Oh are you saving yourself for the Lions tour?" and that kind of crap which I hear all the time. These forwards are constantly abusing the backs and it really fucks me off because they've got no idea what they're talking about. Anyone can bend over and push.

Ironically, the main reason for me choosing Leicester in the first place was the forwards. In 1996 Bath were the better side in terms of running rugby but Leicester had a brilliant pack and as a scrum-half that was more relevant to me. I was first contacted by Darren Grewcock, a scrum-half at the club who is now a leading fitness trainer. I was very flattered, at least until I met Tony Russ, then director of rugby, and heard what Leicester thought I was worth. Russ had made his name at Saracens, who played on a council park pitch, before coming to Welford Road, capacity 16,000. And from afar had seemed a nice enough guy. Yet when I met him in December 1995 he was so condescending towards me that he almost pushed me away from joining.

The initial plan was that Leicester would sign myself, Will and Jim Naylor in a job lot. We played together for the North and we had made a pact to stay together. Russ changed all that. Jim met him and promptly decided he would join Newcastle instead. And when Russ offered me £10,000 to join, as my wage for the entire season, I almost turned on my heels as well.

When I had stopped laughing - bearing in mind I probably earned more than that in the amateur days just on expenses - I spoke to Les Cusworth, a Tigers legend whom I knew from the England set-up, and told him I wasn't getting on with Tony Russ and that I wasn't sure if I was going to go to Leicester. It was a smart move on my part. He put me straight in contact with Peter Wheeler, Tigers' chief executive and a top man, and soon after we met at Leicester Forest East services on the M1 and agreed a £30,000 basic. I signed in March before flying out to the Hong Kong Sevens. When I returned Russ had been sacked. I have not seen him again.

I didn't know anyone at Leicester when I arrived for the first time on 1 June along with fellow new boys Will and Craig Joiner, the Scottish international. I knew that Aadel Kardooni was first-choice scrum-half but nothing more than that. So I went with a completely open mind. The club had impressed me by giving me a car, a Rover 600 turbo, when I had signed in March and I was really up for the challenge. Will, Craig and I were housed in the Holiday Inn hotel and we stayed there for almost three months until we found a place together. It was a surreal experience. The club initially paid for everything, so we were eating carvery every night. We were three young lads basically having a laugh.

My friendship with Will dates back to our time in the North Under-18 side. I think it came from the fact we are both lateral thinkers. At the time we had a different perspective on rugby to most other players. We thought about space whereas a lot of other people were obsessed with contact and tackling. We understood what each other was doing on the pitch. We were, if you like, kindred spirits - and annoying bastards. We enjoyed nothing more than taking the piss out of select Leicester forwards. Guys like Cocker, Rowntree and Garforth couldn't see it half the time which made it all the more fun. But when they twigged it could get quite nasty.

A classic example was in Italy in 1997 when Leicester played Milan in the Heineken Cup. Waisale Serevi, our Fijian star, had been absolutely awesome, scoring a stack of tries in our 37-29 win and famously beating a player four times in one run. Afterwards Bob Dwyer was asked to nominate a man of the match. It was plainly Serevi, everyone could see that. But he gave this huge trophy to Cockerill who had thrown eight line-outs not straight and lost one against the head in the scrum. The rest of the lads knew it was a piss take, but not Cocker. He thought, 'fair play I made that little break, blah, blah, blah'.

After the ceremony we all went out and had a drink in the city and Will got absolutely steaming drunk on wine, port, you name it. He was so out of it that when we went to a nightclub he peed down the opposition flanker's leg. Not surprisingly he was chucked out and so I headed back to the hotel with him for a few more drinks.

It was then Cocker arrived back with his trophy. Somehow Will got his hands on it and started mucking about with it. Basically taking the piss out of Cocker...for a laugh.

Richard didn't see it that way. He got up from his seat and punched Will in the side of the face. I stood up and told him we were all team mates and there was no need for that kind of thing; that he was only having a laugh. But Cocker was having none of it. "You and your northern mate can fuck off back where you came from," he raged. "We don't need you here. You're both shit'.

I congratulated him on his outburst and he turned round and punched me. So I lost it. I started kicking him and throwing punches. Only then did it become comical. He backed off to the marble floor in the hotel foyer, I took a run-up, slipped on the shiny surface throwing a punch, went over his shoulder and landed on my back with my head wedged against a flower pot. Cocker ran off to lick his wounds. I went back to the bar and ordered another beer.

I love Leicester. I love the fact it's so uncompromising. Everybody has the same goal. People talk about prima donnas in sport, and we have some of the biggest names in English rugby at Welford Road, but the club always comes first. Dean Richards insists on that but he doesn't even have to. After an international the England boys are straight back to play for Leicester - last season, for example, Johnno and I turned out against Sale in the driving rain, three days after we'd helped England spank Scotland - not because there's a three-line whip, but because we want to. It's not like that at all other clubs.

Expectation is huge at Leicester. We are now the top club in Europe and we feed off the pressures that brings with it. We like being the team everyone wants to beat as it leaves us no way out. We have to perform. And we have done that. Going into the 2001/02 campaign we hadn't lost a league match at home since December 1997. Our supporters have to take a lot of the credit for that too. If we were playing at one of the smaller grounds every week we probably would have lost one or two of those games. The added buzz you get from up to 16,000 people packed inside Welford Road is fantastic. The secret of our relationship with the supporters is that there are no barriers between us. We have 13 bars at Leicester and more often than not after a game you will find players sharing a beer and a chat with supporters somewhere around the stadium.

Another factor in our success is that we treat every game the same. Whether it be a Heineken Cup final or a routine league match we prepare equally thoroughly, our focus is the same. Peer pressure is so great that the management rarely need to dish out bollockings. The lads will let you know if your standards fall below those expected of you. There is a time for pissing about and a time for training. Once training starts we get down to business. But when we're not training - watch out.

The stag nights at Leicester are legendary. I was warned about them when I arrived but nothing could prepare me for some of the antics we have got up to over the last four years, starting in 1996 when Derek Jelley's do coincided with the club's Christmas outing. It was a fancy dress night and Louise and I turned up as a gorilla and polar bear respectively. All the lads were there but a couple stood out. Johnno came as a rapper, complete with blacked out face, adidas tracksuit and half a ton of gold around his neck. Rob Liley and his wife came as Hitler and Eva Braun. Don't remember looking at Rob, but his missus wore a little bra and leather boots up to her knicker line. We drank for Leicester that night and I ended up getting thrown out of the club we were in after Leon Lloyd got narky when I took a bite out of his burger. As I was deposited onto the pavement this polar bear ran up and punched me in the face. Me, a gorilla. Thanks Louise.

Another belting night was Backy's do. He had booked a barge on a canal out of Leicester and invited thirty of us along. The evening started off quietly enough, but then Wig started running up and down the side of the boat. The driver told him to stop or he'd have to turn around. He then made a phone call and summoned a bouncer. You should have seen the lad's face when he got on the boat and saw the entire Leicester squad, arms crossed, staring at him!

However, the best parts of the evening were still to come. First, Backy was made to snog a pig's head for 30 seconds. Then, after we got off the barge to go to a pub three miles away Darren Grewcock persuaded 20 of the lads to get into a horsebox which he said he'd hitch to the back of his Landrover and tow to the pub. He closed up the horsebox, bolted it and drove off, leaving them there in the height of summer. The boys went absolutely mental, escaping only after kicking a hole in the side.

Johnno's stag do was rather more orderly, as you would expect of the England and Lions captain. He took 40 of us to Benidorm for a mini-break before the England tour to South Africa in 2000 and checked us into a hotel where there was not one person under the age of 60. Everyone was playing dominoes and bridge. After the first night most of the lads wanted to go home. But Dorian, who everyone calls 'rent-a-guest' because he always gets the last call to functions if somebody pulls out at the last minute, saved the trip by getting so drunk on the second day that the police were called. They arrived to find all the lads chilling out and playing frisbee on the beach, assumed they'd been the ones causing trouble and tried to arrest them for being 'peesed up'. Meanwhile Dorian was in the karaoke bar 50 yards away attempting to sing Minnie the Moocher.

I had three stag nights before tying the knot with Louise, one in Cape Town, one in Newcastle and one in Leicester. Each were wild affairs but perhaps the funniest moment came in the North-East where we piled out of a nightclub in such a bad state that we hopped into four taxis, asked for the Copthorne Hotel, then watched as the convoy did a U-turn, came to a stop on the other side of the road and charged us £5 each. How were we to know it was only fifty yards away?!

Wreaking havoc is not restricted to stag nights. On my first New Year in Leicester the squad went out and had a sherbert or two together. I returned home with my friend Ade, who was attempting to woo my sister-in-law Kate. We decided to pop next door and introduce ourselves to the new neighbours who, I was convinced, were swingers. We stripped to our underpants and knocked on Will and Nadine's door. After trying unsuccessfully to yank off Will's chest wig, then spanking Nadine in her full leather cat suit, I went home. They were, I concluded, definitely swingers. Ade had left earlier, saying he was tired. I thought no more of it. I climbed into bed with Louise and was just nodding off when Ade sprang out from under the bed doing his impersonation of Kato, Inspector Clouseau's psychotic man servant in the *Pink Panther* films. He wrapped a phone cord around my neck and shouted "I'm going to kill you." Not knowing what the hell was happening I punched him in the face. Ade left the room bleeding and in tears.

Kato apart, the team spirit at the club is first rate. Yes, Cocker smacked me in the face the first time I met him, and yes the forwards do moan at me half the time, but you learn that that is part of the Leicester way. They do it just to check you don't overreact, that you're not getting precious, that they can still count on you. And all the lads get it. It's not just me.

The real testing ground isn't Welford Road or even the training pitch at Oval Park, however. It's on the team bus. Your initiation when you join Tigers is that you have to try and take the back seat. The seats in the back row are occupied by Cockerill, Garforth, Rowntree and Johnson. The challenge is to dislodge them. More often than not the challenger ends up getting battered, having his clothes ripped off and chucked out of the skylight. Successes are few and far between, but Pat Howard managed it on our pre-season tour to Omagh in 2000.

The new lads had tried and failed so, the heavy brigade, the likes of Paul Gustard and Adam Balding, went back as a group and tried to take it. As the fur flew Pat slid along under all the seats and popped up triumphantly at the back. They were all scrapping and hadn't seen him coming. He had all his clothes shredded just the same. But he had achieved something very few manage. Never mind winning three Premiership titles, a Heineken Cup and never playing on a losing league side at Welford Road, he had taken the back seat. And through brain not brawn - please note, all forwards.

Deano appreciated that achievement as much as anyone because he regularly tries to take the back seat and more often than not fails. In May 1997 he caused a near riot by stubbing his cigar out on Dorian West. We were on the way back from winning the Pilkington Cup final and all hell broke loose. One of the tables got ripped off at the back of the bus, exposing a spike. Someone landed on top of Dorian, the spike pierced his leg and he needed a heap of stitches, both internally and externally. He also got blood poisoning. You still see the scar when he plays. He's got a big red hole in the back of his leg.

The club picked up the bill for that one and there have been a few more besides for damage to Colin's Coaches, but we have a very tolerant, if completely mad, driver by the name of Tone. He's a great fella but he seems to have a problem with braking distances. The most common chant on away trips is "Steady, Tone!!!!!" as he suddenly slams on the brakes.

For all my ambivalence towards forwards as a breed I do admire the loyalty of the lads at Leicester and occasionally get annoyed when I think that loyalty is being taken for granted. I believe you should get paid what you are worth in this game and there are an awful lot of people that get paid more at lesser clubs than some of the boys do at Tigers, despite the fact we are the most successful club of the professional era.

The success Leicester have enjoyed is not purely down to the coaching. A lot of it is down to the players and in ten years time when they are no longer playing I want us all to have more than great medals, great memories and great mates. I don't want any of the lads to be pondering the wisdom of their loyalty.

For the majority of my time at Leicester I've been very happy, which is why I signed a new contract to stay for three more years, on terms which are satisfactory to me. I'm in a great town, we have great support and it's probably my second home in England at the minute behind where I come from. In addition to all that, there are so many fellas I admire at the club, in particular Peter Tom, Peter Wheeler (Wheelbrace), Dangermouse (David Matthews), Tudor Thomas, John Allen and Dosser (Ian Smith). I've never experienced anyone who is as good at motivating players as Dosser. He was awesome when I first arrived at Welford Road.

My regard for Dosser was probably the main reason I joined Leicester. He was coaching England Students at the time and I had always got on with him. All the players respected him. He was like one of the lads yet he still had authority. The way he was treated during the Dwyer years I thought was terrible. He's back now working with the seconds and on the fringe of our team at training, but I don't think he ever really recovered from what they did to him.

To some extent I admire Dean and John Wells as well. When they were playing they were so in a comfort zone it was scary, especially Wellsy. He played for Tigers for more than ten years and in that period he probably passed the ball three times. But he never lost the ball in contact, or so he'd have us believe. Dean and Wellsy were such talented players yet they wouldn't let me do things. If I took a tap penalty they would go ballistic. That has taken three years to get out of them. When I first came I'm sure they thought I was some kind of alien. Taking quick 22s, reverse passing from scrums and lineouts and that sort of stuff. They saw me as a showboater.

But I have always got on with Deano, even though I can't

forgive him for giving me scrum pox during a mass bundle on the team bus returning from a game when he was sweating like a baboon in India. I first got to know him when we were sent together to conduct a coaching session in Norwich in my first week at the club. We met this guy called Smokie, a real huge fella. We had a few beers and a curry, then Smokie started challenging people to arm wrestles. Now I may not be the biggest bloke in the world but arm wrestling is my speciality - and Dean knew this.

He looked at Smokie and said 'my money's on this little fella Austin beating you. If he does you can pay for everyone's curry. What do you say?' Smokie laughed...for about five seconds. Then he got rather annoyed as I slammed his arm down onto the table and Dean dissolved into hysterics. I then started calling him Smoking.

'My name's Smokie,' he kept saying.

'Okay Smoking, I hear you.'

I kept going until he was at boiling point and Dean had to step in and save me. It was a great night. A great way to break the ice between us. Since then Dean has done brilliantly well to lead us to a hat-trick of Premiership titles and the Heineken Cup. But the true test of him will come when his stalwarts have retired. When the cornerstones of this team go we will see if he is truly a great coach/manager. His man management skills are exactly what I need but are not to everyone's liking.

Look at the way he leaves offering new contracts to players right until the very last minute. He lost Craig Joiner because he left it two months too late. He only had to say 'Craig you've had a great season do you want to sign for next season?' and Craig would have said 'yeah'. He wouldn't have had to pay him any more money or anything. Instead I lost a close mate.

Nor does he keep his squad informed about players linked with the club. The press write up that guys like Kronfeld and Carlos Spencer are coming yet we are kept totally in the dark until the signing is announced. We should be kept informed about it. At least that way players who are in the team, would know where they are and could think about their futures. It comes back to my point about not taking our loyalty for granted. But I'm well aware that this works both ways.

What Dean cares about is Leicester winning games on a Saturday afternoon. Anything else is a minor detail. If the team is going well he will not change it, regardless of giving other people opportunities. That proved to be Will Greenwood's downfall. When he had a dip in form I just don't think he was given an opportunity to get back.

Other lads have also suffered, like Glen Gelderbloom who has never let us down. Craig was another case. He scored goodness knows how many tries coming off the bench. He played really well, was a massive impact player, but never got the opportunity to start even in the weaker games, where he could easily have thrown in what was perceived to be his second choice centres, Will and Craig.

For all my observations, no club rugby manager can boast Dean's trophy collection. His record is unparalleled and he can be proud of that. His challenge now that we have won everything is to hold the team together. It won't be easy. But only a fool bets against Leicester.

chapter three

Me and Bob Dwyer

Contrary to the impression I might sometimes give I don't dislike all Australians. I actually like the odd one or two. Bob Dwyer is odd, but he is not one of them. Dwyer coached Leicester for eighteen months between May 1996 and February 1998. From the day he walked into Welford Road until that blessed day he was asked to leave he made my life a misery.

Officially his removal was purely a rugby decision based on the fact that a year after winning the Pilkington Cup and reaching the final of the Heineken Cup, Leicester had done nothing. We had become toothless Tigers. "There was no element of player power," Peter Wheeler insisted at the time. Okay. Let's put it another way then. Dwyer had lost the respect of the squad. Most of all me.

It should have been the stuff of dreams for an aspiring international to be coached by a World Cup winner. A priceless opportunity for me to learn from someone who had been to the very top of the game. As I say, it should have been. Instead, it was purgatory. Dwyer tried to force his way into the hearts and minds of a not altogether useless Leicester squad from Day One. Opinions of players like Dean Richards and Rory Underwood meant nothing to him. His way was the only way.

The older guys saw through him straight away. But I was the only young player who would stand up to him. As with Graham Henry on the Lions tour, he would not tolerate anybody questioning his methods. And as with Henry I would not back down. Both men are like school teachers but at least Henry has the excuse that he used to be one. Dwyer trained as an electrical engineer. Red is live, blue is neutral. Or is it the other way round? I must check with Bob.

I had never met Barbed Wire, as he was hilariously dubbed, until I joined Leicester. When I signed I knew there would be a new coach because I knew Tony Russ was leaving. But that was all I knew. Nor did I have anything against him. I didn't know him from Adam. My concern was to make a good impression at my new club and with my new coach. But it took him no time at all to make an unfavourable impression on me. A couple of months before he was due to start he turned up to brief us on the way things would be. He came into the room and from the off was very vocal and forceful about how we were going to do things his way. He wouldn't accept any slacking. He didn't try to slowly work his way into the heads of all the boys, to earn the respect of players who had themselves been around the block a few times. He tried to force his way in straight away. Quite a few of the older lads, like Deano and Rory, dug their heels in from the start.

I was in great shape, having spent all summer training like never before, and I was playing pretty well, if I say so myself. But he always made a point of saying that Aadel Kardooni, my rival for the number nine shirt, was every bit as good a player as me. I was playing miles better than Aadel yet he insisted on rotating us, him one week, me the next. Just as I was getting overheated by the way he was messing me about he went back to Australia for a month or so to tie up some unfinished business and Ian 'Dosser' Smith stepped in. The lads really responded to him and we started to play some really good stuff.

Perhaps sensing this, Bob came back bringing with him a new assistant coach called Duncan Hall, and basically forced out a man who had given his life to the club. It was scandalous treatment but Bob wielded so much power that he could pull those sort of stunts. He held the purse strings and the Board were seduced by his reputation. He had been the coach of the 1991 World Cup winners - albeit a team which, quite frankly, most people's grans could have coached to win that tournament.

I could not be a silent witness to some of the things Bob was doing at the club. There were other dissidents too. Dean, Rory, John Wells to a certain extent, and John Liley. But I never needed a second invitation to get involved. There used to be an underground fanzine at Leicester and every time I'd fall foul of Bob in some way or other I would find a copy in an envelope marked 'We hate Barbed Wire' left in my cubbyhole, just to cheer me up.

What neither he nor, more recently, Graham Henry could see was that by questioning something he had said I was not being impertinent or a smart arse. I was just putting forward a different point of view. Not saying his way was the wrong way, just pointing out that there were alternatives which I felt should be considered. At that stage I genuinely thought I had quite a bit to offer. I had a lot of different ideas that I'd thought through and which I thought could make us a better team. Bob wouldn't listen, even if I went into his office quietly and said 'look, I've got this idea on this, that or the other'. He should at least have listened.

He was very historical in his coaching, always going back in time for examples of how we should do things. He used to tell me how Nick Farr-Jones did this and Mark Ella did that and how it worked for them. I would respond by saying "Just because it worked back then doesn't mean it's going to work now, Bob. The game has moved on quite a bit". He was obsessed with targets, another area of conflict between us. His favourite phrase in training was 'tackle the tackler'. Not only were you carrying the ball, you had to tackle the defender as well and take him backwards. Bob was obsessed with the power game, whereas I was far more interested in attacking space. That's where we differed. Perhaps if I'd been more receptive to his plans I'd have played better. I accept some of the blame, but I was only 22 and my judgement was clouded by the way he was treating me.

For all our differences it was not until the second year that our feuding spilled into the open. The problem was that Bob was giving me so much shit that I was sometimes taking it out on other players in the changing room, and being quite caustic with my banter. I didn't mean it against them. It was just me trying to handle the fact that the coach, who was in charge of whether I played or not, was really trying to mess me about.

I have since read an interview with him in *The Daily Telegraph* in which he claimed to have been "one of the few people at the club resisting calls to get rid of him (me) because he didn't fit in, either tactically or in terms of attitude." That statement is laughable. He was the one person trying to get rid of me. I had heard rumours that he wanted to replace me with Agustin Pichot, Richmond's Argentine scrum-half. That he had phoned Richmond and offered them me plus money for him. Basically, anything to get me out of the club. He described me as an unstable influence, I think because he couldn't control me. And the more he tried to control me the more resistance I put up.

The training ground row between the two of us three days before his departure was only one of many but it led directly to his departure. He had picked me on the wing to play against London Irish. I hadn't a problem with that, I was quite happy. But on the Wednesday he'd had a massive go at one of our younger players, Leon Lloyd, for knocking a ball on and blatantly bollocked him right in the middle of the training session.

I could see Leon's head drop. So I went over to him and said 'look mate, keep your head up, ignore what he said, he's only saying it to try and get a reaction. Just concentrate on your next job and forget about it'. Andy (Kiwi) Key, who is now Head of Rugby Development at the club, overheard this, or at least thought he had and reported back to Dwyer. Bob said nothing at the time but when I turned up for the team run on the Friday the balloon went up.

We had this move where I had to run round from the wing, then straighten up and offload. I followed orders, went round, took the ball, gave it, only for Bob to shout 'Stop, Stop'.

"Bob, what's up?"

"Austin, I want you to run straighter."

"Okay, no probs."

So we did it again and I ran a bit straighter, offloaded the ball and thought it was perfect. I'd run straighter, taken the defence on and got on with it.

"No, stop, stop," Bob yelled again. "If you can't run in a straight line I'll get someone who bloody well can."

"What are you on about?" I snapped back.

"I've told you to run a straight line. If I tell you to run straight when you come round the corner, run straight."

I couldn't believe what I was hearing. "I'll tell you what Bob. If you think I can't do it why don't you get someone else then."

"Right, you're dropped."

"It's Friday afternoon and you're dropping me from the team because you think I didn't run in a straight line?"

"Yeah, fuck off."

"Right, see you later."

I walked off the training ground, got changed, drove straight to Welford Road and told Peter Wheeler exactly what had happened.

"Look, I've got no idea what's gone on here," I said. "There's obviously been something going on behind the scenes to wind him up because I didn't do anything today and he just went for me."

Wheelbrace paused. "Kiwi has told us all that you told Leon to 'just ignore everything he says'."

"Well that's not true," I said. "If Kiwi had heard the whole conversation instead of part of it he would have realised I was just trying to pick up a young lad's head."

"Oh shit," said Brace.

He then told me I was on the bench the following day and

advised me just to keep my head down and get on with it.

The London Irish game came around. I turned up, didn't really say anything, just went through the team walk-through, put my sub's suit on and went back out onto the pitch while the other lads asked what the hell was going on? The game kicked off and by half-time the crowd were growing pretty restless. We were only just ahead and, to be honest, playing particularly poorly. Bob came down to the touchline where I was stretching and I said to him "Mate, I'm keen to get on and try and make a difference."

He turned and looked at me as though I had three heads. I can't remember his exact words but they went something like "You're not going on this pitch, not now, not ever."

"Oh right. Fair enough."

At that moment something inside of him must have snapped. There were a load of kids up at the front of the Crumbie Stand but he started effin' and blindin' at me. I said "Hold on, hold on. Not here. Not now." I know the pressure of the game was getting to him but it was pretty bad stuff in front of the kids. Sure enough, the following day there were complaints about his language. Unusually for me I had not said anything publicly. Instead I spoke to a few good friends like Peter Tom and David Matthews, both senior figures on the Leicester board, and told them exactly what had gone on. They said they would sort it out.

The following day I went off to England training resigned to the fact that I would either be playing for a different club the following week or Bob Dwyer would be going. It was him or me and, after speaking to the Board, I felt reassured. They wanted me to stay. I had played pretty well and they knew, deep down, that I was a hard worker and someone who would give everything for Leicester. That's why they had gone out and signed me in the first place. They also knew that it wasn't just me Bob was causing problems for. It was young lads as well, like Leon. He spoke to people like they were two-year-old kids rather than grown adults.

Sure enough, by the Wednesday the club had released a statement saying Bob Dwyer had been sacked by Leicester.

When I heard the news it was as though a huge weight had dropped off my shoulders. It immediately impacted on my performance that weekend for England against Wales. I scored a try and we stuffed them 60-26.

In the early days I'd had bad dreams about Dwyer; about attacking him and all sorts of stuff. My sleeping patterns were all over the shop. Why is he dropping me? Why is he not picking me? Why is he playing mind games with me? But by the end he had tried it on for so long and I just had to make a stand. Don't get me wrong, I'm not painting myself whiter than white in this relationship. It was me as well. It was a clash of personalities.

It is the story of my life, ever since I smacked Marvin that day at school, that I have always stood up for what I believe. Later I might think 'what the hell did I say that for?' but at the time I'm not afraid to say what I am thinking.

Dwyer believes he can do no wrong. So it was no surprise to hear him claim the credit when I was picked by England to play on the wing. He claimed that I should "Thank him for resurrecting my England career". Why when it had been he who had wrecked it in the first place?

I was going well at scrum-half. I had played there for England in 1997 and been picked by the Lions in the number nine slot that same year. Then Bob began to mess me around. Play me there one week, the next leave me out completely. I couldn't get any momentum going in my game. His tactic got me dropped from playing nine for England.

It was then that he picked me on the wing against Bath. I had already reached breaking point, so I said "Bob I don't care. From now on I'm just going to play with a smile and get on with it. I'm not even going to talk to you." I had reached the stage where I was avoiding him at training. Not looking at him, not talking to him, not even listening to him. Just hoping that he didn't talk to me. By the very end our relationship had deteriorated to the extent that if he came near me I would just ignore him.

Employing Dwyer is probably the only big mistake Leicester have made since the game went open. I will remember him as the man who brought professionalism in with a bang but in the same breath killed a lot of the team spirit that had driven Leicester on for the previous 100 years. He was a lot more abrasive, a lot more forceful, than any other coach I have ever experienced. And I include Jack Rowell in that. He also knows how to bear a grudge. Even after he left Leicester and joined Bristol, ironically to team up with Jack, he couldn't let our spat go.

By a lovely coincidence the win which clinched Leicester the Premiership title, more than two years after Bob's exit from Welford Road, came at the Memorial Stadium, home of his new team. Bob did not like that one little bit. He had been seated next to our Board in the adjacent box throughout the entire game and at the end obviously wasn't very happy that Leicester had won their second consecutive league crown since he had gone.

One of the members of our Board reached down to shake his hand and say thanks for the game. It was a well-meant gesture but Bob bit his head off. So the tone had already been set when I saw him down on the pitch, after the stadium emptied and went to shake his hand, unaware that he was already consumed by rage. He came at me. I actually thought he was going to punch me. I moved out of the way and started laughing at him. That only incensed him more.

"What are you doing you idiot?" I said.

He came again so this time I took my drink bottle, squirted water in his general direction and said something like "Sod off, see what we've won without you". Then he started at the steward, "Steward, steward I've just been assaulted."

"No you haven't, you've just tried to hit me and I pushed you away with some water."

One of the members of our Board, who will remain anonymous, came up to me and asked what had happened. Barely able to believe it myself I told him and he said "Oh that's brilliant that, I just love that."

The next time I saw Bob Dwyer was in Sydney during the Lions tour when I watched him defend the indefensible. Duncan McRae had repeatedly beaten Ronan O'Gara in the left eye during the match against his New South Wales side in what I can only describe as a cowardly assault. Yet Dwyer attempted to justify McRae's 11-punch attack. It was ludicrous but also educational as it revealed to a lot of people what I already knew: that Bob Dwyer lives life according to his own set of rules.

chapter four

My Nightclub Shame

As I sat in the cells awaiting sentence I hated myself as never before. I was scared, I was alone, and I deserved to be.

For five hours I was banged up beneath Leeds Crown Court convinced I was about to be sent to prison for committing grievous bodily harm. Scrawled on the wall in front of me were messages like, 'Joe Bloggs: seven years for rape - she deserved it', and 'Jack Daniel: 15 years for murder - there will be more'. I half thought of adding my own inscription: 'Austin Healey: doesn't want to be here - shitting my pants'.

I had pleaded guilty to wounding with intent. A year earlier I had headbutted a bloke in a Leeds nightclub whilst completely hammered. He had done nothing to deserve it, other than to have looked less than impressed when I tried to dance with his girlfriend.

It was a week short of my nineteenth birthday and I was in my first year at Carnegie College in the city. My housemate Robin Saverimutto and I had won the student union raffle and the prize on this occasion was a crate of Diamond White and another of Castaways, an orange and passion fruit alcopop. Mix the two together, as we did, and you get a Blastaway, a concoction with a kick like a mule. We drank our prize before hitting the dance floor.

So I was pissed, utterly obnoxious and attempting to make a move on a girl I had never seen before when this tall lad came towards me. I thought he was going to chin me so I hit him first. Better to ask questions later, I thought. Only I had got it all wrong.

I later found out he was a well brought up lad who had no intention of hitting me. But I was in such a bad state that I did not think twice before decking him.

My immediate punishment was to be taken out of the club by three of his mates, pinned against the railings and given a hiding. I managed to throw one of them down an escalator but I still got a good kicking. It was much later that the law caught up with me. Three months, in fact, and even then it was only by chance. I had felt as guilty as hell for what I had done from Day One. Honestly, I had. But I would have got away with it had I not been recognised playing rugby for Waterloo on television.

In the days after the incident nobody had known where I lived. Like so many students I lived in digs off campus. So after getting a few butterfly stitches at hospital I was back home out of reach. And that is how it would have stayed had the policeman leading the investigation not been a rugby fan and happened to see me score a try in a big derby match against Orrell.

I was asked to come down to the local station and was then held overnight. Yet I still didn't realise how grave the situation was. In fact, although I had this dark cloud hanging over me for a year it wasn't until I arrived at court for the trial that it hit home exactly how much trouble I was in. My barrister, David Gee, came over to me and asked 'how did you get here?' I replied that I had driven and he said 'In that case, you should give the keys to your dad'.

'Why's that then?'

'Because I don't think you'll be driving home.'

Those words will haunt me for as long as I live.

I will forever be indebted to John Elliott, the England under-21s' manager, for the glowing reference he wrote for me. Likewise to Deb Murphy, my next-door-neighbour who, as luck would have it, was a QC. But I could not know it was to be my lucky day as I sat in the cell block drowning in self pity. I could only think of Joe Bloggs and Jack Daniel and how I was about to be locked up in the same place as those kind of people.

For five hours I waited for the voice calling me back up to hear my fate. I remember thinking how I had let down not only myself but my family, how I had changed as a person. How my personality seemed to turn nasty with drink. I swore I'd never again let myself get into that position. I was frightened, but at least I was being honest with myself.

I had sat in the dock while pictures of my 'victim' were shown to the courtroom. Pictures I had not seen before. They were horrible. He had a broken nose, his face was a right mess. Only then did I realise how badly hurt he was; how much damage I had done. At no time during the trial did I get the chance to say sorry to him personally. I wanted to apologise for what I had done. I still do.

It was about four o'clock when the voice finally came. I had braced myself for the worst. I was sure I would be banged up for a year. But someone up there must have been looking after me that day. The case put forward by my barrister, allied to my references, saved my skin. "At first I was going to give you a custodial sentence," explained the Judge, confirming my worst fears. "But I've changed my mind and you will serve 200 hours of community service instead."

I was always taught that if someone hits you, hit them back. You know, ask questions later. That was why I found it so hard to live with what I had done to that lad - yet able to justify my actions in head-butting somebody else a matter of weeks later.

This time there was no community service. No let-off with just a rap across the knuckles. I had been sent-off for butting Dorian West, these days a teammate of mine at Leicester, in a match between Waterloo and Nottingham, and the Lancashire Rugby Football Union threw the book at me. I was suspended for 56 days. By the time I was back playing, my Waterloo career was at an end.

But I was able to look at myself in the mirror and say that Nobby had deserved it. Of course there was more to it than that. I'd had a bad game, I was pretty frustrated, I'd been running around like a complete idiot because I didn't want to play for Waterloo any more. Immature, I know. So I didn't need much of an excuse to lamp somebody. But Dorian gave me all the justification I needed and more by gouging me. Something inside me snapped, fortunately not the muscle fibres around my eye. I rolled over and butted him twice and punched him a few times for good measure. We both left the field, Dorian on a stretcher.

Waterloo were not best pleased with me. In fact you can safely take that to be an understatement. But there was no public bollocking. How can I explain? A rugby club is like a family. If your sister punches someone you stand by her whether you think what she did was right or wrong. and then at the end of the day, behind closed doors, you give her a piece of your mind. That is how Sir Alex Ferguson deals with discipline at Old Trafford and that is how Waterloo dealt with me.

They told me to go home and to keep my mouth shut until the Lancashire RFU disciplinary hearing, which turned out to be an absolutely comical affair in a Preston pub. On this occasion my judges looked like fellas who had been dragged upstairs from the pub darts team. I told them that Dorian had gouged me, that I could not see and that the first butt had been an instinctive reaction. I did not even know I had hit him. The second time I was getting him back for trying to pull my eyeball out of my socket.

Nobby and I were okay about it. After the game he had followed me into the shower with a big bump on his head and said, 'What was that for chief, I was only wiggling your eyeball about?' I looked at him, snarled and walked out. He was laughing his pants off.

The disciplinary panel, all smart in their Lancs ties, took a rather dimmer view. 'We can't have this,' they snorted. 'This will not do'. They gave me eight weeks. Looking back I have to wonder how the game has survived this long, let alone progressed into the professional era. Mind you, perhaps I should look at myself first and ask the same question. This was not the smartest period of my life. In fact, I am not proud of myself at all.

I now shy away from violence. If I see a big fight, even if the Leicester lads are involved, my first instinct is to take a backwards step. Unless I see someone getting a good kicking, I just won't get involved. Not out of fear for the repercussions - court action, being named in the papers etc - but because of what I did to that lad in Leeds.

It was during that stressful time that I first realised Louise really cared for me. On the day of my court appearance I wore a suit in lecture while while the rest of my so-called course 'mates' wore tracksuits - yet no-one said anything to me, except Lou. She went out of her way to wish me all the best.

We weren't seeing each other at the time. We'd been through a bit of a rocky period. Yet when I most needed support she was there for me. We got back together soon afterwards. So I ended up a wiser man with a girlfriend who would become my wife. Oh, and I was back in court three months later. In exactly the same court room.

'Bloody ironic', I thought as my first day of community service sent me back to the scene of Judgement Day. I had been assigned to Oxfam in Headingley, near to my college, near to the trendy shops where I liked to buy my clothes. That lifestyle seemed a million miles away as I leafleted houses, asking for old garments which I then had to sort through in the shop. Two hundred hours felt more like two hundred years.

On the first day I was sent out on a furniture removal job. But this was no ordinary Pickfords assignment wrapping crockery in newspaper or lugging pianos down winding staircases. I was back in Leeds Crown Court.

Court business was in the process of being moved to new premises and I and another fella, who has tattoos all over his arms and his neck and who'd also done something bad, had to collect all the old desks to resell for charity.

And you know what made it all the more ironic? On the floor of the room where three months earlier I had expected to pay for my stupidity with a pound of flesh, I left a pool of blood. The lad with the tattoos all over his arms and his neck dropped a desk on me and cut my leg open. It was a deep gash, a seriously bloody deep gash. It was the kind of bizarre moment which stays with you forever.

chapter five

My Stamping Shame

Welford Road, Leicester, 13 February 1999

It looked really bad. And it felt even worse as I flicked the top of his right eye with one of my studs. I could almost feel the flesh tear.

You know what it's like when you do something wrong. Your first reaction is to look around to see if anyone has seen you. The reflex is the same whether you've nicked a jelly bean in a pick n'mix or nudged somebody's bumper reversing into a tight space.

So as my guilty foot returned to the ground I shot a glance at the touchline for any witnesses. As Kevin Putt held his face mine was framed in a Sky television camera lens. Shit.

Time had moved on since my previous brush with authority. Dorian West had by now become a club mate of mine at Leicester and a good friend. I was an England player with Lions experience. But beneath that veneer of respectability my fuse remained short.

For some reason it is my feet which tend to get me into trouble when I become agitated. Rather than use my fists I seem to lash out with my feet. I remember going for Ben Clarke during one game against Bath, kicking him up the backside. But I have always said to myself that I would never kick anyone in the face. Like biting and gouging, that to me is a no-no.

So there I was, ten minutes into a game against London Irish, breaking my own rule by kicking a fella I had never before met and had nothing whatsoever against. Irish called it 'stamping', the authorities settled for 'reckless'. Either way it cost me dear. A death threat and an eight-week ban from the game.

We were playing against a side on a roll. Leicester were top of the Premiership but Irish were up to third. Not only had they won seven straight games, they had twice got away with foul play in the opening minutes of the game. Craig Joiner had been clothes lined by Brendan Venter and then shoed by someone else. There was a definite edge to the game.

But I didn't mean to hurt Kevin Putt. I just wanted to let him know I was there. And when I was shoved from behind with him on the ground in front of me I found myself with an opportunity to let him know he was in a game.

It all happened in a split second. I knew I was going to land on him and I knew that if I slammed my foot down I would inflict serious damage. I honestly didn't want to do that. So I tried to flick my boot in order to minimise any injury but, at the same time, let him know that I could have kicked him in the face.

At no point did I think 'I'm going to kick him in the face and give him some stitches'. That thought never entered my head. But that is effectively what I did. As I brought my right foot down I felt Kevin's face on my stud. It felt horrible and as soon as I'd done it I knew I was in the shit. Kevin had a bloody face which required six stitches. For me it was almost like playing with concussion. My mind was elsewhere, away from the rugby, pondering the consequences of my moment of madness. The game itself was a blur.

I might have been alright had Graham Hughes, the referee that day, seen the incident. A yellow card, a red even. But because I was not punished at the time it meant I was liable for far harsher punishment when committed to trial by video. That is the way our screwy citing system works. But I was still not prepared for what came my way.

When I walked off the pitch at the end I was greeted by Dean Richards and Peter Wheeler who said that they had watched the incident in the Sky van, that it looked bad and that they didn't want me to say anything. That is not my way. I'm not the sort of person who brushes past people with a 'no comment'. I try to be up front. So I apologised to Kevin through the Press, just as I had to his stitched-up face when he returned to the field.

"Sorry mate, I couldn't put my foot anywhere else," I said. "I'm not surprised," he replied, "considering the size of my nose". But my comments were seen as an exercise in damage limitation. Stephen Jones' version of events in *The Sunday Times* was that 'television replays clearly show Healey balancing on one leg and thrusting downwards quite vigorously with his studs pressing into Putt's face...he appears to make no effort to avoid Putt, nor does he appear to be off-balance'.

As high profile players we have a responsibility to kids watching, to sponsors and to the game. I knew I had done something wrong and let the club down as well as myself. So I was prepared for whatever punishment came my way...or so I thought.

Kevin Yates, the Bath prop, had just been banned for four weeks for stamping, recklessly rather than wilfully, on Wasps flanker Paul Volley, who needed seven stitches in his forehead. That was the sort of suspension I would be looking at.

Clive Woodward phoned to ask what I had done and to tell me that I would not be involved in England's game against Scotland at Twickenham the following weekend. He gave me the impression that he already knew Leicester were going to take some action against me. It's amazing how the grapevine works in rugby. Sure enough, Leicester then called me to an internal hearing in one of the executive boxes at Welford Road to hear my side of the story. They concluded that there was no wilful intent on my part but that I could have done more to avoid contact with Putt's face. They banned me for three weeks.

Their action ruled me out of the first half of the Five Nations Championship. I would miss the trip to Ireland as well, not to mention a big Tetley's Bitter Cup quarter-final at Richmond. Yet somehow I doubted that was the end of the matter.

The Press were on my back. *The Mirror* published a close-up of Putt's cut face beside the headline 'Healey gets just 21 days for doing this to an opponent'. The heat was being turned up. A stamping offence carries a recommended ban of three months and London Irish had pressed charges, having branded my explanation "unsatisfactory" and Leicester's action "inadequate". There would be a RFU hearing.

"Healey has always been a competitive beast," wrote *The Daily Telegraph*. "He is forever pressing, forever annoying the hell out of the opposition. For the most part this is a virtue. On Saturday it wasn't. Perhaps the lesson will do him good in future. The fine line is the most important marking on the pitch."

What about Kevin Yates' four-week ban? I muttered to myself as my pursuers closed in on me. Why do they not believe me when I say I did not intend to hurt him? As the days passed I became increasingly frustrated that everyone was discussing the case but there was nothing I could say or do to affect it.

Three days before I was due to go before the RFU at the East India Club in London I had finally taken all I could stand. A letter addressed to me had been sent to the club from some fella in Dublin threatening to kill me if I set foot in Ireland.

It read: 'Healey you scum. When you come to Ireland you're going to get it'.

Fan mail comes with the territory when you are a high profile sportsman. So whether it is a note saying 'I love you, here are my knickers', or 'I hate you, here is a bullet with your name on it,' I normally take these letters with a pinch of salt. In the same breath I don't like to be threatened with death and coming on top of all the other shit I was getting over the Putt episode, it was the straw which broke the camel's back.

I had asked biomechanics at Leicester and Loughborough Universities to take a close look at the video evidence. They concluded that far from stamping, I was trying to remove my foot as quickly and as softly as possible.

That only inflamed my sense of injustice. I wanted the RFU to believe my defence and to accept that I was not a liar. I was quoted in *The Mail on Sunday* the day before the hearing as saying I would retire if they did not. I'm not sure I ever put it that strongly - I take a lot of stick from the lads for claiming I was going to retire - but I probably did use the article to try to influence the disciplinary committee. A lot of good it did me. I got eight weeks.

There is no doubt in my mind that they made an example out of me. It was double what Kevin Yates had received, double what Jason Leonard got for stamping on the chest of Budge Pountney earlier in the season. I wanted to scream 'injustice' from the rooftops, I definitely wanted to appeal. But as I sat on the train back from St Pancras I put my future in the hands of Leicester. "Whatever you want to do I'll do," I told Deano and Wheelbrace.

"You know it's my fault. I got us into this situation. If you think it's right to appeal then we can appeal. If you don't then I'll abide by what you think." I think they respected me for that. For not sulking like some spoilt brat, for not spitting out my dummy. I said it was up to them. I left the ball in their court and went off and trained.

It just so happened that my suspension ended the day before England were due to play Wales in the final match of the Five Nations, a match on which the destiny of the Championship, Triple Crown and the Grand Slam would rest. It could not have been further from my mind. All I was thinking about was getting fitter, faster and stronger than I had ever been so that I could come back with a bang. I was a man on a mission.

I turned to Neil Back for advice. Backy had served a six-month ban in 1996 for pushing over referee Steve Lander at the end of the Pilkington Cup final at Twickenham. He knew what I was going through. 'Stay positive,' was his simple message. He assured me that his enforced rest, if not the circumstances that prompted it, was the best thing that had happened to his rugby career. During his ban he had become turbo-charged, lifting his fitness levels to uncharted heights. I decided to do the same.

Peter Wheeler was a great support to me during this time. He was heading out to Portugal to play in the Henry Cooper Golf Classic and, after hearing that one of the celebrities had pulled out, put my name forward. Not only did I play in the tournament, I joined a week-long training camp with a number of international athletes, by the end of which I was firing as never before. I had lost loads of fat, felt sharp and had a burning desire to get a ball back in my hands. But if I was a changed physical specimen my approach to rugby remained the same.

I vowed not to change my style of play believing, as I still do, that you have got to play on the edge of the edge if you are going to be any good. I had no desire to return to rugby and be only an average player. I don't play sport just to make up the numbers. I never have.

The following week Clive phoned to say he was picking me on the bench for the Wales game to cover two positions following injuries to winger David Rees and scrum-half Kyran Bracken. I thought my nightmare was over, but I was wrong. Not only did I not get onto the pitch, Scott Gibbs scored in stoppage time to grab victory for Wales and rob us of a Grand Slam. An awful end to an unhappy chapter.

chapter six

Counting on Clive

Monday November 21 - Wednesday November 23, 2000

England's most important result since the 1999 World Cup did not come on a rugby field at all but on a carpet in a posh hotel. And the only fans who saw it were the ones keeping the room cool.

It was the key moment in the bitter, at times mind-blowing battle between England's top players and our employers, the Rugby Football Union. A conflict none of us who were involved shall ever forget. At stake was the bond between Clive Woodward and his squad.

We had held our nerve by striking for 34 hours over pay and claiming a victory on the point of principle we had disputed. Now it was time to hold our breath. It was time to find out if we could still count on the individual with the power to make or break our international careers.

Only days before Clive had presided over our win against Australia, the world champions, at Twickenham. The result completely vindicated his methods and the millions of pounds the RFU had ploughed into his blueprint to make England the best in the business. He had put in place a set-up complete in every detail. As players we wanted for nothing in our preparation for internationals. Well, almost nothing.

Just one thing was missing from the RFU. A satisfactory contract for the players. Time and again the Union had stalled on it.

Clive had laid on everything for us - comparing his set-up with Graham Henry's Lions, for example, is to compare five-star luxury with a Bed and Breakfast - but none of that pays your mortgage. So after much soul searching we, as a squad, took the momentous decision to withdraw our labour.

It was never about Clive and yet, ultimately, it was all about Clive.

He had been the one caught in the crossfire, he had been the one who tried desperately to keep the peace, he had been the one who felt personally wounded by our decision to rebel. And he would have been the one left to pick a team of butchers, bakers and candlestick makers that weekend against Argentina had a deal not been struck. It had hurt each and every one of us to go against his wishes. Now we would find out if there was a price to be paid.

Clive had talked us out of doing anything 'stupid' the week before when we had been on the verge of making a protest in the build-up to the Australia game. He had promised that if we agreed not to turn up for training with our sponsored tops inside out that he would get the RFU management board to meet with us the following Monday to sort it out once and for all.

On that Monday, fresh from the euphoria of Twickenham two days earlier, he had kept his word and then tried desperately hard to talk us out of industrial action when negotiations again broke down. He knew we were at the point of withdrawing our labour and he reminded us of our aspirations to play for England and how we were ruining them.

He told us to think about our families. He warned that if we went on strike we would get destroyed in the Press. He was not angry with us. He was emotional but level-headed. Very impressive. For the first time, we realised that he was dead against what we were doing. That he disapproved and did not want us to go through with the threat. The realisation sent a shiver down each of our spines. He had sown the seed of doubt in our minds. Players were no longer so sure which way to go. Not least me.

Without Clive I don't think I would have won half as many caps as I have. I owe him a lot. I don't think any other coach would have had the balls to play me on the wing. Look at the 2001 Lions. It took Graham Henry until the last midweek game to give me a go on the wing. He then looked shocked at what I could do. It was as if he was suddenly hit by the thought, 'Oh God, why didn't we pick him earlier'.

Even after he had said his piece Clive refused to give us up as a lost cause. He left the room but remained outside while we talked it through again. For two hours it was an open forum. "Look it's not about our support for Clive," said one player. "It's not about how much we admire him as a coach or whatever, it's about the fact we're being taken for a ride and if we don't make a stand now in 10 years time the young players will be treated in exactly the same way."

As the debate continued Martin Corry took the role of devil's advocate, asking 'what if this? what if that?' Will Greenwood attempted to supply the answers. He predicted that half the Press would slaughter us but that the dispute would be settled within two days and we would be back playing by the weekend. We could not know at the time that Will was pretty much spot on. As we sat in that room tearing up conference pads to make ballot papers, with Clive sitting outside the door awaiting our decision, we were faced with the biggest decision of our lives. No question. Writing a YES on that piece of torn up paper could, at a stroke of the pen, end our England careers.

Playing for England had been all I ever wanted to do since that day I left my football at home as an eight-year-old and followed my mates down to Birkenhead Park. Rugby's gain was Everton's loss.

It is hard to put into words my emotions when I pull on an England shirt. I feel a responsibility to the country, to my country and a burning desire to do well. The Celts are passionate about their nationalities but all too often nowadays we seem almost to have to apologise for being English. Well I won't do that. I am as proud an Englishman as there is.

As I sat twiddling my pencil and staring at the scrap of paper on the table in front of me I thought about all that. I had worked bloody hard to build my England career. I could remember a time when winning one cap seemed unlikely, never mind the 33 I now had. I was in the 'A' squad where the coach, Peter Rossborough, kept me on the bench for what seemed like my entire life.

I played just one game, against New South Wales. Rossborough never put me on. He kept Andy Gomarsall in the team. I've got nothing against Gomars, I just don't think he's as good as me. Not now, not then. But at that stage I genuinely thought there were people who didn't want me to progress in an England shirt.

One day we were on the team bus playing a game of trivia and Rossborough was getting all the questions right. He was playing the big and clever 'I am'. So I said to him "Who plays football for Scotland and cricket for England?" He thought about it for ages before coming up with some name none of us had ever heard of. I said "No. Kenny Dalglish and Ian Botham". The lads pissed themselves laughing. He shot back: "Who's going to be the next England scrum-half?" I said: "I don't know." He just put both his hands on Andy Gomarsall's shoulders. At that point, for the first time in my life, I pulled back something I was going to say. I was going to say: "Who's not going to be the next England coach?" but I didn't. I wish I had now.

Jack Rowell was coach when I was first called into the senior squad and I can still remember the buzz I felt as I drove down to the session at Henley with the England doctor Terry Crystal, who happened to be my GP when I was at college in Leeds. Jack had called a trial match, Probables versus Possibles I think it was. I played for the Possibles and scored three tries against guys like Bum Chin and Skeletor, sorry Will Carling and Jerry Guscott. I thought 'I'm going to be picked for England this weekend, I've got to be'. How naive I was back then. I had given it 110% whereas the established names jogged about in second gear thinking 'why is this little whippersnapper running about like a blue-arsed fly'. Sure enough when they named the squads I was only on the bench...for the 'A' team.

I kept getting invited back to sessions without ever getting picked. But the 'A' team was great. We used to meet up on Saturday nights and all come down to the Richmond Hill Hotel after playing for our clubs. We would have dinner together and then the coaches would say 'right guys we've got a really hard training session tomorrow at nine o'clock, so straight to bed'. Then everyone, to a man, would sneak out, get absolutely destroyed and not come back in until about five. There were a great bunch of lads in my season with the As. We weren't getting paid and we didn't take it too seriously.

My problem was that Rossborough, I definitely felt, had it in for me. Another factor was that while I was playing reasonable stuff, Orrell weren't a fashionable club. For the selectors to see me play we either had to be on television or playing away in London. I got there in the end but predictably, I guess, Andy Gomarsall got there first.

My debut was against Ireland in Dublin on 15 February 1997. Gomars was picked at number nine and I only got eight minutes off the bench at the end. But I like to think I made my mark. We scored four tries in that time, running out 46-6 winners, and the *Rothmans Rugby Union Yearbook* wrote: 'It was the late arrival of Healey and Guscott which added pace, bite and imagination to the England attack'. It remains Ireland's heaviest-ever championship defeat while our winning margin was, at the time, the biggest in Five

Nations history.

It was a weird feeling to finally achieve my goal. It was as though someone else was running onto the pitch. I stood by the touchline, the Irish heard the name Healey announced over the tannoy, and a cheer went up. They thought it was one of their replacements coming on. My first touch was a put-in at a scrum, my first pass was down by the ankles of Paul Grayson, who had been a team mate at Waterloo. It was reassuring to have Grays there, especially as he somehow held onto my dodgy pass. Had he knocked it on my international career might never have recovered.

(As it was I very nearly didn't recover from the day after, becoming the victim of an age-old tradition that an England new cap share a drink with every player in the side. Being me, the lads all wanted to partake in stupid drinks with me and by 9pm I was collapsed on a couch behind a partition in the hotel, where the post-match dinner was taking place, being violently sick - so sick in fact that the blood vessels burst in my right eye which was completely red for weeks afterwards. Had it not been for the constant supervision of TC, Kevin Murphy and Nigel Henderson - England's legendary medical team - I would have ended up in hospital having my stomch pumped. I survived, although my shoes didn't, thanks to Richard Cockerill filling them with bleach).

I came off at the final whistle ecstatic at having played for England and with a massive craving for more. I didn't play against France next up - England lost and Gomars had a shocker - but the following game I got my first start down in Cardiff where we pummelled Wales 34-13.

I took a gulp of water from the glass on the table in front of me. There was an eerie quiet in the room as we prepared for the secret ballot. I took a deep breath. 'Let's do it', I murmured to no-one in particular. Deep down I don't honestly think we felt we were risking it all. Basically we had a good three-card brag hand and we believed that the RFU didn't really have anything. Or if they did, they were going to have to hold onto it for a long, long time before anything good came of it. So we said 'right, Twickenham is sold out for the South Africa game in a fortnight, there's 50-odd thousand due for Argentina, lets just try and get it sorted. If we leave it until after these two games, we are going to get messed around all the way to the Six Nations and there's no way we can boycott that'.

The vote was taken and it was unanimous in favour of a strike. There was another silence as we came to terms with what we had just done. We consoled ourselves with the thought that the English public would not come to watch an emaciated England team which had no chance of winning. An Englishman is a very proud person and if he thought England were going to get hammered he would not turn up. I wouldn't. Remember our 76-0 beating in Australia? (I do I played in it) That's effectively the standard of team that would have been fielded because the Premiership clubs were full square behind us. If scorelines like that were repeated in the Six Nations people would demand something be done.

Only the real diehards of rugby union would turn up and say this is brilliant because we're back to the real amateur ethos of the sport. And while there may be a fair few diehards still in rugby there are also an awful lot of people who realise that the game has been brought into the real world, a world where we earn money to survive. Those people, the diehards, don't see my bank manager when he wants some money. Nor do they see the living wages some of the younger England lads are on.

For all that, we had put Clive in a really shitty position and we knew it. He deserved to be upset. He told us to go and sleep on it but in the next breath made it clear that he wanted us out of the hotel by 10 o'clock in the morning. It was past midnight and we went to the bar for a beer. A few of the coaches came in and I tried to assure them that what we had done was no slight against any of them. They were as supportive as they could be but left us in little doubt that they didn't think we appreciated the implications of our action. To a point they were right. We were all together in the room and yet we weren't altogether any more, were we?

It was late when I phoned home and spoke to Louise. It was good to hear her voice. I explained that effectively we were being threatened with never playing for England again. Then I called Mum and Dad. As usual they were supportive, agreeing that if the RFU had been messing us around as much as I claimed then we must do what we felt was necessary. They rang off warning me to be careful what I said.

I turned the light off and lay awake trying to make sense of the most extraordinary day I had ever known. Yet it was not my own plight that ate away at me, rather that of Clive and the position we had put him in. He had put together this great package of coaches and players in this brilliant environment. We had just beaten the world champions, things were looking really rosy and all of a sudden the carpet had been pulled from underneath him. He just wanted it relaid, for everything to be as it was.

Of course he was angry. Of course he felt betrayed. But it still wasn't about him.

Johnno would put it best when it was all over, when agreement had been reached that a greater proportion of our England income would be guaranteed rather than left to chance in bonus form. "This was a negotiation between professional players and the RFU," he said. "Clive disagrees with our actions, that's obvious. I can understand his point of view as coach but our point of view is that this is our livelihood. I understand why he is angry but we are in total respect of him as our coach and manager - and that goes for everyone in the squad."

Come Tuesday morning it was far from all over, however our actions the previous day dominated news bulletins on radio and television. Another Amazonian rainforest must have been lost to satisfy Fleet Street's demand for paper to cover the story. Just how big a deal it was to the outside world was only now sinking in. "This is one of the saddest days in the history of the game in England," Clive was quoted in the papers as having said. "The fact that the players have walked out on their coaches, people like Andy Robinson and Brian Ashton and Phil Larder...well those guys don't deserve that treatment. It's really annoyed me and I won't forget it."

It certainly hadn't been forgotten when I got down to reception. Not only did we have Clive's 10 o'clock deadline to vacate our rooms, the breakfast room was out of bounds to us. So we all assembled at Wentworth, where the RFU has membership of the gymnasium. Johnno called Welford Road and spoke to Dean Richards and Peter Wheeler, who told us to stay put until they came down to assess the situation.

I've said for a long time that professional rugby has needed one person with the strength and the ability to pull it back from the precipice. And for everybody to then follow that person. I think Peter Wheeler has filled that role and that when people look back on the history of rugby a hundred years from now, he will be recognised as such. Wheelbrace would certainly emerge as the saviour of this crisis.

It was during the morning that Clive phoned around players. Most of the lads had their answerphones on so just received messages. But not me. Met my phone was on yet didn't ring. I couldn't work out if he'd ignored me because he knew I'd not turn up or because I wasn't in the team. Sadly it would turn out to be the latter.

The Times later crucified him for using bully boy tactics on young lads. The front page of the paper the following Saturday carried a huge picture of Ben Cohen above the headline 'Woodward made phone threats to young players'. Not only did Ben not receive a call - his father had died the previous week - but I honestly don't think any of the calls were meant to be abusive. They were just in the tone of "You've got to be here". We all realised Clive had to do whatever he could to get the team back together.

He would later defend his approach in the Press. "I used some strong language but when you know people very well and they will not support you, you do come out with those sort of words."

It would be fair to say there was a degree of resentment that he was trying to break up a tight unit by picking off people without the group being able to stick together and fight together. But what was upsetting was not so much being told to come back or risk kissing goodbye to your England careers - you get used to emotional talk at the top level of sport. It was more reality hitting home that if Clive, our greatest supporter, was making those calls the situation must be grave.

Nobody doubted how hard it must have been for him to use such tactics. He doesn't play cards and he doesn't bluff. If we were not back by 11.00 o'clock the following morning he would not pick us ever again and it would be up to the RFU - the Game - to decide who they should support, him or us. To this day I don't know what the answer would have been.

One player he did get through to was Mark 'Ronnie' Regan, back home in Bath with his family. "Ronnie," said Clive. "I've picked you for Saturday, will you turn up for training?" There was a pause before Ronnie replied: "Well I don't know, Babs." Clive snapped: "Don't call me Babs". To which Ronnie said: "I only call you Babs because you are my mate. That's what I call my friends." Even Clive could not keep a totally straight face at that one.

The entire squad and management were due to attend a fund-raising dinner for *BBC Radio Five Live* rugby reporter Alastair Hignell, the former England fullback now battling multiple sclerosis, that evening up in London. As things stood it would be a difficult night. But Wheelbrace had an idea. As his car swung into the drive at Wentworth hope arrived with him.

Our argument was that more of our England earnings should be guaranteed. I use the example of the previous Saturday's game against Australia. We won the game on the say-so of the video ref deep in stoppage time. Had he disallowed Dan Luger's try our effort wouldn't have been any less, but our pay would have been. I would have ended up worse off than had I played for a winning Leicester side against Wasps that same day.

A lot of the England squad make very tidy livings. But not all do. One of the younger lads who toured South Africa with us in 2000 was on a £10,000 club contract. This wasn't about getting the top lads a few extra grand, it was about looking after the boys at the other end of the pay scale. It wasn't about short-term gain it was about securing a fair deal for the long haul.

We didn't think it was unreasonable that two-thirds of our fees should be guaranteed with the rest dependant on results. The RFU initially offered us less than half as a guarantee. By the time we walked out their offer was up to 60-40. Close but not close enough. It had become a point of principle for us and we were not prepared to budge.

Wheelbrace spoke to Johnno. What if the RFU agreed to transfer half of the £100,000 bonus on offer to the squad for winning the Six Nations' Grand Slam in 2001 into guaranteed income? It would guarantee us an extra £500 or so a game and it would show good faith on the part of the RFU. It sounded good. Brace said he would put it to the management board.

There were about a dozen of us sitting in the bar area, the rest were on the end of a phone. We agreed to meet in the Glassblower pub off Regent Street, around the corner from the Cafe Royal, where Higgy's dinner was being held. But when we came out we got hit by a mighty barrage of Press. Remember that scene from *Notting Hill*, where Julia Roberts opens the door and is blinded by the glare of a thousand flashbulbs. It was like that. I'd never known anything like it.

It was Higgy's night and we knew it was the not the appropriate occasion to start hurling bread rolls at each other. To be quite honest when we saw someone else with a real problem, ours seemed a little incidental. I bumped into Clive on the way to the toilet and said "I take it I'm dropped then?" He asked me what I meant. "I didn't get a threatening phone call" He started laughing. I knew then I'd definitely been dropped, though I didn't realise at that stage it was from the squad.

At 11 o'clock we had a meeting in a room up on the sixth floor. We were told an offer had been made. Did we want to accept it? Clive had told the Press that we had to be at training at 11am the next day or be axed. So I phoned the Petersham and booked some rooms for the lads. Others stayed at the homes of Lawrence Dallaglio, Phil Greening and Danny Grewcock.

First thing on Wednesday morning I spoke to Johnno. He had a meeting arranged at Twickenham and we should all be by a phone ready for the go-ahead to get to training. At 10.15 the call came. 'Back to work lads'. The ordeal was over, only one question mark remained. Clive?

That night there was a meeting called before our team meal. Clive was there and he looked shattered. I can't imagine he'd slept a wink in 48 hours. It was a first chance for everyone to release their pent-up emotions at the situation we had put each other in; for everyone in the room to get rid of all the bad feeling. It is fair to say there remained a difference of opinion, but I sensed that we were all ready to move on.

Relations were still pretty tense as the players headed out to the local Chinese restaurant. Clive was still far from happy with what had gone on but he at least knew that our support for him was not in question. You can't help like the man. He's the only international coach I know who jumps up and down with the rest of the crowd when his team scores a try. When we see that raw emotion, that genuine excitement, it makes us feel good. It tell us that he believes in us and that wants more than anything for us to be successful. But don't cross him.

In fact, you take your life in your hands if you even play a practical joke on him. I learned that shortly after coming into the England side in 1997. In training I'd put a pair of tracksuit bottoms down the back of my shorts and walked around calling Clive 'Rhino Bum' in front of everyone. He gave me a look but I laughed it off and thought nothing more of it. Then I scored my first try against Wales in our next game and a few days later the girlfriends and wives of all the lads in the squad received a package through the post supposedly sent from me.

In it was a pair of G String knickers with 'I love Austin' printed on them and a note which read: "Just wanted to thank you all for your support at the weekend. As you are aware I scored my first try for England. I think you'll admit it was one of the best tries seen at Twickenham. I know how much you girls admire my play so I thought I'd send you a pair of these knickers each. Lots of love, Austin".

The following week Leicester were at Saracens. I got onto the team bus for the drive south and was summoned down to the back row by the ABC Club (Graham Rowntree, Richard Cockerill and Darren Garforth), all members of the England squad at the time. They were not pleased.

"What the hell do you think you're doing?" they said.

"What the hell are you on about?"

"Sending knickers to our missus? What the hell do you think you're doing?"

They were dead serious. They actually thought I'd done it. They didn't know it was a wind-up. I didn't know what to think. They were on the verge of kicking my head in and I didn't know what they were on about.

I headed back up the bus to my seat and phoned Louise on my mobile. She said that she had received a pair. Then my phone message service called and it was Clive laughing his head off. The penny dropped. "Don't ever take the mickey out of me again, Austin," he said. I tried to phone him back but his answerphone was on. "Clive, it's Austin," I said. "Some time during the rest of your life I will definitely, definitely get you back for this!"

I like to think he and I are pretty much alike, not only in our sense of humour, but also in terms of the way we see the game. He never gets an argument with me at training because when he asks me to do something, more often than not it is something I really want to do anyway. I respect him because I see how emotionally involved he is and how hard he works. The lads talk quite a lot to the security guys down at Twickenham. They get to work at about 6 o'clock in the morning and they say that Clive is often there. Sometimes he's been there for hours. He wakes up in the middle of the night with an idea and goes to work to set it in motion. People who may think he just goes around and watches a few games of rugby are way off the mark. He considers every fine detail.

He is ahead of his time. You know that because so many things he has done people questioned at the time. Six months later they are all doing exactly the same thing. Rugby league coaches, rugby league players, support staff, you name it. All questioned. All successes. He has been given great financial support by the RFU but look what he's built with it. The commercial properties the RFU now hold with the England team are out of this world. Every pound the Union has spent on the England team will bring a return of at least ten times that because of our success.

Over the years he has learnt by trial and error. He's never made the same mistake twice. Slowly but surely that management team has been built up into a very efficient workforce that doesn't make many errors, doesn't leave any stones unturned and, yet, doesn't overkill the players. His mission statement from the beginning was to make the England team so elite that once you are in the squad you never want to leave it. He's definitely achieved that. The question now was, did he want out?

After all the emotional turmoil I had gone through, I was told I was not required against Argentina. All that worry about a boycott and I would miss the game anyway. "We want specialists," Andy Robinson told me in response to my rhetorical question, "Are you telling me I can play every position in the back line yet I can't get a place on the bench?". Luckily for all concerned, mostly me I suspect, he stopped just short of calling me versatile. I can't abide that word.

As a result of my demotion, I was in the car heading home when my mobile rang. The call was from Pennyhill. It was the news we had all been waiting for. Clive had decided to support us for the sake of the squad. More than that he would share some of the blame with the RFU for the crisis. It was clear to me he was holding out an olive branch, that he had decided to return to 'the family', as Phil Greening likes to describe Team England. We could pick up where we had left off.

"I can't hold what has happened against these guys for ever," Clive told the world. "I've got to be bigger than that and move on."

It would not be as straightforward as that, of course. How could it be after such an emotional fall-out? Yet I honestly believe that the episode has made us a tighter group than we ever were before. It is quite unbelievable how strong a unit we now are. The strike experience, traumatic and regrettable as it was, could very well be the making of this England squad.

chapter seven

Euro Kings at Last

Parc des Princes, Paris, 19th May 2001

At various times during my Leicester career I have been accused of selfishly using the club to further my own ambitions with England and the Lions. The thought briefly crossed my mind as I stood on halfway at the Parc des Princes with Tigers trailing Stade Francais 30-27, a minute left in the final of the Heineken Cup and only seven days until I was due to join up with the Lions.

I had come into the game with an injury to my right knee which I really should not have risked. One bang on it and I could kiss my Lions tour goodbye. It might not even have needed a bang. Simply turning too sharply and it could have gone. After 79 minutes it was hurting. Really hurting.

I had so many painkillers inside me I rattled when I ran. Still I could feel the throbbing beneath the strapping which clung to my damaged medial ligaments. For a second I thought of all those 'parasite' jibes I had taken down the years from certain forwards at Leicester.

All week I had imagined this moment. As I lay on the physio's bench first in Leicester, then at the team hotel in Versailles; as I worked with the massage machine in the pool, as I took one suppository after another to try to dull the pain. Last minute of the European Cup final, Leicester down a score, Healey gets the ball...

Then it came my way. I had been switched from scrum-half to

the number 10 slot I had wanted so much to be mine all season. It was the final throw of the dice. We were in a deep hole. The move was a pre-arranged one, Double Suck Option we call it, designed to unlock a drift defence. I was supposed to take the ball and feed Tim Stimpson on the crash. But the lineout didn't go to plan. The ball was tapped back, it bounced on the floor and Neil Back threw it behind me.

I took a step back and caught it and set off at three-quarter pace, trying to pull the defence forward. I did a dummy scissor with Pat Howard, another with Glen Gelderbloom and noticed that David Venditti, their replacement centre, had already set off onto Stimmo thinking I was going to hit him. My shoulders were faced towards Stimmo so it looked likely. Venditti committed himself ever so slightly so I turned the corner and shot through the gap.

I knew their fly-half Diego Dominguez wouldn't have the speed to get there, but I was still concerned about Venditti. Had I been fit I would have been away, but now when I tried to put the accelerator down to go from three-quarters to full speed I started to cramp up just below my right knee. Had I had time to think I might have thought of my Lions tour going down the pan. More likely, though, I would have reminded myself of a pledge I took before kick-off. That whatever happened in the game I wouldn't use my knee as an excuse.

You see, contrary to what some of my team mates have thought down the years, playing for Leicester means a great deal to me. I admit that representing England is my ultimate high, but when I pull on a Tigers shirt I hold absolutely nothing back. Especially when it's the biggest match in the history of a club with a history of playing big matches.

Yes, I had been concerned I could have got injured for the Lions but it was a chance I wanted to take. I'd been on a Lions tour, I'd never won a European Cup. Nor had Leicester. I'd rather win this match than go on the Lions tour if there was a choice to be made. I could cope with having eight weeks' holiday. What I couldn't cope with was not winning the Heineken Cup.

So as I felt my leg begin to seize I took a deep breath. I kept going as hard as I could and managed to get away from Venditti. I then saw that Christophe Dominici wasn't really looking at me so I knew Leon Lloyd was coming up on the outside. Apparently he was screaming at the top of his voice, but there were 47,000 people doing the same. Just in time I caught him out of the corner of my eye. I waited and waited so Dominici didn't know whether I was going to beat the fullback on the inside, then I threw a pass out as far in front of Leon as I could. He ran onto it, somehow caught it and I hit the deck and rolled over in time to see him dive into the corner.

We were ahead by two points but we had led twice before in the game and not managed to press home our advantage. And as Dominguez had already smashed the tournament record by kicking 30 points, from nine penalties and a drop goal, none of us were under any illusions that the game was far from won. Not unless Stimmo could convert from the right touchline. It was a hell of a kick but on his day Stimmo is a hell of a kicker. And this was his day.

He had already landed six out of seven when he struck the ball. "I knew what it meant," Stimmo told *The Daily Telegraph* later. "You put all the self-hatred through your head in case you miss before you line it up, so that if you do miss you've already been through it." But he didn't miss. As the ball sailed between the posts Graham Rowntree turned to the crowd and started playing with his ears. That is always a good sign. We led by four points and we knew we could stop them scoring a try, no matter what - even if it meant someone diving over and biting the ball - because that is our bread and butter in training sessions. We play against each other in those situations. We don't give our team mates an inch so why should we give one to a bunch of Frenchmen.

If I play club rugby forever nothing will top the feeling of euphoria that washed over me as the touch judges' flags went up. I'd played in some great games for Leicester, some big occasions, but what happened in Paris that day blew everything else out of the water completely.

The European Cup had been our obsession for almost as long as we could remember. Certainly since we had faced another French club in the 1997 final. The day is ingrained in my memory because we were humiliated by Brive in a game we had not thought we could lose. We were arrogant and complacent in equal measure. Every mention of Europe thereafter triggered nightmare images of another Frenchman running in another try.

It was as low as I have ever felt in a Leicester shirt. I remember knocking on a tapped penalty and missing a try-saving tackle which nine times out of ten I would have made. Nightmare memories. The whole game went so quickly it was just impossible to get into it. And then there was the build-up, Bob Dwyer's masterplan.

The week started with us doing different photo calls for this and for that. Basically, for any sponsor that wanted to come in on the back of the final. We went down to Cardiff, where the final was to be played, and had to do a live link from the team hotel to East Midlands TV on the Friday night all wearing caps. There was loads of joking around and pissing about. We hadn't really watched any videos of Brive during the week. We hadn't analysed them. Bob hadn't spoken about a gameplan or anything like that.

Then we got to the day of the game and Bob announced that we're going for a team walk at 10 o'clock. We'd never ever done that. We got up and walked out of our hotel in tracksuits, turned right, round the town, back down the high street where all the fans were gathering, and back into the hotel. I turned to the lads and said "What the fuck have we done that for?"

The game kicked off and the Brive boys laid into us with a ferocity that none of our players were used to, even the internationals. The whole episode was born out of arrogance. In the semi-finals we had smashed Toulouse 37-11, who had previously beaten Brive by God knows how many points. This was seen as a walk in the park. It was blatantly not. We lost 28-9, four tries to nil.

We should have been the first English side to lift the European Cup, not Bath. As it was we arrived in Paris four years later not even in a position to become the first East Midlands side to win it, thanks to Northampton's victory in 2000. Nevertheless it was a shot at redemption. The chance to erase that awful memory for the five of us who had played in the starting line-up in Cardiff that day.

The Heineken campaign had begun with question marks placed over our ability to do the business away from Welford Road. We had crashed out in the pool stages a year earlier, beaten in Perth, by Glasgow, and Paris, by Stade Francais. We had also lost at home to Leinster for the only time in a competitive match since December 1997. You could say we had everything to prove.

We started badly, losing our second game on the road at Pontypridd which meant our final trip, to French club Pau, would be a quarter-final eliminator. The game could not have come at a much worse time. For one thing we had been beaten by Harlequins in the Tetley's Bitter Cup semi-finals a week earlier. For another Johnno was suspended.

After the Quins game we'd had the riot act read to us. "Show how much this hurts" yelled Neil Back, standing in at skipper in Johnno's absence. "Go the rest of the season unbeaten." Guess what? We did precisely that, save for a solitary league loss at Gloucester when the Premiership title had already been won and our international contingent were on day-off. Sixteen games in all of which 15 were won, including two quarter-finals, two semis and two finals.

The tone was set in Pau where we produced a textbook performance in what was a very dirty game. My opposite number was Philippe Carbonneau, a player who never lets you down if you want a fight. Sure enough I wasn't disappointed. He stamped on me early on but I kept my cool, an episode which proved a microcosm of the day's proceedings. But we won at a canter, by 20-3. Us scrum-halves are a strange breed in that we seem to live for the fight. If you don't like fighting other scrum-halves you've got no chance. Remember Robert Jones and Nick Farr-Jones on the '89 Lions tour? The Wallabies certainly do. What a classic. Two scrum-halves at war.

Our quarter-final against Swansea was a joke. We expected a really hard game. After seeing them beat Stade Francais I actually thought they were live contenders to go all the way. But we just completely destroyed them 41-10. Half of them I think were thinking about playing England the following week whereas the internationals who play for Leicester concentrate on one match at a time. These Welsh guys had given up at half-time. At that stage they might as well have taken off all their cap players and chucked some youngsters on.

That left Gloucester standing between us and the final. The match was staged at Vicarage Road, the home of Saracens, but clearly not marketed by Saracens, who know a thing or two about getting bums on seats. The ground was only two-thirds full. It might have been a blessing in disguise however as we were shocking, while Gloucester played one of their best games of the season. We came pretty close to losing. Had Martin Corry not stolen the ball on our line in a maul I think we would have done.

We had been our own worst enemies. Just like at Harlequins three months earlier we had felt we were the better team but weren't prepared to put in the work to prove it. As a result nobody played outside themselves, no-one had even a half decent game except perhaps Stimmo and Lloydy. You'd have thought we had lost at the end, so quiet was our changing room. When we win an away game we normally stop off for fish and chips as a treat on the way home but there was no celebration this time, even though we had just won through to the European Cup final. We knew we had to do better, much better.

As we left the changing rooms deep in the bowels of Parc des Princes the thought was still fresh in our minds. But I also had the worry about my knee to contend with. Five days earlier I had been in pieces, unable to walk after injuring myself at Twickenham during our easy win over Bath in the Zurich Championship final; the second leg of our treble. The next day, after 12 hours of physio, I could bend my knee but medical opinion was still that I had no chance of playing.

Jamie Hamilton was told to be prepared to play and less than 24 hours before kick-off he fully expected to. He must have been gutted when I declared myself fit on the Friday night but credit to Jamie that he never showed it. He's a great club man, an awesome fella. Guys like him, Paul Gustard, Lewis Moody and Perry Freshwater are the backbone of the club. Don't look at the internationals at Leicester as the reason for the club's success, look at guys like them. They are the boys who keep the banter flying, who are always around and having a laugh.

Once the game kicked off at no stage did I think we would lose. Even when Dominguez dropped that goal two minutes from time to put them three points ahead. I didn't even bother trying to charge it down, I was so knackered. But also because I knew that we had the character to pull through. I had seen the way we had reacted when Johnno was sin-binned for punching their number eight, Christophe Juillet, soon after half-time.

Stade didn't even look like scoring a try against us. Even down to 14 men they did not really threaten our line. The rest of us lifted our performances and snuffed them out. You usually find when Leicester go down to 14 men that the remaining players step up a gear. That is often when we play our best rugby because we know we have got to move the set-pieces and rucks quickly. So while

Johnno is not the easiest person to lose we held firm.

It was a good punch. It caught Juillet right in the face. But Johnno would have been pretty sick if we'd lost the game while he was off. At least Juillet saw it coming. Johnno had not had that luxury when he had been punched from behind by Richard Pool-Jones earlier. Johnno had come round the side of a ruck and maybe accidentally stood on him. But play had continued and he had thought nothing of it. Then wallop. It's totally out of order to get whacked from behind like that, especially by someone whose only gone to play in a country because he saw a porno film and fancied Emmanuelle.

Only joking. I know *Manon des Sources* is a French classic not a top shelf flick (honest!) and Emmanuelle Beart is not THAT Emmanuelle. All the same the reason Pool-Jones gave *The Daily Express* for his move to France must still rank as the most ridiculous comment I've ever read in the Press. Even I have not surpassed that, and I've had a few contenders. He said that he knew France was the country for him after seeing this actress taking a shower in the French countryside. Here's his exact quote, though remember he had been boozing with his Cambridge University chums. "Everything was a bit hazy. But seeing her nude in such lovely countryside I knew that is where I had to go and I telephoned all the French clubs from the next day on." Amazing.

The article appeared on the day we flew to Paris out of East Midlands Airport and there was a photo of the lady in question. Most of the Leicester lads didn't read the article - they're still learning that discipline - but saw her picture, assumed she was Pool-Jones' girlfriend and were not surprised he had gone to play in Paris.

In which case they presumably thought he had had a row with her before kick-off because he was pretty wound up from the start. Backy and him were going at it hammer and tong as early as 15 minutes, though I suspect it might have been a hangover from the pre-match rumpus.

It was a showpiece occasion, the bear pit was packed and, as with a major international, the two teams had been supposed to walk out together. We waited in the tunnel underneath, me in my usual position at the back of the line because I like to turn the afterburners on for a quick burst as I hit the field. But Stade were pissing around so I just shouted "Fuck them, let's run out". We did exactly that. We then got into our usual huddle on the pitch, pulling each other tight and sucking in the atmosphere. Still no Stade. Eventually they walked out, the cretins, and started walking towards us. We broke from our huddle and, to a man, advanced on them. I was convinced it was going to go off, and I wasn't the only one. Stephen Jones, in *The Sunday Times*, wrote: "By the time David McHugh, the referee, came on shortly afterwards, he had to rush up to stop World War Three breaking out before the first whistle was even blown."

Intimidation is a big part of the game in France and we knew if we let them think they had got the upper hand, either physically or mentally, they would have taken massive encouragement. That was why we reacted. They had misjudged us badly. We are Leicester Tigers. We faced up to them, ready to tear into them if they started anything. At that moment I think they realised they had an almighty fight on their hands if they wanted to lift the cup.

The first half was like a game of chess, both sides jostling for position. Our gameplan was nothing fancy. Kick our way downfield and then steal a lineout. But their lineouts went very well and we didn't steal more than one all game. So we had to change tact. Instead of kicking away possession we kept hold of it and started to build through phases. We knew that if we went through four or five phases there would be holes. We just had to stay patient and keep our discipline. But at the turnaround we trailed 15-9, Dominguez having kicked five out of five penalties for them. He was brilliant on the day but I would say Tim Stimpson was even better.

It just makes you wonder about Stimmo. If he could get his mind right for every game he would be one of the best rugby players of all time, I honestly believe that. Physically he's got everything, but sometimes his mind seems to wander. However, when he's motivated, watch out. I recall a game against Northampton shortly after he had joined us from Newcastle. One of his relations had died the previous day but his family were keen for him to play. He went out and played like I've never seen a fullback play. Ever. He was awesome, making tries all over the place, kicking all of his goals. Just brilliant. It was a similar story against Stade Francais. He seems to pick out three or four games a season where he's simply unbelievable and then had lapses of concentration in other games which hurt his reputation.

Leon Lloyd is another with bags of talent and he too shone like a star for us. It was his try, 30 seconds after half-time following great work by Pat Howard and Geordan Murphy, which got us back in the contest. And of course it was his second score, right at the death, which won us the game. I was voted man of the match but I would have given it to Lloydy. I thought he had a brilliant game and he must build on that performance. He's has the potential to be the next Jeremy Guscott of the England team. He's only 22. Jerry didn't make his debut until he was nearly 24 and Jerry was also said to be a bit volatile when he started. At least Leon has shown he has got fire in his belly and he's prepared to put it about for the lads.

"We can wait for another time to decide whether this really was the greatest club match ever played, although, I have to confess that my initial impression, amid the tumult of a staggering occasion, is that it has to be."

That was how *The Sunday Times* described the final the following day. I wouldn't disagree. It was without doubt the ultimate club rugby occasion. International rugby is great but stadiums tend to be full of home fans, the atmosphere one-sided.

The banter between rival supporters which brings football grounds to life is missing. This time, despite the best efforts of the tournament organisers to hand Stade Francais home field advantage, the split was far more even, the atmosphere electric, quite incredible. It was as though the entire population of Leicester was there. For days afterwards there were pictures in the local Press of French fans wearing glum faces and behind them complete anarchy as Tigers fans celebrated the final whistle.

Johnno had spoken in the build-up to the game about how this occasion was personal, how for all the things some of us have been lucky enough to win with England and the Lions, this was for our city, our fans and the guys with whom we live and breathe rugby day in day out. It was unbelievable, a goal of a lifetime really.

I was very nearly overcome with emotion. I admit I shed a quick tear when I was on the podium, but that may have been because Johnno sent Backy and Darren Garforth up to lift the trophy. I wanted to lift it up. Damn those Cov boys! I can only think that Johnno had become bored with picking up trophies this year and wanted to give someone else a chance.

The other two trophies we had won - the Premiership and Championship - we could bin for all the lads cared at that particular moment. The fact we had won the Big One, meant everything. Climbing up those stairs and seeing all the alickadoos down on the pitch below cheering and clapping was so satisfying: people like Peter Tom, Bob Beeson, Peter Wheeler, David Matthews; their faces all lit up. They had been involved in the club for more than 30 years waiting for a day like this one. To a man they all had a tear in their eye.

I didn't endear myself to European Rugby Cup Ltd afterwards by taking them to task for picking Parc des Princes as a neutral venue, but somebody had to say something as it was an outrageous decision. And better I thought to say so in victory rather than defeat. We were 50 yards from Stade's home ground for goodness sake.

The game should have been played somewhere neutral, not across the road from their pitch. But it was good motivation for us to arrive at the stadium the day before the game and see their players trooping back across the road to their clubhouse for a spot of lunch. Maybe we can play the final at Filbert Street next time.

In our moment of glory I thought it might also be a good time to press my case for a new contract so mentioned to the Press that, having won everything club rugby has to offer, I was going to 'reassess' my career. I explained that it would be difficult to recharge my enthusiasm and motivation. And I mentioned that as Louise and I are both from the north and were soon to start a family, we might move back there one day.

I have known Dean Richards for a long time and the way he deals with negotiating players contracts is to play a waiting game. I just wanted to give him a nudge. Obviously I didn't have any intentions of leaving Leicester. You're not going to leave the best club in the country when you're at the top of your game. But what I did want to make sure was that I was being paid a respectable amount for what I've been giving to the club.

There have been times when I have wanted to leave the club, like everyone has at every place of employment when they've had bad days, but 19 May 2001 wasn't one of those times. I just wanted to strike while the iron was hot, to gently persuade Dean to offer me a contract sooner rather than later. I thought that if I was worth anything it had to be after that game. It was probably the only time I would ever have the upper hand. Any other time Dean would tell me to get lost.

Happily, he didn't as chants of 'Tigers, Tigers' echoed around Paris. He was too busy gasping for breath having been ridden across the pitch at the end of the game by Backy. Both were deliriously happy, as they milked the acclaim of the red, white and green hordes in the far corner of the stadium. so much so that Backy went on local radio moments later without his usual composure.

The fella said to him "Neil, it must feel great for someone of your age, coming towards the end of your career, to win a trophy like this?" Mistake. "Age doesn't fucking well come into it mate," Backy replied. The fella said: "Neil, this is actually a live interview." To which our man responded: "Well, we'll fucking end it there then, shall we?" You see, it's not always me.

I was on a high for a good week afterwards. The Lions tour was fast approaching but I did not want to let this occasion go. From the moment I grabbed the microphone on the pitch at the end to thank our army of supporters, until I packed up the car a week later to head for the Lions den, I was full of it. And I clearly wasn't alone.

The response in Leicester was unbelievable. There were at least 300 fans waiting for us at East Midlands airport on our return and thousands more at Welford Road where we paraded the trophy. Backy, having cleaned his mouth out with soap and water, wheeled the trophy through Customs on his luggage trolley. In the city there were people coming up to me in the gym, people beeping their horns in the street, stopping me at the paper shop. They weren't asking for autographs, simply wanting to say how happy they were to have been there or how amazing it was to watch it on the TV.

Whilst at Mercedes, one of the staff told me that he wasn't a rugby fan, he was a football fan, but he and his mates had all gone over to Paris and had had a blast. I asked if we had converted him to rugby. He shook his head. "Well, not quite. Not yet". I told him that if he was not converted by that game he never would be.

I popped into the Leicestershire county cricket team's dressing room a few days later, during their game with Pakistan, and they were still talking about our game. They congratulated us for putting Leicester back on the European sporting map. Former Leicester City favourite Steve Walsh said the same. He'd seen the second half on TV. Everywhere I went in the city there was enormous pride. It was all over the front and back pages of *The Leicester Mercury*.

Even hangovers don't feel as bad when you've won. It was quite hard to take in at first because I thought of the flip side. Had I given in to the pain of my knee, had I not made that break, had we not scored that try and instead lost by three points. How would we have felt? It had been an unbelievable team effort yet we were only two minutes away from losing. It makes you realise how fine the line is between success and failure.

Part two:

Diary of a Lion's Season

chapter eight

Laying The Foundations

I was dragged kicking and screaming into the Longest Season. It was mid July and there were another 364 days until the Lions were due back from Australia. The campaign stretched out before me like a never-ending road and I panicked. I wasn't ready to go again. The bumps and bruises from the previous campaign hadn't gone. My body was still creaking. My mind was troubled. I pitied myself.

I had tried to switch off, returning from South Africa with England and flying straight to Skiathos for a fortnight with Louise, my wife, Martin Corry and his fiance Tara. But the time was too short. I resented rugby, I resented Leicester for calling us back so soon but, most of all, I resented myself for having gone away for a fortnight and done nothing.

I hadn't been so idle since my Honeymoon two summers before. I wasn't at the standard of fitness I expected of myself and I was annoyed I hadn't got my body back in shape. But I needed to rest, my mind as much as my body. It was going to be a hell of a long season but we'd just come out of a hell of a long season.

I was tired, angry and bitter. I felt 'oh God, here we go again, I need to have a break'. Stan Collymore had taken a shed load of stick for claiming to be suffering from depression; 'an overpaid, underworked wuss', people said. Yet all of a sudden I knew exactly how Stan felt, or at least I thought I did.

I knew there was a lot of hard work to be done but I just couldn't motivate myself to do it. Getting back on the rugby treadmill had no appeal. Louise will testify that for the first time ever I did not want to go to the gym, I did not put any effort into my diet. It was a combination of me being unprofessional and of the unrealistic demands being placed on us. I should have said 'this is my job and I've got to do it'. But I was so worn out that had I carried on I fear I would have burnt myself into the ground.

I suffer from different forms of depression. The worst is if I get dropped. I can't sleep. I lie awake, my mind turning over and over in search of an explanation. This was different, more symptomatic of boredom. It was like 'I've got to do it but I don't really want to'. I was depressed with Leicester because they had just got rid of two of my best mates in Will Greenwood and Craig Joiner. I was turning up for training, doing my bit and then going straight back home. At that stage there was only Martin Corry and Martin Johnson left that I really talked to. I would get home, sit down, switch on the television and fall asleep.

I took it out on Louise more than anyone else and our relationship undoubtedly suffered at the time. I was short-tempered about everything. I was not a good husband, to be honest, and that is one of the things I've always tried to be. She knows when I'm annoyed because I take it out on her. She just takes it and then tries to find ways to get me out of it. But ultimately I have to realise myself what's going wrong before I listen to other people.

I get pretty stubborn at times and assume it is the fault of other people until I get a chance to think clearly for a minute. Then something twigs and I realise I am the one to blame. Louise is brilliant with me and my moods but don't get the impression she is a soft touch. If I overstep the mark she tells me. If I do something wrong she lets me know straight away. She doesn't put up with any nonsense.

As if I did not have enough mental hurdles to overcome I was also seriously pissed off with Pat Howard, who I felt was out to wind me up. Pat is an Australian international centre who had been with the club for two seasons in which we had won back-to-back Premiership titles. And when Joel Stransky, whom I really admired, moved on at the end of the second of those two seasons, Pat took over as our backs coach.

His first conversation with me in his new position was to inform me that he wanted to use me as an impact player in the coming season. He explained that he wanted to keep his young players happy because he didn't want them leaving. That set the tone for our relationship which never recovered. I was absolutely livid, informing him that perhaps he wanted to keep one of his internationals happy because it might be worse to lose an international than it would a young player.

Not long afterwards I read an article in *Rugby World* magazine in which he claimed that he was uncomfortable being a coach because he had been one of the boys the previous season. Utter bullshit. He was completely obsessed by it. At stages through the year he even referred to Leicester as 'my team'.

I would ask 'where am I playing? Can I play 10 this week?' and he would say 'I haven't decided yet'. And I was thinking, 'to be honest Pat I don't really think it's your decision'. I got the impression he was getting a power kick from it. I was all the more annoyed because the previous season I had been consulted about back play. I had far greater responsibility within the team playing 10 and I was voted Player of the Season.

To go from that position of having a really good year to turning up at training and having Pat tell me 'impact player' did my head in. I was under no illusions that I was far from the finished article, I am not that arrogant. But I did feel I had run the plays pretty well and deserved a little more respect from someone with half as many caps as me.

Being me I didn't keep my thoughts to myself. It obviously did the trick. Leicester handed the number 10 jersey to Andy Goode and stuck me at scrum-half! Now Andy is a good player but I have always believed you should earn your place in the first team. At other clubs I have seen players who have had to serve almost an apprenticeship for a year or so and then they get their chance and take it and keep going. I didn't feel Andy was ready to go into the team in the position in which I wanted to play. I thought I was better than him - as did my colleagues, who had never before paid me such compliments.

Better than him as a 10 maybe was right, better than him for the team, perhaps not. But I did not see that. I thought I was the better 10 and I was convinced the team would be better off with me at fly-half. The forwards, however, wanted me to play scrum-half and they transferred that to Dean's thought process. I argued with Dean quite a lot. His theory was that it was better for the team to have a player with a big boot at 10 who could get us into positions from where the forwards could win us the game. He said that I was of more use to the team controlling the pack. I disagreed. He told me to lump it as only he can, with a grin and a shrug of those Honey Monster shoulders. We promptly did the treble.

Experience has taught me that you can never issue ultimatums to Dean Richards, or tell him you've just played 10 for England (as I had in the first Test against South Africa only weeks earlier) and expect him to be impressed. He just says 'so what? what does that count for? You're playing for Leicester now'. I learned very quickly not to call the odds to him. I remember three years ago, just after Bob Dwyer had gone, thinking life would be a cakewalk with Dean in charge. I thought I would be on Easy Street. One sentence from Dean changed all that. "You're on the bench, you missed a tackle last week."

Thanks to Pat and the number nine shirt in my kitbag I went into the season thinking 'I'm shit and unfit'. My morale was in a tailspin. I wasn't interested in playing at all. I'd turn up, pass the ball, go home. I went through a long period where I really couldn't care less about playing for Leicester. I was pretty keen to leave.

Neil Back and I had decided to carry our pre-season training through to the start of October and consequently I was nowhere near the physical condition I should have been for the first few games. I was doing weights on Friday afternoons, thus pretty tired during games. I had basically a five-day training programme which the club knew about but didn't like. They would say things like 'you're not allowed to train tomorrow' and I would go off and do it just the same.

But a funny thing happened on the very first day of the season. From the depths of despondency I stumbled upon inspiration. As so often in sport, one man's joy was another's misfortune. Andy Goode suffered a broken leg in our Premiership match against Wasps at Loftus Road. All that arguing and stress and within minutes of the new season kicking off I was back at fly-half. Better still I scored two tries, the last of which came with the final move of the match, deep in stoppage time, to nick us victory. All that pre-season depression was washed away on a tide of adrenaline.

It was not all rosy, however. I had aggravated a hamstring and I had a long-standing problem with one of my ankles which forced me to play with a silicone pad in my boot. I knew that my Achilles was bad and I was petrified of it rupturing, especially when Thomas Castaignede did his in the warm-up before France took on Australia in November.

I was taking suppositories (massive pain killers) to play every week and was constantly asking the physio to check it. I probably should have rested but I had to carry on because of the way my contract was structured, with most of my income dependant on appearances. With hindsight it was a mistake as it put too much pressure on me to play when I wasn't right. But in the previous three years I had been lucky with injuries. I had hardly missed any games for Leicester.

I was playing well but injury concern was becoming an ever larger distraction. I couldn't accelerate flat out because of my Achilles, I was afraid to do so in case the hamstring went. Looking back, it was probably my ankle which brought on the depression in the first place. I thought, 'I've got this injury, I've got to train, I've got to play, so how am I going to get rid of it'? It was a vicious circle. On top of that were the financial pressures, which hardly helped. Match fees amounted to 30% of my salary. I needed to crash out for a week or two. Little did I know I was about to do literally that.

I'd been playing golf with David Lieping from the Mercedes garage in Leicester who had given me a brand new CLK 320 to drive for the season. I'd only had it three days. Driving back from the course I stopped at a roundabout and all of a sudden I heard brakes screeching. My immediate thought was that was somebody was going to shoot out onto the roundabout, where is he? I looked into my mirror just as I got absolutely smashed from behind.

I had heard about whiplash before but never thought it was serious. I think differently now. At first I was fine, mellow even because I know accidents do happen. I went to the police to report what had occurred and took a cab home. The next day, 24 hours before our first Heineken Cup game against the French club Pau, I was on the slab unable to move.

Turning up at Welford Road on the Saturday everyone thought I was pissing about. But I went out onto the pitch at halftime to do an interview and I could not turn round. The car was battered and my body was battered. Yet the crash actually did me a favour as it gave me three weeks to get myself fixed up. By the time I returned my neck was fine, my hamstring was healed and I was raring to go.

I am not a good spectator but was reasonably content to watch us beat Pau and Glasgow because I knew I wasn't right. That feeling changed dramatically the following week when Leicester went down to Pontypridd on a Friday night and were beaten 18 - 11. As I sat in the stands, powerless to help the boys, I took a load of stick from a section of the crowd around me who seemed to never tire of telling me that 'Leicester are crap'.

Suddenly something triggered inside of me that I was ready to play again. "Let's see what the score is next week when I'm playing," I yelled. Maybe that was an arrogant statement but I knew we had a better team and I was fed up with these people rubbishing us. The pressure was now on to prove my fitness but my masseur Julie Hayton and physio Craig Mortimer did a cracking job getting me right. The daily combination of two hours massage followed by half an hour in an ice bath at home did the trick. I scored the winning try and a drop goal as we beat Pontypridd 27-19.

Two months in and my season was already resembling a rollercoaster ride. Little did I know how many ups and downs were yet to come before the journey ended at Heathrow Airport in late July of the following year. For the time being I was content that while my relationship with the Leicester management was far from perfect, I was playing well and the international season was just around the corner. The world champions, Australia, were coming to Twickenham.

I always had in the back of my mind the thought that Clive Woodward did not care how well I played for Leicester as long as I did not let England down. And because I'd played pretty well against South Africa in the summer I took it for granted that I'd get picked against the Wallabies. That was the start of the next downwards spiral.

I'd had a good tour, Clive had been happy with me and the other coaches had given me good feedback. I felt I'd answered the nagging doubts about whether I could cut it against the very best. It said as much in my end-of-tour report. Mine was very positive. So what was there to worry about? So I marked time until the next game, rather than really driving myself on and asking the coaches for more work.

The great thing with Clive's England set-up is that you can phone these guys up in the week and they will come to your house. They will do video analysis with you. They will take you out on the pitch and train you. I didn't take advantage. I didn't ask Dave Alred to help me with my kicking, I didn't seek extra defensive work from Phil Larder. I just sat back and let it happen. Maybe I was tired, maybe I was complacent...

I don't know exactly when they reached the decision that I should be dropped, but I assumed they had decided to go for size and power on the wings ahead of what I offered. In actual fact Clive thought I'd make a bigger impact against the Wallabies if I came on later when the game had opened up a bit and there was more space. He would be proved right. There would indeed be no space for the first hour.

The dastardly deed was done at Pennyhill Park, the team hotel in Bagshot, on the Monday of Test week. Everyone was assembling outside the meeting room when I got the nod from Clive. As soon as you get that you know you are not in the team. It means he wants a word with you in private and that in turn can mean only one thing. On the Monday of Test week everyone keeps their head down to avoid any contact. I made the mistake of looking up. Clive got straight to the point. "I've decided to..." I finished the sentence: "Leave me out of the team".

He explained his strategy, saying that he was looking to use me off the bench to utilise the space and pick up the tempo of the game. It made sense to a rational mind but my head was spinning. It had come as a complete bolt from the blue, because I'd geared myself mentally to being picked. I was so confident of being picked. I had never considered the alternative.

That is why I made that statement about being the 'fittest, fastest, strongest player, the best back in the country'. I had convinced myself that I was exactly that. It sounds incredibly arrogant but that was my way of building up my self-confidence. Even after Clive's thunderbolt I clung onto that belief as I stewed in self-pity, staying away from the team room and instead ordering a club sandwich and chips alone in my room.

If I was looking for sympathy I had picked the wrong week as the following day came the awful news that Ben Cohen's father, Peter, had died. In an instant my so-called problems dissolved into nothing. I had lost my place in a rugby team. Ben had lost his dad.

I was struck dumb by the news. I felt desperately for Ben and his family. I had just left him upstairs standing in front of the cameras with a smile on his face like a Cheshire Cat. It was his day. Having been dropped in South Africa and been forced to confront his demons for the first time as an England player, he was back in the side. Of course he was still deeply concerned for his dad, who had been in a coma since being attacked outside a nightclub in Northampton a month earlier. But Pete was on the mend. Ben had been to see him the previous night and told him about his England recall. He had been so proud.

The last thing on my mind was that Ben might withdraw and I would get my shirt back. So what? My immediate thought was 'I hope Ben wants to play. I hope he can get through this'. Had it been me I think I would have wanted to.

It would be wrong to say I knew how Ben was feeling but I had had a similar experience a couple of years earlier when my Grandad 'Silver' Sid died on the morning we played Northampton. I was very close to him and I was very upset. I knew he had not been well. I had been to visit him in hospital and spent a while there. He looked terrible and I feared the worst. But I went home and everything seemed okay. Then out of the blue Dad phoned on the Saturday morning and said 'I've got some bad news for you, Grandad died last night'. He started crying down the phone and I too welled up. But then Dad said, 'Enough of this. Go and score some tries for him'.

Clive was brilliant with Ben. He took him to one side and broke the news in the best way he could. He arranged for him to go home and told him not to worry at all about England. That if he felt up to playing the shirt would be waiting for him. As soon as Ben left we had a team meeting at which Clive told me to be ready to play just in case.

That was a really weird position to be in. Of course I wanted to play but at that stage I wanted Ben to play more. Playing for England is a massive honour, but there are certain things that are more important even than playing for your country. That was certainly how Ben saw it. He withdrew from the team on the Thursday night.

I would not see him until he came into the changing room after the game and each of us gave him a hug. But I had wanted him to turn up as late as Friday and say he was playing. He would have done so with my best wishes. But by Friday night I was a definite starter and I had to set about building myself up to prove Clive wrong for dropping me in the first place. For half of the match I felt I was on course.

I had put a good hit on Chris Latham, the Wallabies fullback, and when he ran the same line soon after half-time I was confident of nailing him again. But this time he was a decoy runner. Instead of locking onto the ball he left the pass to Joe Roff. I was slightly out of position, went for Roff and went too early. He brushed me off and went on to create a great try.

It got worse. Matt Perry was injured five minutes later and I dropped back to cover at fullback because he was down. Roff broke through again down my wing where I would have been. I set myself to hammer him but he stepped me again and I completely missed him. Again it was bad technique, but it was my own fault for trying to kill him rather than just tackle him.

Twickenham is a big place but you know exactly where the coaches are sat and when you miss a tackle it feels like the other

75,000 witnesses have gone, leaving the stares of Clive, Andy Robinson, Brian Ashton and Phil Larder burning a hole in your back. You hope against hope that they have not seen it - perhaps nipped to the loo or been talking amongst themselves. You hope the TV has missed it too. I particularly hoped they had not seen that I was growling as I threw myself at Roff.

Mike Catt ripped into me for not being in the line on the outside. I retorted that I had dropped back for Pezza and he shot me one of his looks. I lost it and told him to sod off. A few minutes later I was subbed for blood, Iain Balshaw came on and set up the winning try for Dan Luger. I was watching on the monitor in the stitches room and I thought, 'You jammy bugger, Luger. You're made for the rest of the season'. I saw him later that night and the look on his face said as much. My expression told a different story. A tale of misery, of despondency. It was the look of a man who knew he would not be playing for England against Argentina the following week. First and foremost I'd had a shocker, secondly Ben would be back.

There is no escape when you have had a bad game for England. There is protocol to be observed, formalities to be attended to. So there I was in the post-match function with my parents and Louise wishing I was anywhere else. I was in an absolutely foul mood. People were asking me for my autograph and I was obliging without so much as acknowledging their presence. My Dad tried to talk to me and I told him to leave me alone.

Taking things out on my family before I take them out on other people or myself is a really bad side of my character and one I wish I could eradicate. They are my biggest supporters but occasionally, if I've performed below my own expectations, I abuse their devotion by firing cheap shots at them. I hate myself for it.

I was in a particularly foul mood as I went back to the hotel with the team; snappy, extra sarcastic, a pain in the arse generally. Fortunately Johnno decided that we deserved a treat for having beaten Australia. So he ordered 42 portions of fish, chips and mushy peas from the local chippie and he made me go down to collect them with him. The hotel were brilliant about it. We arrived back with two big boxes and they supplied the bread and butter. We sat in the team room watching *Match of the Day*, eating fish and chips and knocking back beers. It was quite a scene considering we had just beaten the world champions.

It was not until Wednesday of the next week, after the strike had come and gone, that I knew for sure I'd been dropped. I had an inkling because during the strike almost every player had a threatening phone call except me. You didn't have to be Einstein to work it out. Clive broke the news to me and I took it reasonably well as I had half expected it. It was only then that the bombshell dropped.

"What positions am I covering?"

"None. You're not on the bench either,"

The words hit me like a hail of bullets. I was out of the squad for the first time in goodness knows how long. Apart from the time I had spent under suspension in 1999, I couldn't remember being on the outside. What the hell was I going to do?

Clive said he wanted me to stay around and train all week but Leicester had a match against Harlequins on the Friday night in which I said I was keen to play. Clive agreed and so I phoned Dean. He had already picked the side with Andy Goode at 10 but Goodey agreed to step down which was really nice of him. I borrowed Backy's car to get home and shot up the M1 with my mind a blur. Since being initially dropped for Australia I hadn't been sleeping at all well. I couldn't. I was having to put loads of lavender on my pillow. My mind was full of the same question. Why? Why? Why?

I knew all the coaches would be at Quins on the eve of the Twickenham international and I was determined to have a really good defensive game. But my luck was out. Early on I was kicked on my bad Achilles and I couldn't run. My tackling was sound but I couldn't spring, make breaks or kick because it was my standing foot. Dean, who is a top man when the chips are down, did the decent thing by not taking me off. He knew what I was going through. He knew how that would have looked. He moved me out to the wing.

The next day England beat the Pumas 19-0. It was not a classic by any means. When Martin Johnson gets the best attacking player award you've got to figure something has gone wrong. I was not wholly displeased that it hadn't gone particularly well, although I was pleased that the crowd hadn't booed the players onto the pitch as *The Sun's* John Sadler had stupidly recommended in his column.

I was at the game doing some corporate work and decided to show my face at the after-match function. Andy Robinson's wife, Sam, saw me and asked whether I wanted to have a go at him. Robbo looked at me in expectation of getting a gob full of abuse. "It's alright thanks Sam," I said. "It's not his fault, it's mine. I'll sort it out." I think that took Robbo aback. I really don't think he expected to hear me to take responsibility for the situation. But I'd had a little time to think. Mind you I'd also had eight double brandy and gingers.

By the time I rejoined the England squad at Pennyhill Park on the Sunday night, to start preparing for the final fixture of the Autumn series against South Africa, I'd got all the bitterness out of my system. I'd not been able to get a straight thought process for a week, which was why I could not get to sleep, but the Saturday night spent drinking myself into oblivion had done the trick. I would look at fitness first to get back in. Improve that, I told myself, and everything would be alright.

Twenty four hours later I was back in the doldrums. Clive had told me I was not involved again.

I sat quietly through the media team announcement with a face like a smacked backside, chuntering to myself and generally wondering what the hell I was doing with my life. Peter Jackson of *The Daily Mail* just happened to catch me off guard and I unloaded both barrels. "I am angry and confused," I told him. "I was pretty angry at being left out last week but that was a good opportunity to give others a chance. Against South Africa you have to pick your best 22 and not being in it makes me angry.

"If I was playing like an idiot and if the other players were better I could understand it, but neither is the case. I'm not playing like an idiot and the other players are not better.

"I don't really know what more I can do. I'm still the fittest, strongest, quickest back in the squad because the results prove that, so I can't very well train any harder. Nor do I think it's possible for me to make any more sacrifices. Have I done something wrong? Have I said something to upset someone?"

The rest of the lads read it the next morning and banter was flying. I don't think any of the coaches were very happy at what I'd said. To be honest, after I read it nor was I. But at the time it was what I was thinking and they all know I'm quite emotional and I tend to go off the top board.

I don't think the coaches would ever take a player to one side and lecture them. They put the onus on us to sort ourselves out. If you do that you earn greater respect. Clive says a lot of things off the cuff to players in team meetings purely to get a response, so that subconsciously you look at yourself and work on your game. The squad might wonder why he has said what he has but the individual almost always knows.

Anyway, the day the article appeared I sensed the coaches were looking to me for my next reaction. When I said I'd stay for the week and train I think they realised I had turned the corner. I trained hard and was fully supportive of the other lads. Then at last a break. Mike Catt was injured and doubtful for the game with a popped rib cartilage.

His fitness test involved having to run and tackle Martin Corry ten times. I sneaked down to the pitch and watched from behind the trees, as I didn't want to give the impression that I wanted him to fail. Catty crumpled on the first tackle, Will Greenwood was immediately called into the team and I found myself back in the 22. I've never felt so good about being on the bench.

England beat South Africa 25-17, Will scored a great try and then had the decency to cramp up, allowing me the last five minutes. It was not long but just enough for me to make a tackle on Japie Mulder and to come away knowing that I was back on track. My attitude was better and I was being more honest with myself instead of living out a kind of fantasy in my mind that I'm the best player in England, the best back, blah, blah, blah. It took fifty units of alcohol to kill off that fantasy. It was well worth the hangover.

chapter nine

Back in Favour

Sport has a nasty habit of knocking you down just when you think you have cracked it. Dan Luger was 'the man' after scoring the try which beat the world champions in November. Against Australia that day his season was made. Mine was in ruins. Or so I thought.

By the end of the season I'd be forced to revise my assessment. Injury would mug Dan's ambitions both with England and the Lions to the point that he would manage only seven minutes' game time in the Six Nations Championship - having missed the previous year's tournament in its entirety - and two warm-up games for the British Isles in Oz.

At the start of February he was not to know this and neither was I. He remained in pole position while I sat idly in the pits like a spare car at a grand prix. I had at least heard whispers that I was coming back into contention for a wing slot because the coaches had not been satisfied with the way the attack had been going.

You can end up getting hurt if you place your faith in the rumour mill, yet I was feeling a lot more positive about my opportunities and chances to play in the Six Nations, because I felt that while size was a major factor in selection against the southern hemisphere teams, skill was going to be of greater premium against Six Nations opposition. Sure enough, I was called onto the bench for our opener in Wales. I was back in on merit and I was confident of getting a run. But the eighth minute was certainly sooner than I expected.

Over the autumn I had undergone a change in attitude. I was now willing to listen and willing to learn. I no longer thought I knew best. I had fully come to terms with the fact that my inadequacies were actually down to me and not the coaches, helped by the constant reminders of Phil Larder, our minister of defence.

I lost count of the number of times Phil played back my missed tackle on Joe Roff for the benefit of the entire squad, as if he revelled in my humiliation. Whenever an Australia shirt appeared on tape I knew my embarrassment was just around the corner. I felt he overdid it, but Phil likes to beat things into you like that. The fact that my defence against Wales was sharp I suppose justified his approach, though it pains me to say it.

The build-up to the game was bizarre. Before we journeyed down the M4 Ben Cohen revealed that he had received death threats from some Welsh idiot and then when we got to the Principality we found the entire Wales team waiting to confront us in the away changing room at the Millennium Stadium.

People who hide behind anonymity are pathetic. If people want to make threats why don't they make them to your face, then see what happens? If somebody wants to send me a letter give me your address and I'll send you one back. Ben is a young lad who had just lost his father. Whatever nutter sent him those letters is a sick coward. At the end of the day it wasn't important to him, after what he had just been through. He had also had his flat burgled. But it was a worry he could have done without.

Clive put his mind at rest by telling him that he too received hate mail from Wales. "I've had letters where all the bits and pieces are stuck together," he told *The Mirror*. "Where people have cut letters out of newspaper headlines rather than use their own handwriting. It's like something out of a film. There are some very strange people out there."

Security in Cardiff was higher up the agenda as a result of the episode yet it failed to bar the reception committee awaiting us in the bowels of the Millennium Stadium when we arrived the day before the match for a look around. Standing growling at us were the Welsh team - life-size cardboard cut-outs of each and every one of them. Maybe it was designed to psyche us out. Certainly the excuse made by one of the stadium staff that they had been left there by accident did not add up. It was only when Matt Dawson started karate-kicking them in the head that Mr Jobsworth went ballistic and agreed to remove them.

The match itself was a triumph for my old mate Will Greenwood, who became the first Englishman in more than a century to score a hat-trick of tries in Cardiff (I'm told the last was Howard Marshall in 1893). A more interesting statistic, I feel, is that he became the second Englishman to score a hat-trick of tries in the Six Nations Championship. Behind me.

To be fair it was a great performance and I was chuffed for him after the year he had spent out in the cold with both Leicester and England. Will thanked his 'lucky' bleached hair, which just goes to show how much of his rugby is played in his mind. A lot of people reckon that rugby at the top level is 50% physical, 50% mental. Looking at Will, it's hard to disagree.

In Dan Luger's case, the problems on that day were 100% physical. He took a bang on his neck and his championship was over. Out of the blue I was given a chance to re-establish myself in the side. We won 44-15, England's highest score and greatest winning margin in Cardiff, and I felt I played my part.

It had been a good day. Thomas Castaignede and Ieuan Evans both went into print to say that they had just watched the best team in the world in action, and it was not Wales. Ieuan described our performance as "frightening at times", whilst Thomas went as far as to say: "I think if a World Cup was played now they (England) would win it." Even Graham Henry, the Wales coach bound for bigger if only marginally better things with the Lions, admitted: "That was as good a performance from a European team as I have seen for a long time." Satisfied with life, I returned to the changing room feeling I was part of the team again.

There is no longer an intimidation factor playing in Cardiff - if anything the magnificent Millennium Stadium helps us as it is such an exciting place to play - but there certainly was on the team coach back from the post-match dinner later that evening. We were heading down one of the main streets when the coach became surrounded by a couple of hundred drunken Welshmen chucking donor kebabs and abuse at the windows. It was shocking really.

As a squad we were not going to be intimidated and we stood up and yelled back at them, beckoning them towards us. That is when it really kicked off. Some of the mob began to head-butt the coach and hurl bottles and cans, and then the coach knocked one of them over. Thankfully we were only doing about 10mph, because we had no police escort and we were seriously surrounded, when the wing mirror caught one of them in the head. He was so pissed that he had walked straight out in front of the bus.

Immediately we hit the brakes and Clive and team doctor Terry Crystal got off to have a look at him. They found a bloke so drunk that he was oblivious to what had happened. He would have a headache in the morning, but he would have had one anyway.

Clive wanted to know he was okay but got a gob full of abuse for his troubles. "Get out of our country", the usual garbage. Clive's assistant, Nathan Martin, is a former Royal Marine (a body of men whose dedication, organisation and honesty have inspired me since my visits to their Lympstone base with the England squad) and he and the rest of us were on the steps of the bus ready to pile in when all of a sudden three police vans screeched round the corner, a load of coppers jumped out and the confrontation was fairly quickly diffused.

Back at the hotel we jumped off the bus and someone suggested we go out for a drink. I laughed, bearing in mind there was what appeared to be a full scale riot going on in the middle of town.

By comparison, Italy at Twickenham was a mild-mannered affair. For the first time since the previous summer in South Africa I was selected for the starting line-up, with Jason Robinson called up to make his debut in the matchday squad.

Jason has got bags and bags of natural talent and when he switched codes the previous autumn, joining Sale Sharks from Wigan, there was little doubt in any of our minds that he would be fast-tracked into the England set-up. Nonetheless there was some surprise at the speed with which Clive had chosen to integrate him.

But I didn't see him as a threat, confident that there were things in rugby union I could do that he could not. Sadly making the Lions' Test team wasn't one of them! But at that time he could not possibly understand the game thoroughly as he was still new to it. And I say that with the greatest of respect to him.

Clive handed him his first cap all the same, four months after he had crossed rugby's great divide, with 35 minutes left on the clock. But to be fair he looked a bit lost. Much was made of him not receiving a single pass, let alone scoring a try against a tiring Italian side, and various conspiracy theories were put forward. But there was no anti-League snub, no resentment at the speed with which he had been capped. It was purely and simply that things didn't go his way.

In rugby league, wingers tend to stay quite wide and come in on maybe the first or second tackle to give the forwards a break. Apart from that they don't roam the pitch as much as they should do in union. On a few occasions that day I came across from the opposite wing and got inside the pass before Jase. That was not done on purpose, to abandon him out on the touchline, it was simply that I knew where the ball was going. But he's a quick learner and the following game against Scotland, just a fortnight later, he was popping up at the base of rucks and mauls and taking people on.

For the second year running we beat Italy by an emphatic scoreline; our 80-23 victory constituting the highest score and biggest winning margin in championship history. Jonny Wilkinson also made the record books for his 35-point haul and I was pleased to add two tries to my hat-trick in Rome the previous year. But there was still work to be done as for the second year running Italy had enjoyed the better of the first quarter before our fitness and structure told.

It did us no harm that our next opponents were Scotland because we owed them one from a year earlier when we had blown up at Murrayfield and lost another Grand Slam chance, and all of us were well up for the game. But there was no guarantee the fixture would even be played due to the outbreak of Foot and Mouth disease which was sending shockwaves throughout the countryside.

Ireland, who had won their opening two games against Italy and France to emerge as our main rivals for championship honours, had postponed their trip to Wales on the advice of their government, who argued that going ahead with the game would increase the risk of the disease being spread from the UK across the Irish Sea.

The Rugby Football Union monitored the Irish situation carefully and sounded out the Ministry of Agriculture, Farms and Fisheries (MAFF) before deciding that England should proceed with their campaign against Scotland. Thank God, because we were ready for payback time. Moreover, Catty, Will and Iain Balshaw all had points to prove after coming in for criticism from former Scotland captain Finlay Calder in the build-up. Those three were outstanding, Scotland didn't manage a try and were sent home tae think about a record 43-3 hammering.

As a consequence of the Dublin postponement we had a month off Six Nations duty waiting for France to come to Twickenham in April. The spirit in the camp remained buoyant, even if the uncertainty caused by Foot and Mouth allied to threats from club owners not to release players for rearranged internationals if they clashed with the end-of-season play-offs, caused a bit of concern.

But we remained focused, assembling for an extra couple of days training with England in the gap week. Then some of the boys headed out to Spain on a training camp with England fitness advisor Dave Reddin while the Leicester contingent went off to Portugal. These were not holidays, rather an attempt to maintain our focus and our momentum. Having blown two Grand Slams in as many years we did not want to risk wasting another great campaign. Ian Jones, the former All Blacks lock playing for Gloucester, had said before the championship kicked off that England must win the Grand Slam to be taken seriously in the southern hemisphere, and he was right.

Nevertheless when the time to play France finally arrived, we struggled to get back in the groove. We had played mind games in the build-up, mentally rehearsing the playing of the game with the aim of developing our concentration. The idea eventually is that we should be able to visualise and play a whole game perfectly in our minds.

We obviously still have some way to go with that one because for 40 minutes against France we were pretty dire while they reproduced some of the dazzling stuff which had accounted for New Zealand on the same pitch in the semi-finals of the World Cup. Fair play to them, they really gave it a go early on. They played very wide, very quick and we didn't handle it particularly well. I think everyone in the team missed a tackle in the first half, which is almost unheard of.

I think there is a confidence in the team now that we can overcome whatever is thrown at us. The lads go into a game convinced that we are not going to lose. It is just a question of how we are going to win. That is what it feels like at least. People may call it arrogance, I don't think it is. It is just a confidence that everything behind the scenes is right.

All the coaching is sorted out, every fine detail is looked at.

Nothing is left to chance or overlooked. And when you get to the games you know you have got this armoury of moves or structures or patterns that we can flexibly adapt to. We had all this stuff two seasons ago but we were not able to switch it between one game and another. Now people are so rehearsed in it that we can change at the flick of a switch.

Sure enough, when we came out after half-time we were a completely different side and we destroyed them. Jonny Wilkinson kicked 18 points to overtake Rob Andrew and become England's leading points scorer (407 in 27 appearances). And I was well pleased to have executed an overhead kick which put Mike Catt in for a try under the sticks. Geordan Murphy had tried it for Leicester in a Heineken Cup game against Swansea but it had not come off. Mine did and we won 48-19. A record victory for the fixture, as it had been against Wales, Italy and Scotland.

With the Ireland match rearranged for October, there was a strange feeling in the camp. According to the calendar France were our last opponents. The championship should have been over. As we were unbeaten we should have had the Grand Slam, the Six Nations Trophy and the Triple Crown safely under lock and key. We had none of them. Beating France had instead felt like winning a middle game in the championship.

I was back in the team but I hadn't been particularly overjoyed with my performances in the Six Nations, save for my second half against France. I thought I could have given a little bit more. I'd done just enough to stay in. For me to stay in next year I'm going to have to do a little bit extra. Make sure my defence is better, improve my ball carrying, make more breaks, be stronger and quicker.

The main lesson I took from the campaign is that if I leave a pitch breathing I have not played particularly well. If I leave the pitch and it takes me 10-15 minutes to get my breath back then I can say I've done alright. I was shagged after the French game. I had 18 ball carries in the second half and about 14 offloads. I think I did alright.

The problem I'd had with Leicester all season, besides my non-relationship with Pat Howard, was that I was also not speaking to Andy Goode. We'd had a fight earlier on in the season and I'd had enough of what I perceived to be his misplaced arrogance. He would say things to me in training like 'You just concentrate on making sure you get the ball in my hands'. And he was doing it quite cleverly so that no-one else could hear. Whereas I was just telling him to shut up in front of everyone. So I got it in the neck for having a go at him.

Our scrap had occurred in training back in August and it ended with him needing hospital treatment. It was just a flare-up, there are loads of those in training at Leicester every week. He was trying to strangle me to get the ball off me. My arms were trapped and I couldn't get his arm off. So I punched him in the face. That did it. Paul Gustard came over and grabbed both my arms and Goodey, bless him, slugged me back in the face.

So that was the fly-half and the inside centre that I, the scrum-half, wasn't really talking to. I wouldn't even talk to Goodey when I was putting the ball into the scrum. I did ask Pat why they were picking him instead of me but that got me nowhere. Pat came out with all sorts of rubbish like 'I didn't take the ball to the line properly' and that 'Goodey's kicking was better than mine'. I responded by saying that my defence was better than his and that I could break down defences on one leg better than him. Pat wasn't listening.

My feud with Goodey went on until we played away at Northampton in March. We stopped off at a pub on the way back and I said 'look, it's time we buried the hatchet. Let's just get on for the sake of the team'. We would have shaken hands but we were both pissing at the time. The following week we beat Newcastle at home to clinch a hat-trick of Premiership titles.

That, too, was unsatisfactory. Unlike the Six Nations there was a trophy to collect but due to Sky television's scheduling we had to kick our heels all afternoon waiting to hear how Wasps, the only side who could catch us, had fared at Bath. We had been given a 12.15 kick-off.

You've got to admire Sky for pumping money into the sport but we should have played at the same time as the Bath-Wasps game which was live on TV. Then at least at the end of the game the 15,000 people who were at Leicester, as opposed to the 7,000 at Bath, could have enjoyed the celebrations together. Instead, only about 2,000 were left inside Welford Road when news of Wasps' defeat came through and we were presented with the hub cap, sorry the Premiership Shield.

Nonetheless it was great to win it for a third successive year and the team picture was a hoot as my Dad almost gatecrashed his way into it. Freddie Tuilagi didn't even get that close. He'd got his timings wrong, gone home to change for the presentation, and not made it back in time. Fortunately there was a lifesize cardboard cut-out of him in the club shop.

Despite our high spirits we emerged from the league campaign feeling we still had a point to prove at the end of this never-ending English season. We were through to the final of the Heineken Cup and we had won the Premiership yet the powers-that-be wanted to call the winners of the all new-look end of term play-offs the English champions.

It was a scandalous decision, made purely and simply in an attempt to inject new life into a season which had ended so early for our Premiership rivals. Initially we weren't that fussed about the Zurich Championship but when we heard that the Premiership would not decide the English champions we changed our tune.

Some of the lads suggested we boycott the Championship in protest. Even the coaches and Peter Wheeler were in favour of that at one stage. Another suggestion was that we win and then don't go up and collect the trophy. But after beating London Irish in the quarter-finals we thought we might as well do it properly. After all a treble sounds better than a double, wouldn't you say?

chapter ten

Making the Cut

The Lions is the pinnacle of your rugby career. That's what everyone has always told me. Only I didn't see it that way before my second tour of duty with the British Isles.

I make no apology for the fact that four years after first pulling on the red shirt, the famous red shirt, I had still to discover the true magic of the Lions. For me white is the colour. The white of England. As I looked ahead to Australia and the ten-match challenge stretching out before me I was no more excited or inspired than I would have been by an England tour.

Perhaps it was because I hadn't started a Test match for the Lions, but I felt a greater pride wearing the England shirt than that of the Lions. I tried to rationalise this in my mind. The fact I was able to draw more energy and more enjoyment from playing for England, and wondered if it was to do with the bitterness I felt at not making the Test starting line-up in South Africa last time around.

That might have been a contributory factor but it is probably more down to the way I feel inside. I am English first and a Lion second. When I get asked on landing cards and other forms whether my nationality is British I write English. It upsets me that the Scots, Welsh and Irish all have such passion about being who they are while England, to a certain extent, seems to have lost its own identity. Playing for England means the world to me, the Lions probably not quite as much. Close friends with whom I discussed this after returning from South Africa thought I was barking mad. But the plain fact of the matter is that while I never had ambitions to play for the Lions, I dreamt of playing for England.

For all that a wave of relief swept over me when the contract arrived from the Lions for my perusal in February. It meant little, of course, other than I had been included in the preliminary squad of 62. I would have been bitterly disappointed not to have been. But it was exciting to receive my first correspondence on 2001 Lions-headed notepaper.

There were few surprises to be fair. The media made a fair bit about the omission of Scotland captain Andy Nicol and a potential rival of mine for the scrum-half berth. But at no stage did I expect him to be in. Jason Robinson was another to miss out. Again no great surprise to my mind. Not because I didn't rate him, only that he was at a very early stage of his rugby union career and for him to have been named so soon would probably have caused more negatives than positives to the squad. I remember team manager Donal Lenihan remarking that "If we were to name him in the squad now it would put too much pressure on him. He should be allowed to go away and learn the game." Those were wise words in my opinion and I think Jason was ultimately the beneficiary of them.

Donal recognised Jason's latent rugby talent but took the pressure off him by publicly acknowledging that the tour had "possibly come a season too early for him". By also leaving the door ajar for Jason by insisting he was "not out of the reckoning" he presented him with the best of both worlds. Jason had nothing to lose and everything to gain.

Selection, at that stage, didn't really matter one way or the other. There had been plenty of players picked in the tour party in 1997 who had not featured in the longer squad; Neil Back and Tony Underwood to name but two. I don't think anyone took too much comfort from being in the 62. There was too much else going on.

Personally I was concentrating on trying to play well for Leicester in order to keep my England place, which I had just won back after being axed in the autumn. Those were my priorities. I am a great believer that good performances mean you get picked, not pieces of paper.

At the back of my mind was always the prospect of a summer in Australia and the chance to make amends for my nightmare against the Wallabies at Twickenham when playing for England the previous November. But it certainly wasn't keeping me awake at night. It was not until April, when those Six Nations matches which escaped the Foot and Mouth epidemic had been completed that thoughts turned to the Lions.

The squad announcement was due on April 13 but was pushed back ten days to allow the Irish lads who had managed only two Six Nations games, due to the Foot and Mouth restrictions placed on movement in their country, to play in a specially arranged fixture for the benefit of them and the selectors. With England business over until the autumn and Leicester well on course to complete a hat-trick of Premiership titles, Lions selection was now at the forefront of my mind. From being pretty cool about selection I was suddenly desperate to be picked; more than anything for the recognition of my performances over the season. Recognition that it hadn't been a waste of time which, at one stage, I thought it had when I was playing at scrum-half for Leicester and had been dropped by England.

For three or four nights prior to the squad announcement I dreamt about the Lions. Flashbacks to key moments in recent Lions history. David Campese gifting the series-winning try to Ieuan Evans in 1989; Jerry Guscott's try in Brisbane which had brought those Lions back into the series the previous week; the dodgy penalty award against Dean Richards which robbed the 1993 Lions of victory in Christchurch; Willie John McBride's '99' call when it cut up rough in South Africa in 1974 and, of course, Matt Dawson's lucky try against South Africa last time round. Each an episode locked in immortality.

As I lay awake at night I wondered whether I would get the chance to star in one myself. I was pretty nervous, probably more out of a fear of rejection. It did not make it any easier having been given an inkling by Andy Robinson, after England's game against France a fortnight earlier, that I was to be considered as scrum-half. Could I believe him? In this age of wind-ups and practical jokes I couldn't be sure.

The only thing I knew for certain was that Martin Johnson had been appointed captain, because I had played a mind game with him the day before the announcement and won. He walked into training smiling and I said, "I know something about you". Johnno replied, "How do you know?" I told him that a little bird had told me. "Told you what?" he countered. "You know very well," I said. He caved in. "Yeah, I got the call last night, I'm captain." I paused. "So am I vice captain then?". He laughed.

Johnno is a good mate and I was genuinely thrilled for him. He is one of the best captains of all time and I know what that honour means to him. The way he has led Leicester over the past few seasons has been nothing short of inspirational really. He has been great to play with and for, because while he is on the one hand very stern, he has also got a great sense of humour. He leads from the front but is quite flexible in the way he captains the team. What particularly impresses me is the way he takes a lot of the pressure off the younger lads. It's something he's worked on over the years. He doesn't intimidate them, they just respect him. Decision day for the rest of us followed 24 hours later and coincided with a defensive session Leicester had arranged. To be honest most things coincide with some training session or other that Leicester have arranged. We never seem to stop. I thought we would have five guys picked, perhaps six. I thought we were probably due that sort of quota the way our season had gone. We ended up with only three.

Fortunately I was one of them, along with Johnno and Neil Back, but I couldn't help feeling for Martin Corry, Dorian West and Tim Stimpson. I was gutted for Cozza, who is a great mate and who had enjoyed another great season. He has lived in the shadow of Lawrence Dallaglio in the England squad for a good few years now. But I really thought his ability to play blindside, number eight or lock would count in his favour.

Dorian had also given himself a great chance by breaking into the England side for the Six Nations, although he was concussed against Scotland at just the wrong time. Stimmo too had played awesomely at times, but had perhaps not been consistent enough. Had he got his head right throughout the entire season and been highly motivated for all games I'm sure he would have made the tour because he has got immense physical talents and is an awesome goalkicker. Without him, Leicester would not have won three consecutive Premiership crowns. I think I can say that. We certainly would not have won the Heineken Cup. In some respects I think he has been hard done by. People seem to get a downer on Stimmo and move off him. Once that happens, it's very hard to change those perceptions.

My own feelings on Lions D-Day were purely practical ones. It's quite late in the season to be told what you are doing in the summer. With England the tours are mapped out years in advance. And with squads of 40 players you usually have a fair idea whether you're going to be involved. It was not until the last week in April that I knew what the summer had in store for me. Lions in Oz rather than England in north America? But once it was decided I think I probably played some of my best rugby of the campaign. The heat was off. I could relax and let my game flow. I was on the Lions tour, my wife Louise was expecting our first child. All was right with the world.

The British & Irish Lions 2001

Meet the Cast

Neil '*Backy*' Back	*(Leicester, England)*
Iain '*Balsh*' Balshaw	*(Bath, England)*
Mike '*Catty*' Catt	*(Bath, England)*
Colin '*Charvo*' Charvis	*(Swansea, Wales)*
Ben Cohen	*(Northampton, England)*
Lawrence '*Lol*' Dallaglio	*(Wasps, England)*
Jeremy '*Dangerous Brian*' Davidson	*(Castres, Ireland)*
Mattew '*Daws*' Dawson	*(Northampton, England)*
Phil '*Phyllis*' Greening	*(Wasps, England)*
Will '*Shaggy*' Greenwood'	*(Harlequins, England)*
Danny '*Grewy*' Grewcock	*(Bath, England)*
Austin '*Oz*' Healey	*(Leicester, England)*
Rob '*Hendo*' Henderson	*(Wasps, Ireland)*
Richard '*Hilly*' Hill	*(Saracens, England)*
Rob '*Howlers*' Howley	*(Cardiff, Wales)*
Dafydd '*Daf*' James	*(Llanelli, Wales)*
Neil '*Jenks*' Jenkins	*(Cardiff, Wales)*
Martin '*Johnno*' Johnson	*(Leicester, England, Capt)*
Jason '*Leopard*' Leonard	*(Harlequins, England)*
Dan '*Luges*' Luger	*(Saracens, England)*

Robin McBryde	*(Llanelli, Wales)*
Darren '*DM*' Morris	*(Swanasea, Wales)*
Scott Murray	*(Saracens, Scotland)*
Brian O'Driscoll	*(Blackrock College, Ireland)*
Ronan '*Rog*' O'Gara	*(Cork Constitution, Ireland)*
Malcolm O'Kelly	*(St Mary's College, Ireland)*
Matthew '*Pezza*' Perry	*(Bath, England)*
Scott '*Scotty*' Quinell	*(Llanelli, Wales)*
Jason '*Jase*' Robinson	*(Sale, England)*
Tom Smith	*(Brive, Scotland)*
Mark '*Tayles*' Taylor	*(Swansea, Wales)*
Simon Taylor	*(Edinburgh, Scotland)*
Phil '*Vicks*' Vickery	*(Gloucester, England)*
Jonny Wilkinson	*(Newcastle, England)*
Martyn '*Nugget*' Williams	*(Cardiff, Wales)*
Keith '*Woody*' Wood	*(Harlequins, Ireland)*
David '*Dai*' Young	*(Cardiff, Wales)*

The Replacements

Gordon Bulloch	*(Glasgow, Scotland)*
Martin '*Cozza*' Corry	*(Leicester, England)*
Scott '*Gibbsy*' Gibbs	*(Swansea, Wales)*
Tyrone Howe	*(Dungannon, Ireland)*
David '*Wally*' Wallace	*(Garryowen, Ireland)*
Dorian '*Nobby*' West	*(Leicester, England)*

The Management

Graham '*Emperor Ming*' Henry	Head Coach
Donal Lenihan	Team Manager
Andy '*Robbo*' Robinson	Assistant Coach
Phil Larder	Defensive Coach
Dave Alred	Kicking Coach
Steve '*Blackie*' Black	Conditioning Coach
James '*Doc*' Robson	Doctor
Mark '*Carcass*' Davies	Physiotherapist
Richard Wegrzck	Masseur
Alun Carter	Video Analyst
Joan Moore	Admin assistant
Pat O'Keefe	BaggageMaster
Alex Broun	Media Liasion Officer
Anton Toia	ARU Liasion Officer

chapter eleven

Coming Together

Week One, Saturday May 26 - Friday June 1

I suppose it all began for real in leafy Hampshire. Tylney Hall, an 18th century mansion house turned hospital turned school turned pricey hotel. Lovely place for a blind date. And meeting up with the 2001 Lions for the first time was a bit like that. I knew the England lads, of course, and those Celts I'd toured with in 1997. But I didn't know the boss.

I still remember the day I heard Graham Henry had been appointed to coach the British and Irish Lions. I also recall the reaction of virtually the entire England squad. We were on tour in South Africa, having breakfast by the pool at our plush hotel in Johannesburg, when the news reached us. I think the word 'disbelief' pretty well sums up the reaction around the table.

After all, England had won the Six Nations Championship and we were on our way to a share of a Test series against the Springboks. For the first time in years a European side was causing the Big Three of Australia, New Zealand and South Africa to sit up and take note. And the reason for that was Clive Woodward, for my money the best visionary in northern hemisphere rugby. From a perspective of how to play the game and how to create a professional environment in which to bring the best out of the talent at his disposal, I believe he's world class. Oh, and he's also British and a former Lion.

And yet amazingly he was not even approached for the job which instead went to a New Zealander. I thought he was the best man for the job but the Lions committee didn't even talk to him. John Jeffrey, a former Scottish Lion, was quoted in the Press as saying that Henry's appointment "makes us the laughing stock of world rugby". The only possible explanation I could find for the decision was that what Clive is achieving with England is a long-term project. The Lions is not. It is a goal which has to be achieved in little over six weeks. Different discipline, different man. We'd see.

Let me be clear. I had no problem whatsoever with Henry, personally speaking, at the outset. I found him to be a top bloke, a really nice fella. But he is not British and I know how I would feel if I was asked to coach the All Blacks. I know, because I was asked to play for another country before I was selected to the England squad. My Grandad, Silver Sid, was Irish, born in Cork. Word got out. When Ireland approached me I was flattered by their interest but I took my decision based on one question which I asked myself. Could I sit in an Irish changing room before an Ireland-England international and say 'let's smash these English bastards?' The simple answer was no, I couldn't.

So I thought of Henry. He's not from the northern hemisphere, he's not British by blood, he's certainly not in the same kind of bracket as Clive, Ian McGeechan and Jim Telfer. Cut those guys in two and I suspect, like a stick of Blackpool rock, you would find British Isles written right through them. In Graham's case, a Kiwi would fly out. For people like myself and Keith Wood, our rugby stems from passion. I was concerned with that passion being stifled by a Kiwi, albeit one who proclaimed, "Every New Zealander wants to stuff the Australians big time."

My concerns ran deeper than his nationality. From an early stage I didn't believe in the way he coached us. I'm more about space and expression, like Brian Ashton, England's backs coach, who encourages you to play what you see. Henry is big on structure. A lot of his philosophy is based around targets. Attacking people rather than attacking space. I wanted to see him expand us. At this stage I couldn't tell him he was wrong because on such a short tour the end result justifies the means and I thought we'd win no matter what. But it did worry me that if it did all go pear-shaped. Henry could move on as a Kiwi whereas we as players would forever live with the consequences of letting down our countries.

I travelled south from Leicester with Johnno and Backy, Johnno doing the driving. We chatted about general things, rather than the Lions in particular. To be honest we were all a bit tired. Since the announcement of the squad I'd hardly had time to draw breath. Leicester had played right up to the previous Saturday, seven days earlier, and as that game was the Heineken Cup final we took a few days to come back down to earth. People see us exclusively as players but we also have everyday lives to lead. And when you leave home for seven weeks that takes some organising.

It made matters worse that my house was being decorated and I could not find anything. One day I lost it completely and declared war on the mess in the house. I grabbed the leaf vacuum in the garage, switched it to 'blow' and set about blasting the dust out of the house. I must have looked a complete fool.

It was a relief to finally get packed and on the road to Hampshire. Saying goodbye to Louise before a tour is never easy. This time was harder still because of her pregnancy. Our first child is expected the week before Christmas. The last couple of days before you leave are the toughest and you reach a point where it is better just to go. I know Backy found it particularly difficult as he had never before left his daughter Olivia for so long. On this trip there was the added apprehension of not knowing some of the lads in the squad. You are being thrown together with people who previously you have played against and wanted to hurt and humiliate in games.

I shouldn't have worried. Take, for example, Robin McBryde, the Llanelli hooker, who for some reason I was a bit concerned about. I had this preconception that he was some sort of psychopath. I couldn't have been more wrong. He turned out to be one of the nicest, funniest guys on the trip. The same was true of Rob Henderson who I roomed with at Tylney Hall. But there were a couple of drawbacks. Hendo smoked like a chimney and he and snored like a blocked up chimney. As for sleeping, he rarely did. He was like Count Dracula, wide awake at night with the television on very loud.

There's no question I benefited from having been involved in the previous tour because I knew what to expect. It's pretty hard when you're new to it, especially for young lads like Ronan 'Rog' O'Gara and Simon Taylor. They both seemed pretty nervous. Timid even. So I had a word with Ronan, telling him that he looked like I felt in 1997. I think he appreciated that. I also told him that just because other fly-halves were seen as being ahead him in the pecking order it didn't mean it would work out that way. That was the mistake I made in '97 when I kind of accepted that was the way it was going to be. Bad move, but like Rog and Simon this time, I was young and it was my first tour. My advice to them four years on was that if they forced their own personalities on the tour it would come through and they would be successful.

Those words were as applicable to me as to those lads. On the squad list I was listed at scrum-half, number three in the eyes of many, notably Jerry Guscott, behind Rob Howley and Matt Dawson. Jerry had warned me to take slippers and a lot of reading material because I'd have a lot of spare time. He did so at the Belfry after we had both played in the B&H Pro-Celebrity golf day and I was seated at a table with him drinking water while he got shit-faced.

"Have you sorted your reading list out?" he asked.

"What?" I said.

"For the tour. Have you sorted your reading list out? Because you ain't going to be playing much rugby are you?"

"We'll see, won't we."

A few days later Leicester destroyed Bath at Twickenham in the final of the Zurich Championship, I played pretty well and and I happened to bump into Jerry afterwards.

"About that reading list," I said. "I've just halved it. After that performance I reckon I might get a couple of games."

A week later he was watching me again, this time in the European Cup final. Leicester won, I made the break for the winning try in pretty much the last minute and then picked up the Man of the Match trophy.

"Jerry," I said. "I've decided not to take any books. I hope you were watching today. I think the selectors were and I'll probably play four or five games."

Behind all the joking I knew he had a point. I was seen by many as cover for scrum-half, fly-half and wing. But I was determined to prove him wrong and everyone else who banged on about my versatility. There is no word I hate more in the English language. In fact, from now on, I will refer to it as v*********y. People think it means you can do a lot of things but you can't actually do any of them all that well. Like being able to play different sports to an average capacity. As a result you end up on the bench. That's great for the management as it gives them options. An ace up their sleeve. Specialists on the field, Jack-of-all-trades in reserve. But for all the talk of rugby now being a 22-man game, players still measure success by making the starting line-up.

History has not been kind to v*******e players. Most have tended to lose out, certainly out of starting line-ups. How many supersubs can you remember? David Fairclough at Liverpool is one. I can't think of any others. I've always believed I have the ability to play three different positions at international level - scrum-half, fly-half and wing - and play each to international standard. What's more I felt I'd gone a long way towards almost achieving that over the last couple of seasons.

I'd improved my scrum-half abilities to the point that I like to think I would have been up there with Daws and Kyran Bracken as first choice for England by the end of the season, depending on who Clive wanted for a particular game. At the same time I'd been selected on the wing all season in the Six Nations and proved I could play fly-half at international level when filling in for Jonny Wilkinson at short notice in South Africa. Jonny is still in front of me because I can't kick like he can, but there are a lot of things that I can do.

To be a v*******e player you have to be skilled in rugby terms, not in positional terms. And I get so annoyed when I've had a really good game at, say fly-half, and someone writes 'Healey again proves his versatility by playing fly-half'. I think, 'Hold on a sec, I've played there 30 or 40 times, I'm not v*******e any more. It's just a different position'.

When I met up with the Lions I knew there was a very real possibility that I would fall between two stools. Make that three. But I was determined that wouldn't happen. My confidence was still sky high after the Heineken Cup final and when Henry revealed that he thought I could be the surprise package of the tour, I felt good. He went as far as to predict that I would stamp myself on the tour. What could he have meant?

The atmosphere in the Lions den was a little bit cagey to begin with. Even I, the one they call Mr Gobby, the Leicester Lip and Motormouth, was a bit subdued. Why am I called those names, by the way? So the management turned again to Impact, the motivational team who had done such a good job bringing us all together four years earlier through a series of teamwork-building activities. They help make a squad close and accurate and they don't waste any time. They compress probably four weeks of team bonding into five days, which is unbelievably crucial on a tour like this where time is so short.

There was dragon boat racing and a relay in which I had the misfortune to be picked in Ben Cohen's team for a race across stepping stones. Misfortune, because we decided to go with Ben's idea of belt-strapping the stones to our feet (we borrowed belts from anyone wearing trousers, including Syd Millar), rather than just putting them out and running down them like the rest of the teams did. Then there was the Giant's Ladder, a massive wooden structure we all had to scale. It looked impossible but teamwork got us all to the top, including Lawrence Dallaglio and Phil Vickery. It was one of our best achievements on the whole tour and it taught us a valuable lesson. The Lions were a scratch team given seven weeks to come together, get to know one another, go to the other side of the world and beat the best side in rugby. If we worked together, all pulling in the same direction, we had a chance. If we didn't...

And yet for all the Impact exercises we did, the activity I felt actually brought us closest together was the good old fashioned night at the pub which we had two days before we left. The following day we were as one. Each of us did a presentation about our values for the tour and it was clear everyone was pulling in the same direction. There were no hidden agendas. The only agenda was to win the Test series and be remembered as one of the great Lions teams.

Our first training session hardly overburdened me with expectation. The first thing which struck me was how hectic it was and how little attention to detail was paid. England is so much more organised. The difference was remarkable. 'Stop comparing everything with England, Austin', I told myself. But comparisons were inevitable. Consequently, so were my misgivings.

I couldn't do full contact because of my knee and when the management read out the teams for the first two games, against

Western Australia and the Queensland President's XV, I was listed as injured along with Lawrence, Jonny, Johnno, Iain Balshaw, Jason Leonard and the boy McBryde. So I knew I would not be starting a game before we got to Brisbane for the Queensland Reds game a fortnight in. I was cool about that, knowing the Reds game was the first major challenge of the tour and it would be a good stage on which for me to stake my claim for a Test shirt.

Our first full day together coincided with England playing the Barbarians at Twickenham. How strange to see England shirts running around without the familiar faces in them. Still I thought some of the younger lads did well, especially Leon Lloyd. The previous weekend he had scored two tries for Leicester at Parc des Princes in the Heineken Cup final, including the last-minute winner, so his confidence was understandably high. It can only be a matter of time before he forces his way into the full squad providing he carries on doing what he's doing. He has great physical attributes and a good rugby brain. He just needs to work on his distribution and up his workrate.

The one guy I really felt for during the game, which England without their 18 Lions only lost 43-29, was Tim Stimpson who had a horrible afternoon against Jonah Lomu. I know from experience how difficult it is to tackle Lomu and Stimmo did not have much joy. Worse still, Jonah got him big time, picking him up and throwing him to the ground. Stimmo is a great player and for someone to do something like that to him is pretty immense. It just makes you realise the full force of Lomu. Will Carling famously labelled him a 'freak' after he ripped England to shreds in the 1995 World Cup. I think 'freak' is a bit strong, 'gifted' would be more accurate. There has never been anyone like him and I don't think there will be again.

Tackling Jonah is phenomenally difficult because you can't go round his legs. I've tackled him probably three times in my life, all three times when I got him round the collar, then got him round the waist, almost like a lion bringing down a buffalo. You just can't stop his legs from moving. His legs are so strong that if you put your arms round them and squeeze he will just break free.

Yet when you see Jonah coming your instinct is to go low. That's probably the worst thing to do. If you stand in front of him you've got no chance. Your only chance is to move to the side and then hit him from the side. If he runs straight at you and puts his leg out in front there is only one place you're going and that's backwards.

I remember when England played New Zealand in the 1999 World Cup when, with the match finely balanced at 16-16, Jonah got the ball. He ran through Jerry Guscott, who didn't even try, then fixed me in his sights. It was make or break time for me. 'Knock down Lomu here and you're laughing,' I told myself. So I put everything I had into hitting him low and just squeezing my arms. Even if I only got one leg I was determined to hold onto it. I hit him as hard as I could around his right thigh, got my arms linked, which usually means you're going to drag a person down, squeezed as hard as I could and thought to myself 'job done. I've got him', next thing I know his heel hits me in the chin and he's gone. I looked up, saw Daws come across, grab him by the shorts and start sliding; Dan Luger arrived and jumped on his shoulder. But Jonah was still going. By the time Lawrence got to him he was over the line.

Stimmo has been in and out of England favour for longer than I can remember and I felt for him as Lomu ran riot two years on. He had been a hero the week before in the Heineken Cup final, a villain this time. But that happens in sport. It has happened to the very best. Look at David Campese screwing up in Sydney in 1989, throwing that pass to ground which enabled Ieuan Evans to score the series-clinching try. That is one of my first memories of the Lions and I know Campo hasn't forgotten it either because he made an advert for Bundaberg Rum, the sponsors of the Lions series, which poked fun at his blunder. He should have dummied and gone himself, but he probably realises that now.

Campo was a fantastic player, a genius on the rugby field who was always doing the unexpected. This might sound rich coming from me but I just wish he'd let his rugby do a little more of his talking because he was always slagging off the northern hemisphere and England in particular. I'm no shrinking violet and in some ways we are pretty similar, but I think it's wrong for somebody to insult another country so relentlessly and for so long. I sometimes wonder how Australia would react to even a single dose of Campo's medicine from somebody English? Just a thought.

chapter twelve

Popcorn and Honey Traps

Week 2, Saturday June 2 - Sunday June 10.

My welcome to Australia was two blondes, with big boobs and long legs knocking on the door of my hotel room in Fremantle. South Africa had given us Zulu dancers on the airport runway four years earlier. Australia laid on a honey trap.

I mustn't blame the whole of Australia. That would be unfair of me and out of character. I'm not one for sweeping statements. So let's say a rogue element in the Perth area saw half a chance to turn up the heat on us in the few days before the Aussie rugby fraternity found their voices and took up the attack. It was the night before our opening game of the tour against Western Australia. As I always do on the eve of a match I went out to buy some popcorn. Popcorn is an essential part of my pre-match ritual. Don't ask why. I just always have popcorn the night before games. The first place I tried was closed, but the cinema obliged. I walked back to my room in the Esplanade Hotel and began packing all my kit that was not going on to Townsville, the second leg of the tour, at the weekend.

That was when the honey trap appeared at my door. At least, I can only assume that's what it was. Two girls in short skirts, high heels and revealing tops claiming to be looking for free tickets for the game. I told them they might find some tickets downstairs, but that wasn't what they wanted to hear. They asked if they could come in and watch *Big Brother* on my television. I said I was too busy packing and that there was a TV in reception. They replied "Okay, we'll go to the bar and wait until you've finished. Then we can have a drink." I told them not to bother because I was going to bed. They said it was a shame because I had nice legs.

Thanks for the compliment girls, but no thanks. I'm married and Lou is pregnant. I was polite but didn't give them the attention they wanted. They turned on their stilettos and vanished down the corridor. A few minutes later I looked out of my hotel window just in time to see them being picked up by a man in a white BMW. My first reaction was that I couldn't believe newspapers would go to such lengths to catch us out. That it was a pretty sad state of affairs. But I had no reason to suggest that the papers were out to get me. Not here in Australia.

I thought no more of it and when my room mate Iain Balshaw got back we started playing cards. I took him to the cleaners on a blind hand. He was gutted but I had to teach my monkey a lesson. He will behave from now on. Then Alex Broun, our media liason officer, popped his head round the door with a word of caution. He had got chatting to two well-proportioned girls in reception and they were definite plants. One of the girls had told him that she was a weather girl on television and gave him her card.

An hour later he returned, grabbed the remote control handset for our TV and gasped "You've got to see this". We all thought the weather girl was on TV in some porn film. She wasn't. It was the weather that was on. Alex felt we should see how hard it was raining in Tokyo where Australia were playing Japan at football. The lads ripped the piss out of him.

Six nights in Oz and we still hadn't played a game. The lack of competitive action was starting to strain on a few people. The lads just wanted to play now. We needed a game for the banter to come back. Less than a week from arrival and we were already tired and fed up of being flogged in training.

Trying to crawl away from Dad's haircut

Born to support Everton

You can see why I was called Melon Head

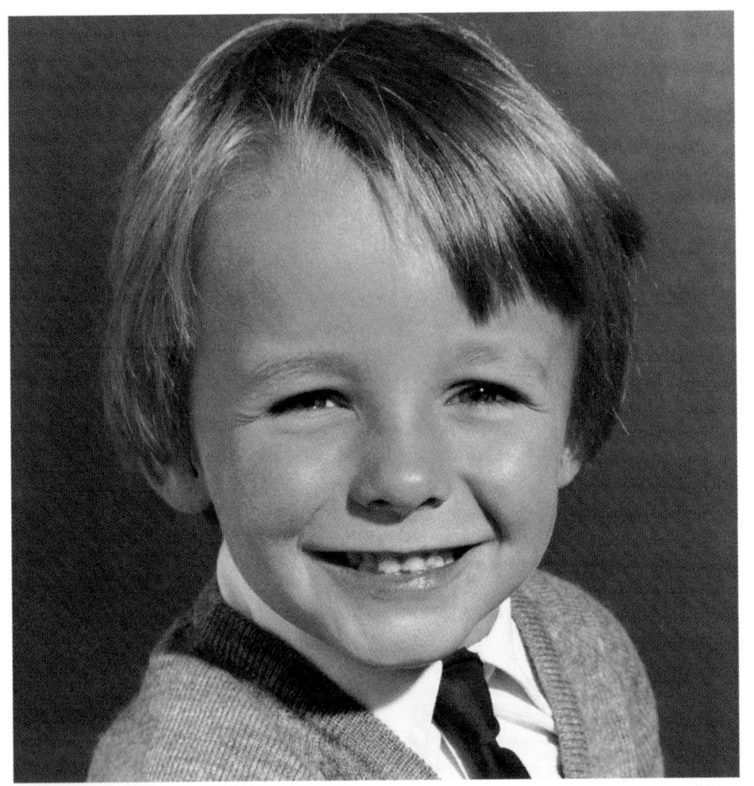

Butter wouldn't melt

Birkenhead Park v Hoylake Mini's. Another easy win

Mum and Dad help collect my degree

Our happy day

Celebrating a fun and successful Lions Tour

Knackered after Lions v Transvaal '97

These three burglars escaped to play for Leicester. Johnno, me and Will Greenwood

Greenwood does star jump as Healey scores v Scotland

I think I need smaller pads

Having a discussion with Ben Cohen - he took exception to me calling him 'Bowl Head'

A typical night out
in Leicester

Holidaying in Portugal with close friends

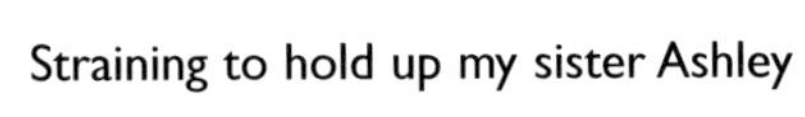

Straining to hold up my sister Ashley

Simon and I controlling our monkey Ade

Botchy Boys - Will Greenwood, Craig Joiner and me at Craig's wedding.
Can you guess what we had on under our kilts?

My finger was stuck. Honest

At Lake Louise, Canada
after the tour with my wife, Louise!

Above: Hopefully this pass hit the fly-half. I think Dai and Jason look more concerned

Left: Over celebrating that try v ACT

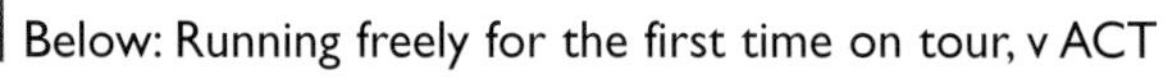

Below: Running freely for the first time on tour, v ACT

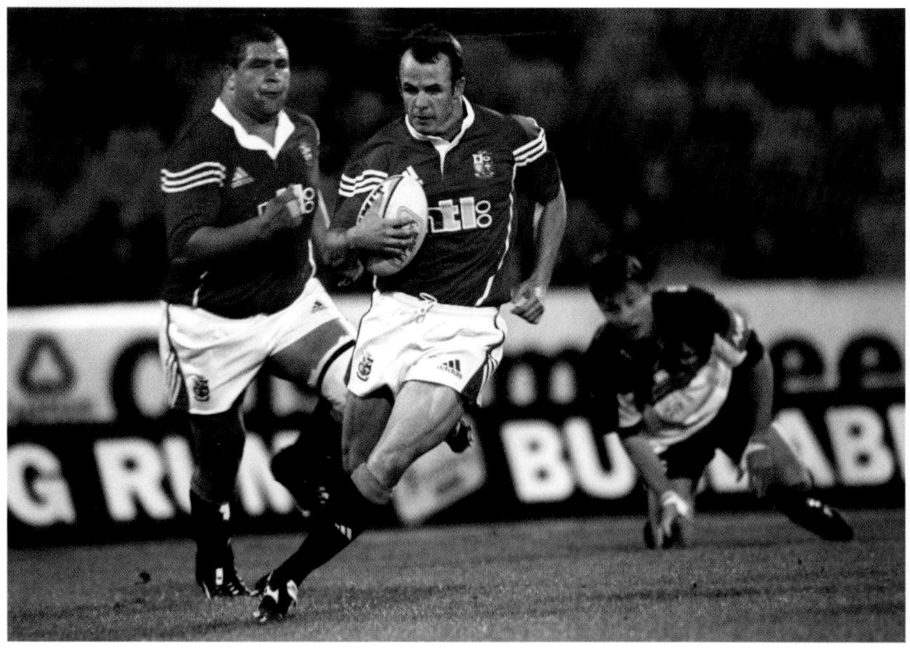

Above: Something else that went to my head

Our best achievements will always feel special

Three trophies - what a season!

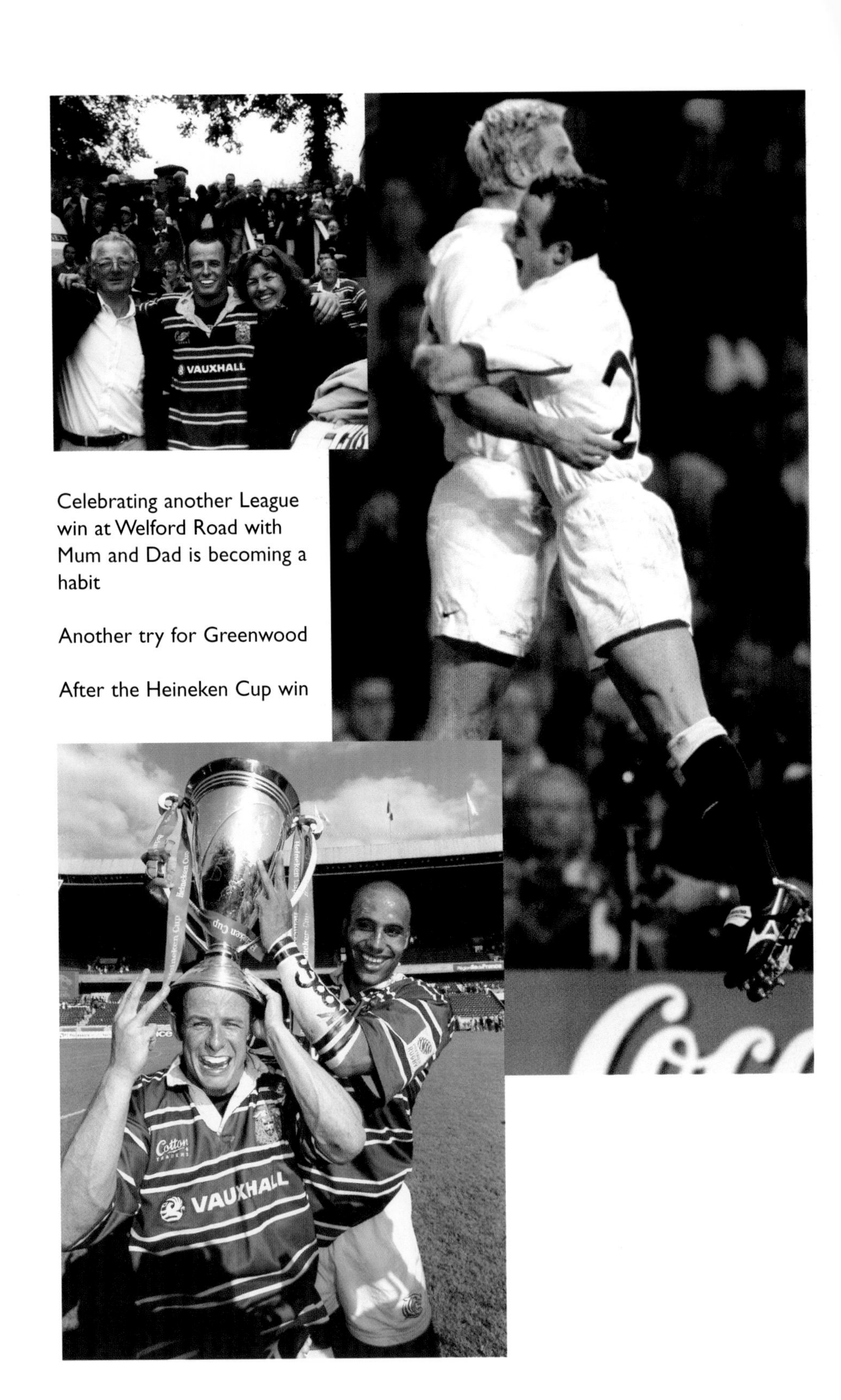

Celebrating another League win at Welford Road with Mum and Dad is becoming a habit

Another try for Greenwood

After the Heineken Cup win

Cozza auditions for modelling job

Lifting the Calcutta Cup, March '01

Heineken Cup Final 19.5.01 v Stade Francais, getting Leon Lloyd involved

I had to lean out of the cart to counter balance the weight of Dorian West

It was a shame I didn't get the chance to play on this pitch

Our anthem is strong, emotional and highly motivating - it makes you proud to be English

Having a laugh with Richard at post Six Nations game dinner

Healey motors on, changes gear, blah, blah, blah. The car references over the years have been truly inspirational

SUNDAY

From almost the moment we landed in Perth, Henry's regime has been a shock to the system. Having popped a sleeping tablet on the long haul Down Under I had a few drinks on arrival to help me sleep all through the night before our light jog this morning. Only the management changed their minds. What was billed as a light runout became two full contact sessions. More than that, the management decided that to help the lads get over the jet lag we would train at 7.15am. Can I be the last to thank them. For the benefit of future tours let me make it clear that it didn't help. My alarm woke me. I could have done with an extra two hours' kip.

If it was a shock to my system then I had to feel for Neil Jenkins. In the very first session he needed ten stitches after Jeremy 'Dangerous Brain' Davidson clumsily tried to run over him. Jenks went off for repairs and I stepped into the fly-half slot in Team Two. Things went quite well. I kept pace with the game. Not bad with a dodgy knee. But by the time we had finished our second session in the afternoon, following two hours shuteye and no lunch, I was completely wasted and crawled back to the hotel for another profitable game of cards.

MONDAY

Daylight brought no respite. In fact Day Two was worse. The training schedule was as punishing as Day One but without the rest, fun or cards. Two days in Australia and I am bored and exhausted and my knee is killing me. At Tylney last week Donal was asked what he thought was the difference between the 1997 tour and this. He replied, "We've been together three and a half days and haven't even been to the pub." Everyone laughed. But the gag has quickly worn thin. I've had enough training to last me a lifetime and I'm not alone in feeling that way. The boys have joked about ringing the bell and travelling around Australia backpacking. I phoned home and spoke to Louise, who was suffering with morning sickness. Touring is not all fun and games. We were both tired and fed up. I have always found touring hard when people are sick at home, ever since my gran, Lil Healey, died while I was on tour in Australia with England under-21s in 1993. My parents didn't tell me until later because they didn't want it to distract me. That's how seriously Mum and Dad take my England career. But it has left me apprehensive whenever people I care for back home are unwell.

TUESDAY

I have only been with the Lions for eleven days (including Tylney) and already I need a break. Help arrived this morning when I was given the day off by our medical team to help my knee recover properly. Instead I was assigned the job of scribe. I was put in charge of noting down and naming all the team calls in the different areas of the pitch. The session went well, probably because I watched most of it, and I came away convinced that the team was starting to take shape. But there remains precious little to do and precious little time in which to do it. We have a swimming pool in the hotel, a computer room supplied by shirt sponsors ntl, the odd Gameboy, a pack of playing cards and a video camera.

Ah, the video camera. Rob Henderson and I had given it a go at Tylney Hall last week, mimicking John 'Bentos' Bentley, who had made as big a name for himself off the pitch as he did on it with the 1997 Lions in South Africa. Anyone who has seen '*Living with the Lions*', the critically acclaimed video account of that trip will be familiar with Bentos Tours. He spent what seemed like half the trip pointing the lens of a video camera in our faces, or indeed at his own, and talking gibberish into the microphone. He would pop up in the most unexpected places and say, "Now then, what have we here?"

Thanks to Bentos I became known as 'Mr X the Invisible Wanker'. Being on tour for eight weeks you get a bit frustrated so I was having a bit of a tug in the bathroom with the door locked when all of a sudden it sprung open - Bentos had picked the lock from the outside - and before I knew what was happening I had a camera filming me. By the time I had put myself away he'd scarpered down the corridor and three other lads grabbed me so I couldn't catch him. He went straight down to lunch and announced to the rest of the squad that there would be a special screening. I had to think quickly. So I broke into his room, turned the place upside down, eventually found the video camera, blacked out the offending footage, rebuilt his room, then put the camera back.

Half an hour later he had got the whole squad together. They'd all heard about it and were winding me up big time. Then Bentos started the video. The lads saw him sneaking into my room whispering 'I know the bastard's in here somewhere, I'm going to catch him out'. They saw him open the door but just as it swung open the screen went black. I wet myself laughing. Bentos went ape.

We could do with some laughs like that on this tour so Hendo and I today decided to try to recapture the spirit of '97. Actually, it was just an excuse to take the piss out of Bentos who, in South Africa, had made a rule that he wouldn't talk to me after 4 o'clock in the afternoon because he found me so annoying. He would say, "Austin, it's 4 o'clock, I'm not listening now". It deflected from the fact that, for my money, he was the biggest nause of that entire trip.

The first scene of 'Bentos, The Sequel' found the great man in pensive mood. "Here am I sat on the toilet waiting for the squad to be announced". The action then moved to a fish and chip shop somewhere in Western Australia. "Here am I in the chippie. I'm having to pay my way around Australia. I'm making the chips". Hendo interrupted. "Scuse me mate can I have a cod and chips?" "Sorry," said I, I mean Bentos, "Must go. Good luck with the first game. Hopefully I'll be selected for the second game and I can show some of my magic there".

It is clear that the punishing regime is getting to us - well certainly to me and Hendo - and we still have three days until our opening game against Western Australia at the WACA cricket ground. I know I won't start the match but I have been selected on the bench. So after destroying Will 'Shaggy' Greenwood on the games at the local arcade over lunch, I headed to the gym with Lawrence Dallaglio as we both needed to work on our injured knees. I felt good for having put in the extra work, especially when heading back later we passed some of the lads in the burger bar.

WEDNESDAY

Newspaper column day. My agent has negotiated a twice weekly deal, for me to appear in *The Guardian* on Friday and *The Observer* on Sunday. I meet Eddie Butler, the *Observer's* rugby correspondent, and he puts words to my thoughts. As a safety net, I have the right of veto on the finished article. At this stage I'm still not sure about Eddie. He seems a decent enough fella but I am slightly concerned that he turns up for our interview with neither a notebook nor a tape recorder. Still, the columns have been amusing so I'm happy enough.

Not that there is any controversy around, just sweat and knackered bodies. It is all about hitting tackle bags, hitting scrum machines and then hitting the sack to try and grab enough shut eye to get you through the following day which you are pretty safe to assume will be spent hitting tackle bags and more scrum machines.

THURSDAY

Today ended with the Honey trap but began with a shocking warm-up. We had a team run at the WACA first thing and Steve Black, our fitness advisor, had people running around all over the place. He claimed to have choreographed our movements. I think he made it up as he went along. Blackie is a nice bloke and a good motivator but he's not in the same league as England's Dave 'Otis' Reddin when it comes to any aspect of fitness or pre-match preparation. Otis is 100% organised and motivates the person to motivate themselves. I can only think Blackie had a problem sleeping, which is why he gives us all a side of A4 inspiration every day.

Training went okay but still left me with the feeling that the pace and the width of the game would have to go some to catch up with England (God, there I go again). I suspect that both Phil Larder and Dave Alred have noticed this but I don't know what they can do to change it. It has to come from the head coach. I am convinced that pounding forwards and big backs with territory will not be enough to beat the Aussies. I really hope I am wrong.

Meanwhile, the lads not involved against Western Australia had another full contact session, during which Phil Greening twisted his knee and probably ruled himself out of the tour. I feel really bad for Phil because he's been quite lively since we arrived. That said, he probably doesn't fit the Test mould. He thinks about the game, you see, and attacks space instead of channels! There was a lot of talk about who would come out. Both Johnno and I made a case for Dorian West, but Backy seems to know it will be Gordon Bulloch.

FRIDAY

Last night was a shocker for me as I had an asthma attack. It was only a mild one but I got no sleep. I couldn't breathe normally. It was probably the result of coughing up phlegm, cold dust and the dreaded air conditioning. I overdosed on Ventolin so it failed to work properly. I went to breakfast and on to the team walk-through but I still couldn't breathe at all well. I had been confident that a dose of exercise would bring me out the other side of the attack. It didn't. I was still very short of breath.

Thank God for Dr James Robson. The doc gave me a vibration massage to get the phlegm off my lungs and bronchials. Then a Salbutamol nebulisor sent me way out there on a relaxed scale. Unless you have asthma you can't understand how horrible the tightness in your chest, shoulders and throat makes you feel. Underwent the treatment at 1 o'clock. Thirty minutes later I awoke feeling like a human being again.

Refreshed, I met up with the squad and saw Shaggy looking really focused. I was so pleased to see him back in a Lions shirt after what he went through in Bloemfontein four years ago, when he was knocked out in a crashing tackle. To my mind Will struggled for 18 months after that, though he will deny that. He wanted to play but he didn't want to get hurt and that is probably the worst situation to be in as a rugby player. Trying to hold back and prevent getting hurt is virtually impossible. That is probably when you play the worst and get hurt the most.

He had been through a traumatic experience, one that I saw happen at first hand. We were playing our penultimate midweek game in South Africa against Free State and Will was playing like a God, as he had been all tour (I actually thought he should have been the Test centre). It was just before half-time and I was shouting for him to pass to me and he didn't. I was thinking what a greedy bastard he was. Then he went down, knocked unconscious by a major tackle by a guy called Jaco Coetzee. It was not immediately obvious what trouble he was in. He was looking up, his eyes were wide open and he was blowing a raspberry. I thought he was taking the piss out of me so I called him a dickhead. Then I realised that he wasn't. So we kept him there on his back and checked he hadn't swallowed his gumshield or his tongue.

It was when the doctors came on that he started to fit. And then he swallowed his tongue. I had told him to cut his sleeves off before the game. He had asked me if it was cold out there and decided to not to cut them off. With hindsight it was a bad decision as he got whipped by the corner of his sleeve. It wouldn't have happened had the fella not had something to grab hold of.

We didn't know how bad it was. We just thought he had been knocked out. We came in at half-time and I went straight up to the doc who told me he was fine. That put my mind at rest. It was not until I saw it on the video later that I realised how serious it had been; when they took him into that room and they could not get him round and they were going to give him a tracheotomy. Seeing his mum and dad there shakes you up a fair bit, I can tell you. They were very concerned, as you would be if one of your children was hurt and you were powerless to help. They were in other people's hands at that stage.

It was one of those accidents that can happen to anyone. Unfortunately it happened to my mate Will. The next time I saw him was in the foyer of the hotel. We had moved back to Durban and he had stayed the night in the hospital. When he rejoined us the next day a load of lads went down to meet him. He was blatantly shaken up and had a bad headache. He is definitely scarred by the experience and I would estimate he lost two years of his rugby life due to a combination of that and his subsequent groin injury.

It's not really been until this season that he's properly got over that concussion. Since rejoining Harlequins from Leicester he has looked superb. He was more responsible than anyone for beating us in the Tetley's Bitter Cup semi-final back in January but I always felt he had a Lions demon he had to get out of his system. Pulling on the shirt again I hoped would do the trick.

Match one details

Western Australia 10, British and Irish Lions 116

Lions: O'Driscoll; Cohen (Henderson 66), Greenwood (Balshaw 56), M Taylor, Luger; O'Gara, Howley (Healey 59); Morris, Wood (capt, McBryde 73), Vickery (Leonard 63), Grewcock, O'Kelly, Hill (S Taylor 40), Back, Quinnell (Davidson 43).

Scorers - Tries: Quinnell 3, Luger 3, Howley 2, Back 2, Balshaw 2, Greenwood, Grewcock, M Taylor, S Taylor, Healey, O'Driscoll. Cons: O'Gara 13.

Everyone looks forward to the first game on a tour, but never more than on this occasion. We had all had enough of training. I think that showed in the way the lads played. We won 116-10, the biggest victory in Lions history. Our 18-try haul was another best. And we did it despite a quite extraordinary speech by Graham Henry beforehand.

It was the first pre-match meeting of the entire tour and Henry basically announced that he wasn't one of us. He told us that the fellas down here in the southern hemisphere don't think we're skillful enough, don't think we're athletic enough and don't think we're committed enough. "And I should know, because I'm one of them." The lads sat round and thought, 'there's nothing like setting your stall out early'.

It didn't get much better when we got into the changing room and Blackie started gobbing off and shouting out instructions. Most of the guys couldn't be bothered to even listen. It was almost like a football changing room where everyone is shouting and motivating each other. A rugby changing room is generally a lot quieter, apart from music perhaps. The lads chill out and concentrate and focus. With people shouting all the time it makes it a lot more difficult.

Every player prepares differently. Some listen to a Walkman, some (like Jenks) are sick, some bang their heads, others get changed straight away and go out and warm up and have a proper stretch. I go in, clean my boots, sit down, read the programme for a bit, go and check the pitch, then get changed, put some deep heat on my calves, have a stretch and go back out and warm up.

While Blackie banged on about 'trigger words' and all this stuff that the coaches like to hear, Henry paced the room quietly, pausing only for the occasional personal word with a player. He stopped in front of Jenks and Scott Quinnell, whom I was sitting between, and whispered 'just like France', referring to the great performances they had turned in against France in the Six Nations. To me he said something like 'talk a lot - I know you find that easy'.

I didn't feel at all nervous before the game. It just felt like another game and as such it was no major concern to me. For some strange reason I didn't feel any apprehension or honour or pride about playing for the Lions in their first game. That will change later on, I'm sure, when the opposition is of a higher standard.

Obviously I was keen to get on the park, because I love playing rugby, because my last game had been a European Cup final and had been thoroughly enjoyable and because I needed to get out there and run off my asthma. I got on for the last quarter and at first found it both difficult to breathe and incredibly hard to keep up with the pace of play. I made a few passes and a few tackles. It wasn't exactly a hard game.

Then I scored the try which brought up our century on one of the most famous cricket grounds in the world. I went down the blindside expecting someone to tackle me. My plan was to offload to Hendo but no-one touched me so I went straight through, sold a half dummy and waited for the fullback to come back, but he never did. It's called a Fijian dummy. You show to pass, he thinks you've thrown a dummy, then comes back to you. But he took the dummy hook line and sinker. I went on moved up a gear to third or fourth and cruised in. I then spent the walk back to halfway trying to get my breath back.

We were in a bit of a no-win situation but you have to play pretty well to score 116 points against any side. There was a fair bit of white line fever and back in the changing room everyone was pretty happy with the performance. Everyone except Phil Larder, our defensive coach, and Simon Taylor. Phil was seething at the two tries we'd conceded whilst Simon discovered he had torn the anterior cruciate ligament in his knee and his tour was over. Simon said "I will go home to Edinburgh and cry into my pillow for a few days." To a man we all felt sick for him. He's a nice lad and a good rugby player. He is also the second player we have lost to injury and we're only at the end of our first week out here. I only hope the coaches take that on board and reduce the training load.

With a game under our belts the rest of us feel a bit better about life. After arriving back in Fremantle at 10 o'clock a load of us went out for a pasta. I had two beers and probably would have stayed out but for the training session called for first thing in the morning. What a nightmare. So I headed back to the hotel where the doc gave me half a dose of the nebulisor and I glided back to my room and into a state of unconsciousness.

SATURDAY

The justification for early morning training was that the main part of the day would be spent in the air, travelling to Townsville on the north east corner of Australia, five and a half hours flight time away. Fair enough, as long as the flight wasn't delayed.

My alarm call came at 7 o'clock and I chucked a bowl of cereal down my throat before meeting at 7.15am and heading out to the local pitch for a quick 90-minute session. It was memorable for Andy Robinson coaching support lines and angles - and for him having a go at me about my depth and my timing. He may be a coach and a very good forwards coach but come on! If he needs advice he should just ask!! From the training ground we raced back to the hotel to pack. I am fed up of rushing around like a trainee doctor in *ER*.

I consoled myself with the thought that I could at least relax on the flight. But I arrived at the airport to find that the plane was screwed. All of a sudden no-one seemed to be in quite such a hurry. Can we get another plane please? They did, but only after we'd sat around for hours. Simon was going to come with us to Townsville but changed his plans when he learned about the delay and headed straight home.

The only good news from a day which eventually ended in the hotel casino an hour after our charter flight touched down at 2am is that Martin Corry has been called up from Canada. It will be good to have him here. Maybe he should have been here from the start, but he's missed the mindless training and instead been on what sounded a great tour with England. Good to have him here. What odds he makes the Test bench?

SUNDAY

I have swapped my monkey Balsh for Jenks. He's a top man and he rose even higher in my estimation when he told me about the time he shared with Jerry Guscott on the '97 Lions tour and started to try and have a chat with him. Jerry, he claimed, looked over the top of his book and said, "Look, if you want to talk phone up one of your Welsh mates!" I'll leave you to work out what I think of Jerry. On second thoughts let me tell you.

Remember, Jerry is the guy who told me to bring slippers, books and a pipe because he said I wouldn't get much playing time with the Lions. He is also the guy who took the mickey out of me in front of all the England lads in 1999 on the day before I was to mark Jonah Lomu in the World Cup match at Twickenham. He had poked fun at how I was going to be hanging onto Lomu's shirt and be dragged along the floor like a rag doll.

With all that in mind let me say that Jerry was a great talent, but a very lucky talent. The ball bounced right into his hands on numerous occasions. He had great speed but didn't make many tackles. He wasn't the best kicker of a ball yet dropped a goal to win a Lions series. He's also one of the most selfish people I've ever met. He really didn't give a stuff about anyone else in the team. There, that's better.

Jenks, on the other hand, is a true legend, the nicest bloke you could ask to meet. He is very proud of his 'little viking', his 17-month old daughter Georgia. He showed me some lovely pictures of her. She looks like him, especially dressed in her Adidas gear and Wales shirt. It made me think about the baby Lou and I are expecting. Jenks says it's hard to tour when they're so young, that he really misses her and that it hurts him to miss any part of her infancy. Hopefully I'll have a healthy six-month old baby this time next year. I bet I feel the same as Jenks. But playing for England means so much to me that I'll probably pay for the family to come with me.

chapter thirteen

Tackle Bags and Dreams

Week 3, Monday June 11 - Sunday June 17

Live your dreams in North Queensland. That's what the blurb said on the tourist guide I picked up in the foyer of Jupiters Hotel and Casino on the morning the side was picked for our third match against Queensland. Ten minutes later I heard I was on the bench for the third game running. Live your dreams? This tour is turning into a bloody nightmare.

MONDAY

I made a mental note to start eating a bit better as I stared at my breakfast. My diet is going out of the window but I'm so tired that I can't be bothered to do anything about it. We had a team run at Dairy Farmer's Stadium, the 30,000-capacity home of the North Queensland Cowboys rugby league side and the venue for tomorrow's game. After that we had to train with the squad to play Queensland on Saturday. Full on again. The only saving grace for me was that I got to wear the green bib so nobody was allowed to touch me. What joy! Nonetheless, I was knackered when I got back to the hotel and slept for two hours. Then it was off to Dai Young's team meeting. Dai is captain of the midweek side and a top fella. He spoke well but I can't look at him because I know it will make us both burst out laughing.

This time I managed to escape without cracking up and went in search of popcorn at the local Hicks cinema. 'Back to the Future' will be showing soon! Despite my popcorn habit I'm actually not superstitious. I just have a certain routine which I follow. Popcorn and Dyoralite in water (to try and get some elecrolytes into my calf muscles) the night before a game, then on matchday I have a shave to try and freshen myself up and become as alert as possible. I also eat as much as I can. I like to have bacon butties but I have struggled over here because there only seems to be streaky bacon.

It's not only my body I look after. Everything about my day is organised in advance. I have a pair of trainers, an undervest, a tee shirt, a pair of shorts and socks which I always wear on matchdays so that I don't have any unimportant decisions to make that will distract my focus. This process is just designed to make my preparation for matches very precise. So that come matchday I have everything with no bearing on the game sorted out so I don't even need to think about them. I like to avoid surprises.

Unfortunately the Lions management have been running into them, one after another. Henry had a beer thrown over him as he gave a television interview in Perth, which was pretty embarrassing for the Aussies, not least John O'Neill, the chief executive of the Australian Rugby Union, who was watching at the time. Then today the Mayor of Townsville failed to turn up to a reception billed as the 'Mayor's official welcome to the teams'. Happily I dodged that one and instead gave Matt Dawson an almighty battle on the table tennis table, winning 27-25, 21-19. I guess I just step it up against Daws when I get to the big points.

TUESDAY

Matchday dawned and I felt physically drained so I had a long lie-in before going straight to my morning matchday snack. When I'm with England I'm always the first player up because I like to get in two meals before kick-off. But England normally play in the afternoon whereas the Lions go hunting at night, so there is no great rush. My typical matchday platter consists of Special K with strawberries, a bowl of fruit, four bacon butties and beans, six pieces of toast with organic jam and a couple of muffins. My other rule is that I stay awake in the five hours before kick-off to make sure my brain is alert, while constantly sipping a water-Lucozade mix.

Match two details

Queensland President's XV 6, British and Irish Lions 83

(Dairy Farmers Stadium, Townsville, June 12)

LIONS: Perry; James, Greenwood (M Taylor 65), Henderson, Robinson; Jenkins (Healey 65), Dawson; Smith (Leonard 57), McBryde (Bulloch 9), Young, Davidson (O'Kelly 67), Murray, Charvis, Williams, Corry.

SCORERS - Tries: Robinson 5, Henderson 3, Charvis 2, Young, O'Kelly, penalty try. Cons: Jenkins 5, Perry 4.

For a lot of the lads this was their first start of the trip (I only wish I could say the same), two and a half weeks after meeting up as a squad in Hampshire, and they were under pressure after the first game to put in the same sort of performance. Maybe that's what stuffed up our first half, at the end of which we were lucky to lead 10-6. The preparations seemed okay, everyone was very eager, but that was the major problem.

Donal had given us a good, aggressive team talk in the changing room beforehand. We had all clapped and then run out onto the field yet come kick-off there were all sorts of problems in terms of our continuity. A lot of guys were chatting and not going through with their calls. Playing as 15 individuals rather than as a team is probably the best way to describe it.

It's hard for everyone to get a fair crack of the whip in such a short tour - the 37-man squad is the biggest in Lions history for a ten-match tour which ranks as the shortest - so I suppose it was understandable that people would look to make the most of their time on the ball. But rugby is a team game and we needed to remind ourselves of that fact during the break.

That done, it was plain sailing. We scored a very early try through Colin Charvis to settle us down then added five more in the next 17 minutes. I came on at fly-half with 25 minutes to go and things got even better. I was pretty pleased about that. The first thing that happened was that Hendo told me to kick it. We were in our own 22 but I told him to shut up. I said, "Look at the scoreboard, look at how many Lions supporters are in the crowd. We want to score some tries." The next thing he knows he's scored underneath the posts. From then on I just laughed at him and said "I bet you're happy we didn't kick it now, aren't you?"

Everything I called we seemed to score from. Things were going particularly well. We were running well, supporting well and I think they were just dead on their feet. We were on fire in the last 20 minutes and any time you score 73 unanswered points in a single half, no matter who you are playing against, you've done well. I certainly felt very satisfied and almost vindicated. I said I could play 10 in that game. It was good to prove it. I also knew that the Leicester management would be watching and as I am keen to play fly-half for Tigers, I think it gave me a little more bargaining power.

The headlines belonged to Jason Robinson. Fair play to him, scoring five tries on his Lions debut was pretty impressive, even if four of them were run-ins. However, one was down to a couple of great steps by him. 'Safety first' Hendo also had a good game, scoring a hat-trick, yet he didn't get any press at all because of Billy Whizz. That pretty much sums up his cards on this trip to. He's had really good hands but someone has always had just slightly better.

We went out as a group for a beer in Townsville but there were too many Lions fans out for us to relax properly. It was more of a signing session than anything else. It would have been nice to have a beer and relax with the lads but that's part and parcel of being a Lion I suppose. The support and adulation that follows it all is unlike anything you experience anywhere else. Mike Catt's missus, Ali, is from Townsville so I spent the evening in tease mode, calling her a Hillbilly. Her friend got annoyed and abused me. She had cowboy boots on and had a bit of straw coming from her mouth! The pub was called Mad Cow.

Returned to basecamp with Shaggy and Daws at 3am, two hours before a couple of the President's men. Shane Drahm and Nathan Williams had the misfortune to bump into Queensland coach Mark McBain as they arrived back from a nightclub and he was on his way to catch a red-eye flight out of Townsville. Both should have been in the Queensland squad against us on Saturday. Not any more.

WEDNESDAY

My two appearances for the Lions had totalled 39 minutes, during which time we had scored 12 tries. Worth a start, I felt. Henry obviously disagreed. He showered me with compliments and then stuck me back on the bench for the Queensland game.

I hadn't been too fussed about being a sub against the Queensland President's XV, though I did make a note in my diary 'better start soon or will get very fucked off'. But while I had known it was coming, from our first full day at Tylney when the teams for games one and two were named, I fully expected to get a start in game three.

When I was again left out I felt exasperated. I was tired and confused. I was not wanted for the first big match of the tour, yet I'd been praised to the heavens by the management for my twenty minutes against the President's XV the previous evening. "I don't think anybody would be happy with not having a start yet," Henry told the Press. "That's a natural reaction from a competitive rugby player. But having Austin on the bench gives us a lot of options. And when he comes on he gives us a spark. He gives us vision. He is a winner."

Townsville is known as Hicksville to the boys. There is a population of 130,000, a tropical climate and just off the coast lies the Great Barrier Reef. Some would say a nice place for a holiday.

But as we need no reminding we aren't on a holiday. We're on a treadmill.

I had been excused contact at morning training because I popped a rib last night and my knee was also sore. But I was back on duty at the lunchtime press conference where I was asked if I'm pissed off to be substitute again? No, I said, you get used to not being given half a chance to stake a Test spot claim. I was seething inside, convinced the Lions don't want me to play on this tour so they can stick with the team they picked before we flew out, but I answered all the questions without slagging anyone off or without telling anyone how dreadful this tour is compared to the last one in 1997.

It seems I've been given the role of tour joker - I don't mean prankster - and I don't find it very funny. When there are a few injuries or someone is tired they send for Austin. Henry plays his joker. Memo to coach: I wouldn't mind an opportunity to step in from the start at some stage. Henry has said I will definitely start next Tuesday against Australia 'A'. I better, because if they change their minds I'm out of here.

I was not sorry to get to Brisbane this evening and check into the Sheraton, which is a nice hotel. On the way into town from the airport the driver of our bus said he hates being called Drives. Big mistake, Drives! I grabbed a quick bite to eat and then fell into bed at 7.30.

THURSDAY

Woke at 10 o'clock to learn that I'd missed the biggest night of the tour so far. A large group of lads had escaped. No names obviously but I hear they came back at 6.30 pretty pissed up. Apparently they went for a quiet drink which turned into a shot necking night. Just as well for them that they took their fun while they could get it because there was bad news waiting for us all at breakfast. On what was supposed to be a day off I went downstairs to find the lads in kit. Two training sessions for the non-Queensland squad had been called and we were told we had an analysis session at 4.30. What a shocker.

The problem with this tour at the moment is that there's been too much training and too much chat. The lads just want to chill out and play rugby. All this talking has driven a bit of a wedge between the coaches and the players. The lads are pretty aggrieved at the way we have been treated so far. I'm sharing with Daws and our room has quickly become the place to be for the disaffected. If someone wants to have a moan they know where to come. Today's change of plan meant that Will Greenwood had to cancel golf which he'd arranged. He was gutted. So we decided to use the time that we had to go and watch Neil Back, Richard Hill, Jonny Wilkinson and Martin Corry walk in a shark tank on the Sunshine Coast. It took us an hour to get there but it was well worth it. While the lads went through a quick training session on diving in a pool I peered at the sharks. They looked very scary. The lads were told not to touch them - no shit!

I walked across to the aquarium tank which had a glass tunnel running through it. The sharks look a third of their actual size from there. But I saw them from the top where the boys got in and they were huge. I'm scared of fish so these put the fear of God into me. Still, I felt it was my duty to make the lads feel even worse so I asked the staff to drop some food into the tank first. They looked at me as though I had a death wish before explaining that if they fed the sharks first the boys would be eaten. Nice.

Afterwards we had a nice lunch on the beach before two of our support staff, Beth and Louisa, crashed into each other, damaging the front of one of the two cars we had with us and the back of the other. I think I could claim for whiplash but we were only doing 10mph at the time. Women drivers! Back to hotel in time for game analysis then out to the casino, where I played craps with Daws. We had a good laugh taking the piss out of two croupiers: Larry and his love handles and porn star Pete. Both men were out of a time warp. The micro chip will be a great innovation here in about 20 years!

FRIDAY

What the hell is going on? Team run at Brisbane Grammar School ground today lasted two and a half hours, the day before a game. They are coaching for the sake of it now. The boys who aren't involved tomorrow got beasted and then had an afternoon session. It's depressing for the squad to get so hammered. A lot of the boys are walking zombies, very close to 'ringing the bell'.

I sat in the hotel foyer trying to make sense of it all. I am at the top of my game but I'm not getting picked so what is the purpose of me being here? There has to be more to life than having your arse run out of you. Life doesn't start and end with the Lions. If they don't want me others do. I want to be fit for Leicester and for England.

The coaches are saying because it's such a short tour that we've got to get all this training in now so that when we get to the Test matches we can taper off. Fine, but they don't need to coach us in how to win rucks and mauls. They shouldn't have selected those people in the first place if they didn't think they could do it. The same thing with defence. I don't mind doing technique a couple of times a week, but not every single day and sometimes twice a day. It's just becoming mindless. The problem is that there are five different coaches each saying "I need 20 minutes doing this. We've got to do it to make sure we win the next game". But if they all get their 20 minutes that's 100 minutes. It's too much.

Clive Woodward and Brian Ashton are visionaries and I headed to Australia thinking Graham Henry would try and take that role. I was wrong. He is largely obsessed with structure. Structure and patterns. Quite honestly, a lot of the English players took a backwards step when they heard him speak. It wasn't like 'you make your own mind up', it was 'this is where you are going, this is what you are doing'. I suspect that attitude will lead to many hours more on the training field than we are accustomed to with England. Not being funny, or arrogant, but English players have had to go back three years of their evolutionary development to incorporate his style.

Don't get me wrong, I think Henry could be a good coach but in terms of where players in the northern hemisphere are I don't think he should be coaching like he is. I think he is behind the times. He sees targets and patterns. He doesn't look for space. We have been told that our gameplan is to attack 10 and 12.

The English lads appreciate how Clive works with and manages his coaches. Much more attention is paid to training sessions. Everything is mapped out so there's no stage where you're just doing things for the sake of it. Everything is done for a purpose. There's no time wasted. That's why the English players are all fresh as daisies when they get to an international. Here in Oz we are completely fucked because there is always some coach or other wanting to do a little bit extra. I can only think that they feel some players are not up to scratch in their specific disciplines.

In 1997 it was different because we didn't get beasted so heavily and we had a lot more time to socialise. But here, certainly among some of the squad, there's a discontent based on the over-training and the lack of time to do anything else. In South Africa we were given time to bond together properly so that it felt we were a part of something special long before we won the Test series. Here you can't go out for a drink for fear of being too tired for training in the morning. And there haven't been many days off. The time that has been free people have been so tired that they've slept. Right now, the only common theme between the two trips has been the great medical staff. James Robson (doc), Mark Davies (Carcass) and Richard Wegrzyk are a superb team.

What the coaches need to do is get back on our side. That's the most important thing. If the players lose contact with the coaching the whole thing can fall apart. When we had a day off the other day and they called two training sessions I reckon there were quite a few lads who were close to breaking and saying 'fuck this, I've had enough'. I, for one, was deadly serious about packing it in. My knee was really sore, we had been training every day, doing contact every day and I couldn't really step out of it because I was picked to play at the weekend. Louise is forever telling me on the phone that I sound tired. I thought about my mates out in Aya Napa on holiday drinking and partying and wondered what I was doing out here. I'm a professional sportsman, and this is my job, but sometimes you would like to be normal.

The only thing that keeps me going through the low times is the fact that all my family have saved up to come over here. Had they not been coming I probably would have said 'fuck it, see you later,' left my kit in the room, taken a few clothes to travel round Australia and gone. I don't know whether or not I'd have lived to regret it. I don't really deal with 'what ifs'. I don't see the point. Yes, I could be in the Test team, achieve such and such and be renowned throughout the country. But if I come home so pissed off with everything that has gone on, that feeling will outlast any adulation.

All the rest of the boys have been very supportive of one another. We have taken the view that we are all in it together. But there is still no change. There was a senior players committee meeting the other day and they decided that at most we should train once a day. The following day we trained twice. I don't think there's any point having a senior players committee.

SATURDAY

For all that I thought we'd hammer Queensland by 50 points. The lads had prepared well in training, the team run yesterday had looked good and I had got my lucky popcorn, albeit after an hour-long search. I've stuck with my pre-match rituals, even though I've not been playing in the games, just in case. Still it was something of a non-event for me because, while Queensland provided the first major challenge of our tour, and a lot of people expected me to play a part in it, I'd been told that I wouldn't feature unless there was an injury.

The lads were nervous and excited about playing but my emotions were pretty non-existent. For the third successive game I'd woken up on match day feeling like it was just another day, whereas I wake up at home when I'm playing for Leicester or England and the day feels special from the moment I open my eyes. My mind was more focused on Tuesday night in what would probably be a bigger game still against Australia 'A'.

Match three details

Queensland Reds 8, British and Irish Lions 42

(Ballymore, Brisbane, Townsville, June 16)

LIONS: Balshaw; James, O'Driscoll (Robinson 61), Henderson, Luger; Wilkinson, Howley (Dawson 48); Smith, Wood, Vickery, Johnson (capt, Murray 83), Grewcock, Hill, Back (Charvis 77), Corry.

SCORERS - Tries: James, O'Driscoll, Henderson, Luger, Hill. Cons: Wilkinson 4. Pens: Wilkinson 3.

I was very relaxed before kick-off, convinced we were going to give them a spanking. As it turned out I almost got one first - from my room mate Cozza. He is a typical forward roomy: bossy, likes his sleep and always wants to be in control of the TV remote. So I nicked the remote and turned the TV onto a ballet. Cozza, who had done brilliantly to get selected to start his second game in five days since arriving on Tuesday, was furious but I told him that ballet relaxed me before a game and that he should try and be a bit more cultured. He reacted by going next door, borrowing their remote and using it to switch over to a music channel. He then turned the volume up before returning it next door. But while he was away I turned the ballet back on and carried on as if nothing had happened. "The TV must be broke," I said. He looked at me with his psycho death eyes, as if to say, "do you want to die?" Suddenly I remembered where the remote was and handed it over. He's 18 stone and 6ft 6in and I didn't want to have to hurt him before his big game.

The team walk-through was held on the same patch of grass at the Botanical Gardens which we had run round in 1998 following the 76-0 debacle against Australia on the Tour of Hell. I looked for a sign saying 'Welcome all happy tours' but I couldn't see one. I then headed off to appear on a live sports show on Channel 7 with Colin Charvis.

Back to Ballymore in time for the game and the early argy-bargy. Queensland tried it on up front, big mistake. Johnno, Danny Grewcock and the other forwards stood their ground and then took total control. Mainly from Queensland mistakes, but who cares? We only created two tries in the first half yet the game was won by half-time. We allowed Queensland back into the game in the second half though they didn't score a try until Matt Dawson had one of his kicks charged down. Afterwards quite a few of the boys went out and got pissed. I, on the other hand, had nothing to celebrate so had a lemonade and quite an early night. The post-match food had again been shit. I'm losing weight and putting on fat.

SUNDAY

I hate travel days. Packing up and moving on is a nightmare. Living out of a suitcase does my head in after a while. The flight to Sydney was okay but the England netball team were on board and they asked us for our autographs which I found a bit strange. They were also not as tall as I would have expected. I went to college with two girls who played netball for England and they were massive and not in this squad. It was only later that I found out they were the mixed England team. Arrived in Sydney and played football in the airport car park while we waited for everyone. The bus got us safely to the Manly Pacific hotel - thanks Drives! - and we jumped out to admire the amazing oceanfront view. This is more like it. The tour can start now.

chapter fourteen

Driftwood and Planks

Week 4, Monday June 18 - Sunday June 24

I read it in the Aussie papers so he must have said it. Graham Henry, speaking before the game against Queensland, made the following statement. "If we have a split camp, with A and B teams if you like, I don't think that's good for the unity of the side. I think you have to look at the big picture. It's not just the 15 on the track who are going to win the Test matches. It will be the whole tour party of 50 pulling together."

Four years ago in South Africa the Lions had remained together from start to finish. None of us involved in that victorious tour had any doubt that the old saying was correct: united we stand, divided we fall. So for once on this tour I was in total agreement with my coach. It couldn't last of course. Less than a week later Henry revised his opinion. "We might just have to concentrate on the Test matches rather than other games. We think we need to put our eggs into the Test basket now." The midweek side had lost 28-25 to Australia 'A'. But Henry's remark had done the greater damage to morale.

MONDAY

Manly is an awesome place when the sun shines and the surf is up. It almost makes you feel pleased to be on tour. If the Aussie dollar was stronger it would be a great place to play and live. Sadly my positive mood could not survive training which today was a complete joke. One of the major problems on this tour is that midweek games have been played on a Tuesday, whereas in South Africa we played on Wednesdays. That has made even adequate preparation impossible. There are big games on Saturdays and we then travel long distances on Sundays so, more often than not, we can't train then as a team. And because Monday is the day before the game you can't do too much then either. The upshot is that the midweek team has found itself going into games diabolically under prepared.

This morning we only had about 20 minutes as a team doing our own thing because we had to spend most of the session running plays against the Saturday side who are preparing to play New South Wales at the weekend. The coaches are not giving us as much of their time or effort. The split between the Saturday and Tuesday teams has become very evident. The midweek boys are now known as Dai's Driftwood, because driftwood floats aimlessly down rivers just going with the flow. Pretty accurate, eh?

Why don't we name the Tuesday team before Saturday night so we can get through a little bit of work? I'm really surprised no-one in management has thought of this. The announcement is so late that players have to go to two training sessions not only with no firm idea of what position they're going to be playing but without knowing whether they're going to be playing at all. This stems from bad management and we need to sort it out because it's certainly become a huge problem.

In the short time we had today our lineouts were awful. We'll need to spend more time on them tomorrow. After all, we're up against a side containing ten Wallabies who have been in camp for 12 days preparing specifically for this one game. We have had 20 minutes. The backs don't look too bad but Mike Catt, who has been fighting a losing battle against injury since Tylney, is really struggling with his calf. He is so desperate to play and the ultimatum he has been given from on high means he will have to at

Gosford tomorrow. It's sad really. He's at least 10 metres off the pace. Jenks is struggling too. His knee is swollen big style. To be quite honest I don't think one person on this trip is 100% fit. Had two hours sleep this afternoon before watching one of Alun Carter's motivational videos. It did nothing for me. I looked at Daws while it was on and both of us burst out laughing. Purchased popcorn from Manly cinema, beat Daws at table tennis then went to bed.

TUESDAY

My first start. Isn't that amazing? Best player on the tour and I only get to start the fourth game! Quite remarkable. Quite unfortunate too, as it turns out. The Lions hadn't lost a non-Test in Australia for thirty years. But this was an accident waiting to happen given our chronic lack of preparation.

The build-up to this game was shocking. One session together the day before the game. It didn't help that not all the forwards knew all the calls. I was a bit dismayed by that. Then we were put through almost a mini training session in the team walk-through, hitting pads and stuff, which I thought was unnecessary, didn't exactly inspire confidence and certainly didn't keep us fresh for game time.

But that was not the end of it. We were informed that because the changing rooms at the stadium were very small that we should get changed at the hotel in Gosford, which is something I hate doing. And I didn't. I asked for my kit to be sent down to the ground, which it was. We then got to the changing rooms and they were huge. It would have been quite easy to stay down there and get ready for the game. As it was we turned up an hour and a quarter before kick-off, and things were slightly rushed.

I wasn't apprehensive personally. I'd had a good stretch in the hotel, a bit of a dance to our music. I was pretty focused, looking forward to the game, my first chance at scrum-half. Where I was nervous was up front because I knew our lineout wasn't going well. I was concerned that Jenks, at fly-half, was struggling with his bad knee and I would have to be very accurate with my passing because I knew he wouldn't be able to reach any 60-40 balls. I also knew that Catty was in all sorts of trouble. I think he knew in his heart of hearts that he had no chance of getting through the game.

As if we didn't have enough on our plate Eddie Jones, the opposition coach, had gone into the Press to accuse the Lions of foul play against Queensland and to urge the referee, New Zealander Paul Honiss, to keep a close eye on us. His claims that the Saturday side were guilty of 'indiscriminate rucking' were completely out of order and angrily rejected by Donal but I had to wonder whether it would prey on the ref's mind. Come the game we were pinged 24 times.

Match four details

Australia 'A' 28, British and Irish Lions 25

(North Power Stadium, Gosford, June 19)

LIONS: Perry; Cohen, Greenwood, Catt (M Taylor 44), Robinson; Jenkins (Dawson 59), Healey; Leonard, McBryde (Bulloch 54), Young (capt, Morris 68), Murray, O'Kelly (Davidson 54), Dallaglio, Williams, Quinnell (Charvis 29-43).

SCORERS - Tries: Robinson, Perry, M Taylor. Cons: Dawson 2. Pens: Jenkins 2.

People were pretty hyped up before hand and then we went out and got absolutely blitzed for the first 20 minutes. They had picked a huge team. Their pack was massive. As for some of their backs, the square jaw lines on some of them beggared belief to be honest. Thank goodness our defence, though we didn't win many collisions against these big fellas, was pretty awesome because our lineout was all at sea and we lost Catty, as I feared we would, when his calf gave way on the stroke of half-time.

But at 15-6 down we were still in the game. Our line had held firm thanks to some awesome cover defence and with it our morale. I was hurting though, having been knee dropped after Will

Greenwood had thrown a pass on the floor in front of me. I was left with a dead bum. While I could still accelerate I couldn't sprint at top speed because I couldn't pick my knees up. Several times during the game I'd seen gaps and been unable to go through them.

I also upper cut their flanker, Peter Ryan, who had been stamping on Will, when he fell on the wrong side at a ruck. You expect a shoeing when that happens but the fella then kicked him in the top of the head so I dragged him over by the scrum cap and punched him in the face. It was between me and him, but some guy called Justin Harrison, the plank, stuck his four-by-two in, chasing me in search of retribution. I ran towards the touchline inviting him to hit me in front of the touch judge so he'd get himself sent-off. With hindsight, it was a stupid thing to do. The way the decisions were going that would never have happened.

At half-time we were still in the game but we were just not winning any quick ball and when they finally breached our defence on the hour we were in a hole. I saw Daws appear on the touchline as a sub and I thought I was being taken off. But as I was running off Daws yelled 'You're playing 10, they're taking Jenks off'. We had Ronan O'Gara on the bench, a specialist fly-half, I felt for him. When the coach takes off a player in your position and moves someone else across it doesn't bode well for the rest of your tour. He's a top fella and a good player, Rog. It's a shame he hasn't had many opportunities to show himself.

Given our predicament I made a conscious decision to take the ball on myself and try to win some quick possession for the lads. It worked and we started to get some pattern going with the forwards running into their backs. Mark Taylor went over for us, then Matt Perry, then Jason Robinson. Had I given a diagonal kick to Ben Cohen slightly more weight the result could have been different. But it needed another five yards and with their fly-half kicking almost everything we finished three points short.

Emotions ran high after the game. Having said before the tour that we were going to be the best Lions team there had ever been, we had failed...after just four games. You feel responsible for the whole 37, not just the 15 that are playing and I felt pretty gutted. I came off and kicked the ice bucket over. I wasn't used to losing. Leicester and England don't make a habit of it. As if we didn't feel bad enough Donal weighed in with his disapproval, saying we hadn't performed properly as a Lions team and we were a disgrace and all that sort of stuff. A few of the lads came pretty close to snapping with him. I know I did. I didn't appreciate the words he was saying having come off that pitch breathing out of my arsehole, having given everything and only been beaten by different interpretations of the tackle law.

How else can I account for the way he penalised us at two consecutive rucks? At the first Mal O'Kelly was stood over this fella trying to rip the ball off him and the ref said 'no, no, you're using your hands'. Moments later Mark Taylor took the ball in and one of their players was stood up over him trying to yank the ball off him. We had players all around him so it was clearly a ruck but the ref pinged Mark for holding on. It was just completely ludicrous. All that whingeing in the press before the game by Eddie Jones about us cheating and being physical and lo and behold we got completely reffed out of the game. It was very disappointing. We went to the after-match function which was a dire affair. Australians patting themselves on the back everywhere you looked.

WEDNESDAY

Woke to the feeling of pain. I'm a physical wreck. My body is so sore and battered and my ego is bruised after losing. I needed to relax, yet last night's team had to help prepare the Saturday side and I'm on the bench again. Training lasted two hours - another short session - and was hugely depressing because Dan Luger suffered a fractured eye socket in clash of heads with Backy has been ruled out of the tour. Luges was looking really sharp and it was a freak accident. Backy has got a hard old head. He chose the wrong person to bump into at the wrong time. Sums up his last two years really. He is a huge loss to the tour and to our prospects of winning the Test series because he would have been pretty influential.

With Catty also confirmed as leaving the tour I returned to the hotel feeling pretty down. I needed to get out to clear my head of all the frustrations I was feeling so I suggested to the Stiffs that we head into Sydney. There was a big group of us, about 20. We started at Doyle's restaurant in the Harbour and then we went on to a bar called The Establishment, where I met my old mate from Hong Kong, Ian Shaw, and shared a commiseration drink with Catty and Phil Greening, who was also on his way out of the Lions' den. That was when things started to turn to serious.

I started buying Dr Peppers for all the lads: half lager, half coke and a depth charge of amoretto. Because it was my call I had to drink one in front of them so they knew I wasn't trying to make them ill. I was quite pissed by the time I decided to call it a night at 1.30am. I spent the entire ride back to the hotel yelling at the taxi driver to 'go faster' whilst on the phone to Louise who was telling me to 'shut up'. But I was in a funny mood and after making a few phone calls outside on the beach to catch up on the gossip from my mates Si, Ade and JP back home I went into the hotel and saw Donal at the bar.

I think he was quite pissed too so I started to try and wind him up. I was no longer drinking but the earlier alcohol had freed up my inhibitions and made it easier for me to speak my mind.

"Donal, this tour is shit. When are we going to have some fun? It's been crap so far. Nowhere near as good as the last one. We haven't had a team day out together yet."

He looked at me quizzically.

"And while we're on the subject Donal, why haven't you picked me? I'm by far the best player on this trip and you haven't even picked me in Saturday's team."

By this stage I think he realised that I was starting to take the piss. And I hadn't finished.

"This tour is crap. We want to have some fun and get pissed. When you went on tour with the Lions in 1989 and captained Donal's Donuts midweek team, you got pissed loads of times and had a cracking laugh. I think we need to knock the training on the head a bit, relax and have a bit of a crack and get some smiles on people's faces."

He looked at me, said "good night" and went to bed.

THURSDAY

It was nothing to do with my rant at Donal, but we had the morning off. Golf was arranged and after my alarm had rang at 8.30 I set about waking up my playing partners, some of whom had only just got in after one last drink with Catty. Played with Mark Davies, Lawrence Dallagllio and Will Greenwood. Managed to get 18 holes in but had too much of a hangover to play well. Got back to the hotel but food was again so poor that we headed out for lunch at a cafe on Manly seafront. Walking back with Shaggy we bumped into the forwards coming out of the hotel for their line-out session. Andy Robinson looked at me as if to say 'where have you been?', then said "We're at Manly Oval" and gestured me to follow. I didn't see the wind-up. My backside was killing me, it was cold and he had me walk all the way there to do nothing. One-nil to you Robbo.

The team meal had been set for Doyles but as most boys don't eat seafood the lads splintered off into cliques. No-one had a good word to say about Henry, who I have now re-named Emperor Ming. The boys are tired and agitated with the way things are going. They are happy with each other, in fact it's as good a bunch of fellas as I've been on tour with. But the tour as a whole has been an ordeal. A lot of lads just want to go home. But at least Catty's replacement Scott Gibbs has arrived. It will be good to have him in the midweek team.

FRIDAY

Surprise, surprise, my old mate Bob Dwyer has joined the

chorus of Wallaby whingers. First it was Eddie Jones accusing us of foul play against Queensland, who were far more guilty than we were, now Barbed Wire has pointed to "a lot of illegal things" which he reckons we get up to at the breakdown. Add Rod Macqueen to the mix, alleging that we are guilty of breaking scrum and lineout laws. When we first arrived the Australian RU president had come to meet us in Fremantle and promised that everything in his power would be done to make us feel welcome. It feels like quite the opposite. And if all that isn't enough to be getting on with, my relationship with Henry has plumbed new depths. He basically doesn't talk to me any more.

I'm run down at the minute. I have got scrum pox coming on my face. The tour thing is beginning to destroy me. If my family weren't coming out I'd be with Catty, Phillis (Greening) and Luges who are having the time of their lives. It's not just me I feel sorry for. Balsh is not getting the opportunity to show what he's all about. Henry's structure prevents players like him and me from expressing ourselves.

After our team run at the Sydney Football Ground, I had a sleep in the afternoon then just chilled. I'm utterly disenchanted. I feel like talking to the English coaches and telling them that it is nothing to do with them but I can't motivate myself at the minute to play for this team. I just want to get going on my two-year plan for the next World Cup. I'm all rugby-ed out at the moment. I desperately want to play for England against Ireland in October but I feel that no matter how hard I try I'm getting nowhere with the Lions. I won't make myself available to tour New Zealand in four years time unless they are better prepared with a visionary coach like Brian Ashton, Clive Woodward or Dean Richards.

SATURDAY

The tour erupted into violence tonight and it is a safe bet that Ronan O'Gara's battered mug will be on the back of every newspaper tomorrow. His left eye was beaten to a pulp by Duncan

McRae, who played for Saracens last season, and he needed eight stitches to stop the bleeding and close the wound. Rog's face was in pretty bad shape to be honest. He had tried to clean McRae out at a ruck, perfectly legally, and McRae went beserk. Rog was pinned down and McRae punched him not once but 11 times. It was completely over the top, disgusting and I thought McRae showed what a coward he is.

Match five details

New South Wales 24, British and Irish Lions 41

(Sydney Football Stadium, Sydney, June 23)

LIONS: Balshaw; James, O'Driscoll, Greenwood (O'Gara 25, Perry 59), Robinson; Wilkinson (Healey 83), Dawson; Morris, Wood (McBryde 87), Vickery, Johnson (capt), Grewcock, Dallaglio, Back (Hill 80), Quinnell (Smith 60).

SCORERS - Tries: Robinson 2, O'Driscoll, James, Wilkinson. Cons: Wilkinson 4, Dawson. Pens: Wilkinson 2.

I remember at Leicester last season, just before Johnno broke his ribs, that he'd thrown his body weight around. I'm sure had he stayed on the pitch tonight he'd only have lasted a bit longer. Had he not been sent-off he would have found himself with some severe problems from the rest of the squad. A few of the boys were quite keen to go and find him afterwards and sort him out but nothing came of it. Hopefully he'll get the opportunity to come over and play in Munster. I think if he does probably the entire tour party will go and watch that game. I haven't a clue what provoked it but McCrae has a small man problem and needs to get himself sorted out. I saw him after the game and shouted abuse at him. I was amazed he had the front to show his face at the post-match function after what he'd done.

Bob Dwyer, the NSW coach spoke for him. And what a performance he gave at the press conference. I went along to watch him in action and I have never heard such rubbish in all my life. He blamed Danny Grewcock for starting the trouble, claimed the Lions had thrown more punches and that McRae was retaliating to a swinging arm. I don't think the press could believe what they were hearing. Bob plays the media well normally but this time he went too far. I was asked what I thought of Bob's comments. I said I thought they were ludicrous and completely in his character. The things he came out with were just mindboggling.

As far as I was concerned NSW came out to try and rattle us and to physically dominate us (I'd never seen four players sin-binned together before until Grewy and Phil Vickery went off with two of theirs as the balloon went up after McRae's sending off). There's been a bit of an agenda since we've been out here to rough us up a bit. If there's any more of that in the next couple of games you may see the old '99' call come back in where the entire team piles into whoever starts the fight. All of us, when we saw what McRae did, united together and wanted to pile into him and anyone else who tries it on with us. What happened tonight has galvanised us as a squad. When we wake up tomorrow a lot of people will be a bit sore but we will all feel a lot tighter as a squad.

We are forever being told we are a dirty team, totally because of Australia's perception of the '89 Lions. We have done nothing to deserve it. What they can't understand over here is that we play a very physical game in the northern hemisphere. They take that physical presence as a sign of violence when in actual fact it's just the norm for us. They have got us all wrong. Spiro Zavros, who writes a rugby column in *The Sydney Morning Herald*, said this week that "northern hemisphere rugby favours 6-3 scorelines, played on muddy fields with set-pieces becoming dockyard brawls." Mind-blowing! Has he watched a game in England in the last five years?

The game was a bit of a disaster for me personally as I was injured before kick-off. We were forced to warm up on the cricket ground, which was a good five-minute walk from our changing room. I was in charge of the defensive line. I was moving them forwards and backwards when one of the forwards pushed me and I slipped and fell right onto the bruise on my backside. I was in bits. I had to go straight back to the changing rooms and get painkillers and some ice, before I could suit up. As I went out I wasn't able to run for ten minutes until the painkillers started to kick in.

Things generally went pretty well for us, although Balsh had a few problems at fullback and Pezza may have played himself right back into Test contention. Jason Robinson again played very well. He's really starting to get to grips with the game and is a great natural talent. I still think that maybe the Australians will find him out and isolate him and turn him over because his ball retention is not that great just yet. I hope I'm wrong. On the other wing Dafydd James played alright. He's having a very steady tour and seems to be in the Test team already. I find that quite remarkable. He's a good player and a nice fella, but I've not been considered on the wing at all, not even in training, which upsets me bearing in mind I've got more caps than all the other wings left here put together.

Johnno had a good game. He and Grewy were very physical and they seem to be the driving forces in the team at the moment. Scott Quinnell played very well, as did Backy. Lol's tour ended after he hurt his knee which is another big blow to the squad but personally I think he's made the right decision. The last thing he wants to do is risk his entire future. The Lions is a big thing to a lot of people but he's got a family to provide for and he loves to play rugby. We have now lost five players - eight is apparently the Lions record - and we're still a week away from the start of the Test series. It's a case of players trying to play injured. That stems probably from earlier on in the tour when everyone was knackered and there was too much training and not enough time to prepare for the huge confrontations ahead. The Aussies are probably in the gym every day, training and getting fit for the Test series.

I still think we're playing too structured a game which doesn't allow us to utilise or visualise opportunities and space. Several overlaps went begging. Had I been on the wing I would have been running in with steam coming out of my ears. As it was I came on with about eight minutes to go, made four tackles, missed one and put in a couple of kicks. But we didn't have any ball. We were constantly defending. Every time we had the ball someone would turn it over. It was shocking. Our defence was relatively strong but there is still room for improvement throughout our entire game.

After the game ice, ice, ice for everyone. It will be a miracle of modern science to get through this Test series with no more players flying out because quite simply there are just not enough fit bodies around. People are really struggling. Donal made a very good 'backs to the wall' speech. He talked about how the Aussies were trying it on with us and how all it would achieve would be to bring us tighter together. He used examples of how previous Lions tours had overcome adversity to achieve great things and said we would do the same. Hope he's right. Got back to hotel and popped into the nightclub next door with Daws and Balsh. Had a few waters then left at 1am knackered after my eight minutes of rugby.

SUNDAY

Dwyer's case was so compelling that McRae got seven weeks and the Lions were totally exonerated by the disciplinary panel. Spent the morning packing for Coffs Harbour, our next port of call, and trying to fathom how my stamp on Kevin Putt two years ago was more serious than McRae's offence (I was banned for eight weeks). Couldn't work that out, nor how I came out on tour with half-empty bags which are now full. I'm having to jump on them to close them now. Coffs Harbour is another Hicksville with nothing but golf courses and a saloon. Played cribbage with Daws on plane, 10p a point. I ended up £1.70 down. Sat in front of management whilst they were planning the week and selection. Henry doesn't listen to anyone. Robbo was making good suggestions and being ignored. I gave my sandwiches to Donal and said that just because

I gave him my food I didn't want it to effect selection. I don't think it will somehow.

Arrived at the hotel. I'm sharing with Backy, who is so tidy it's scary. He knows where all his kit is and never needs to unpack. By the time our bags had caught up with us a training session had been called. We had to be quick because we only had 45 minutes of light left. So we went out and did lineout practice. More structure. Balsh was named at 15 in the side to play NSW Country Cockatoos to give him confidence. He doesn't need confidence, he needs someone to distribute the ball to him and a team which agrees with the gameplan. What gameplan? We only have structure. No heads up rugby. The structure and targets here are completely the opposite to the vision and heads-up rugby of England. Attack space, create space. Henry can't spell space.

chapter fifteen

Against all Odds

Week 5, Monday June 25 - Saturday June 30

MONDAY

What an unbelievable day. Ming has completely given up on the Tuesday team in a blatant way. This morning's training session was supposed to be our team run-through. Henry called over Dai Young, our captain, and asked him to rehearse some of the first Test line-out options against the rest of the lads as part of our team run. Dai brought the Stiffs together and said "We'll do our stuff first, then the Australian lineouts that Graham wants."

Henry came over and told Dai to do them immediately. We then played all of Australia's options against the Test squad in full speed grip touch for 30 minutes - we scored two tries and, to be fair, tore them apart. After the second try Henry stopped the session, so we had no chance to do any of our own stuff. The team to play NSW Country tomorrow left the pitch in a state of complete disbelief - thoroughly fucked off. What is our motivation to play this game if they can't be bothered to put any effort into our preparation? What the hell is the point of the midweek team?

The importance of the Lions has diminished for a lot of this squad and for Henry to do that to players' morale is a disgrace. He has already said publically that he has given up on the Tuesday games and is concentrating on the Tests. He has destroyed the squad spirit. There is a huge split in the party, yet the lads get on really well together and most of the coaches do too. There are a lot of cliques on this trip but all the cliques get on with one another. There are no divisive factions between groups of people. Take Henry out of the equation and we could have a happy and successful tour.

Why pay for Impact and team building if you're going to come here for the first two weeks and not give anybody half a day off? I think Donal is a good manager, I think he's a decent fella. The one problem is Emperor Ming. At this point I don't see how we can win the Test on Saturday because of the gameplan and because the boys are out on their feet from overtraining.

My mood didn't improve when I saw that the Aussie press had implicated me in a sledging row. They said that I had claimed to have been the victim of sledging in the match against Queensland a week ago. They then accused me of accusing Queensland hooker Michael Foley of saying 'You Poms are shit, you shouldn't even be on this pitch with us'. Not content with that they then turned it into a war of words by getting Foley to slag me off. There was one major problem with all this. I had said nothing of the sort. They had picked up Backy's comments in *The Mirror* and attributed them to me. I had been accused of something I had absolutely nothing whatsoever to do with. I asked Alex Broun, our media liason man, if I could do anything about it. I was seething that I'd said nothing, had words put into my mouth and then been accused of starting a war. He said that he'd speak to the journos responsible. I decided not to hold my breath.

Decided I needed to get away and relax so I played golf with Daws against O.D and Rob, the cameraman and producer of the Lions' fly-on-the-wall documentary. We played an awesome course and Daws and I played some awesome golf. We had four birdies and an eagle and took $350 off them each. We had a great laugh with them. For a few hours all my troubles seemed so far away. Then we were hit by a bombshell. On the way back from the course

I got a call from one of the lads telling me that Anton Toia, our Australian Rugby Union liason officer, had died while swimming in the ocean outside our team hotel.

I just couldn't believe it. Anton was a good fella, all the lads really got on with him and he worked his arse off for us. All evening meetings were cancelled because we were all in a state of shock. Hugh Llewellyn, our Adidas kit man, took it really badly. He had become a really close friend of Anton. To be fair we all had. I feel like this tour is cursed. It's certainly going off the rails. The only positive is that Dorian has been called out which should be a breath of fresh air to the squad.

TUESDAY

My backside is still very sore and today didn't help. Went to the team meeting at 10.45 and sat around doing nothing as most of the other boys were twenty minutes late. The timekeeping on this trip has been shocking. In England we work to Lombardi time - fifteen minutes early to every meeting. Just another detail the management has neglected. But if that irritated me it was nothing to the way I felt when Jerry Davidson pulled away my chair just before the meeting started and I landed smack bang on the bruised part of my bum. The pain was severe and I had a real go at Dangerous Brian. On this trip he has clipped more people in training than anyone else.

The upshot was that I couldn't do the walk-through on the morning of the game. Instead I had treatment from the doc, then at midday had an injection to stop the pain and reduce the inflammation. It was the first time I'd ever had a jab to play. Strange, when the game meant nothing to me. The needle went into my other cheek and hurt like a typhoid jab, but it did its job as the pain temporarily subsided, allowing me to play.

Match six details

NSW Country 3, British and Irish Lions 46

(International Stadium, Coffs Harbour, June 26)

LIONS: Balshaw; Cohen, M Taylor, Gibbs (O'Gara 49-58), Howe; Jenkins, Healey; Leonard (Morris 58), Bulloch, Young (capt), Davidson, O'Kelly (Murray 72), Charvis, Williams, Corry (Wallace 57).

SCORERS - Tries: Cohen 2, Gibbs, Healey, Young, Charvis. Cons: Jenkins 5. Pens: Jenkins 2.

It was a dreadful game, even though I got over the line for one of our six tries. There was no passion in our performance. Perhaps not too surprising. The support for us was tremendous, but the stadium was small, the opposition were poor, the home referee was diabolical and we felt de-motivated by the path the tour has taken. When Steve Black stood up in the changing room beforehand and admitted the coaches had let us, the midweek boys, down it was impossible to disagree. He basically admitted that they had messed us around all week, that they'd let us down, treated us like second class citizens, spent too much time with the Test team and not prepared us like they should have done. He said that we didn't owe them anything but we owed it to the Lions shirt to go out and do the business. Henry stood behind Blackie and made some glib remark. He gave the impression he was immune to all criticism.

It's amazing how bored players get in small towns where there is nothing to do. We end up either playing cards or making up stupid games. Tonight we played corridor bowls with golf balls for more than an hour and a half before Hendo claimed a victory of sorts. I then went back to my room to find out that Backy had been ruled out of the Test with pulled oblique muscles. Making the first Test was a massive goal he had set himself. He knows this is his last Lions tour and he was bitterly disappointed. He is quite obviously more motivated than me to play for this team.

WEDNESDAY

This day had been billed as a focal point of the tour. From Tylney onwards all the meetings had come to the same conclusion that we as a squad had to be together and focused on the day the team for the first Test was named. Well, as a bunch of guys we are desperate to beat Australia but waiting for the announcement the suspense was minimal. The majority of the room knew they didn't have a chance because they hadn't been given any opportunity of staking their claim.

The squad isn't split. It has been pulled tighter together by adversity - Anton's death, Ronan's beating by Duncan McRae in the New South Wales game and the spate of injuries we have endured - rather than by the methodology of the coaches. We are all in it together but a lot of the boys have lost their individual purpose for this trip. If there is nothing to play for how do you push yourself to the maximum? Being in the midweek team is like being a temporary teacher - you are just there to keep things going.

I had sat down with Will Greenwood and correctly picked the 22 last night, starting with me on the bench. It really wasn't difficult once I knew that Backy was out. Cozza is in and deserves his chance. He has done brilliantly since coming out. Donal read out the names before Phil Larder stood up and told us that this team was better equipped to beat Australia than England had been in November last year. He gave a very passionate speech on defence and I got the distinct impression that the management are nervous about the weekend. Later, I asked Phil if he truly believed what he had said. He replied that he thought the squad needed a bit more confidence. I took that as a 'no'.

Again I was unable to train because my backside is still killing me. I just want it to go away now. We left Coffs Harbour for Brisbane without me having seen any part of the place. How typical of touring these days to go to somewhere nice and see next to nothing but the training pitch and the hotel. How my battered body could do with a couple of days R&R. However, glad to be heading back to Brisbane because Louise is flying in and hopefully having her around will relax me and somehow make me able to enjoy the rest of the trip. We've reached the business end of the tour now and I'm going to try and be more positive. At least that was what I pledged to myself before Donal stood up on the bus ride from the airport into Brisbane.

Journeys to hotels are when keys are handed out and you find out who you are rooming with. I got Daws, which should be a laugh and I was just congratulating Joan Moore, Donal's administrative assistant, on the smooth running of the day - all our gear had arrived before us - when Donal spoke into the microphone. "You've got the day off tomorrow lads, relax, play golf, whatever you want...but at 3.30 there will be a team meeting followed by a run through."

The lads stormed off the bus spewing and I told Joan she had fallen at the final hurdle. None of us can believe our day off has been broken up. I went out with Daws, my sister Ashley and JP O'Reilly, one of my Leicester teammates, for a couple of quiet ones to try to cool down. We had been looking forward to playing golf on an awesome course. I know we need to be prepared but my attitude has gone from motivated to mischievous with one dictom. A month into the tour and my prospects are bleak. I haven't been given an opportunity to play on the wing, Jonny's a goalkicker so I can't play 10 and Howley's playing at 9 and he was picked before we left England. I've tried so hard to stay positive but I just can't escape the conclusion that the Lions is no longer my pinnacle.

I know it's sacrilege to say that but it's just the way this tour has made me feel. Representing England is top of the tree at the moment because it has been made so elite that I am desperate to stay in that environment. This Lions tour has never tried to compete, that's what I can't understand. It's been like stepping into the tardis and going back to play for England three years ago. If our fitness advisor Dave Reddin had been here he wouldn't have let us train like we have. He would have advised the management that if you do that to them you're not going to be successful. Otis is very organised, an expert in his field, highly driven and he believes fitness is the answer to winning games. He's also very lucky because he's going out with Isabel, who I can only think is very short sighted.

THURSDAY

A poor decision yesterday and another one today as we were taken to train in the Botanical Gardens. The Australian team hotel is right across the road and there we were going through our secret moves. We can only hope that they were not peeping through their net curtains. Surely Henry knew they were staying there. I felt really disappointed that the senior players did not have the ability to stop the training. It was not for the want of trying but their pleas fell on deaf ears. The lads need a rest. I went to the casino and lost money. A great day it wasn't. Bed. I can't take much more of this.

FRIDAY

The day before the first Test and I finally lost it with Henry. We were at Ballymore preparing for a three-hour training session and had just had the warm-up when we came together in a huddle, circling Ming in the middle.

"Are you ready then lads?" he said.

Everyone replied "Yeah, let's go".

He then turned to me and straight to my face said "Austin?".

"Yeah, I'm ready".

"About fucking time."

It came completely out of the blue and none of the lads could believe what he'd said. So I turned on him.

"Who do you think you're talking to, you prick?"

There was a pause. He looked at me and I looked at him. Then he spoke.

"Right then, let's go".

Why did I speak to him like that? Because he spoke to me out of turn. I had done nothing wrong. He is the coach, he's not my schoolteacher or my dad. Various players came up to me and told me not to let him get under my skin. Some of the other coaches even told me to stay cool. But I reached the point two weeks ago where it would not bother me if I was sent off tour. Louise arrived today and I'd just go travelling around Australia with her and have a good time. Phil Greening, Mike Catt and Dan Luger are having the best time they've ever had in their lives: travelling, seeing the country and not going anywhere near a tackle bag.

I left training totally disillusioned and convinced Henry has got it in for me. Louise came round to the team hotel and I told her what Henry had said in training. She told me to keep my mouth shut and to get on with it. She stayed for a while to sleep off some her jetlag before I took her down to reception at 6 o'clock to get her taxi. Who should walk into the lift but Ming. I introduced him to Lou. He said hello and then gave me a look which said 'what is she doing here the night before a game'?

The Captain's Meeting was scheduled for 6.15 and, frankly, I was not in the mood. But Johnno spoke well; he's a real leader. Alun Carter then produced a good video and the combination of Johnno's words and some stirring action highlights lifted me. In an instant the tour started to almost feel important again. I found myself almost looking forward to the game, (even though I'm only on the bench), almost desperate to play. I said back in April when I was selected that I wanted to play in the Tests. Now, just in the nick of time, that desire has helped me to turn the corner. I'm going to step up my attitude and efforts from hereon in. I will get into the starting line-up.

Returned to my room to be greeted by a bullshit note from Blackie asking each of us to write a 'positive motivational message' to each of the other players in the Test match 22. "A short statement will suffice, it can be about anything you want," he wrote. "Just let your colleagues know how much they are valued and respected." I screwed it up and threw it at Daws and then we chatted about his Tour Diary which is being published in *The Daily Telegraph* tomorrow. He read it to me and I have to say I thought there were a few risky comments about the management, given that it was coming out on the day of the first Test. But he only said what a lot of people are thinking.

SATURDAY

It needed to be something special to get me excited about being a 2001 Lion and Willie John McBride provided it with his pre-match speech. I hadn't thought a great deal about the Lions concept up to that point, I had been too busy training, too busy drawing unflattering comparisons between the Lions set-up and that of England. Maybe that was naivety on my part. It was only after hearing Willie John, then seeing thousands upon thousands of Lions fans at the Gabba today, that I questioned my judgement.

My conclusion, based on a brilliant performance by the lads against all the odds and seeing the passion of fans who have travelled so far to support us, is that I have probably been wrong to have had such a downer on this tour. I stand by every criticism I have made of Henry, his coaching philosophy and his management style, but the reaction of even my friends back home, who are totally excited by what's going on, has shown me how big a deal this is for people.

I had been pessimistic about our chances purely because of the structure we'd been coached to play by Henry. I didn't believe it would work. In fact I didn't believe it had a chance of working. But the lads completely ignored the gameplan for probably the first 25 minutes of each half. They got the ball wide to Jason Robinson and Dafydd James and we saw some exhilarating play from 15 obviously very talented players. It was great to watch.

The tone was set by Willie John when he spoke to us at the hotel and presented each of us with our jersey. I have met him a few times but I never saw him play. I just know his name. It has a certain aura about it. The Lions and Willie John McBride go hand in hand. And yet he said he was humbled and honoured to be asked to come and speak to us. He said he didn't know why he'd been asked, but that he just wanted to get across what it would mean for us to win not only to him but for everybody else in the British Isles. It wasn't so much what he said as the way he said it. He sat down amongst the circle of the team and didn't raise his voice at all. He didn't have to. The passion in him was unmistakable. He just spoke very softly and just went through what he thought it meant to play for the Lions. He said it was a great honour and one that should be enjoyed and remembered. He spoke about how hard it was going to be physically and he tried to assure us that the pain would be worth it. It was easily the best speech of the tour.

I looked around the room. The eyes of every player were glued to his. Then Graham Henry spoke. "Right fellas, let's talk rugby". Players looked at their watches, the ceiling, the floor, anything but his eyes. He shouted a bit and started to gee up the players. But we were already geed up by what Willie John had said. Far better to talk about the passion and the emotion than the rugby because we know about the rugby.

We left the hotel through the back door because you couldn't move for fans in the lobby. There were still at least 300 cheering us out onto the bus but that was small beer compared to the numbers at the Gabba where everyone in the ground seemed to be wearing a Lions jersey. It was awesome.

Match seven details

Australia 13, British and Irish Lions 29

(first Test: The Gabba, Brisbane, June 30)

AUSTRALIA: Latham (Burke 41); Walker, Herbert, Grey, Roff; Larkham (Flatley 51), Gregan; Stiles, Paul (Foley 51), Panoho (Darwin 61), Giffin, Eales (capt, Cockbain 65), Finegan (Lyons 73), Smith, Kefu.

SCORERS - Tries: Walker, Grey. Pen: Walker.

LIONS: Perry (Balshaw 41); James, O'Driscoll, Henderson, Robinson; Wilkinson, Howley; Smith (Leonard 73), Wood (Bulloch 74-81), Vickery, Johnson (capt), Grewcock, Corry, Hill, Quinnell (Charvis 62).

SCORERS - Tries: Robinson, James, O'Driscoll, Quinnell. Cons: Wilkinson 3. Pen: Wilkinson.

Ref: A Watson (SA). Sin-bin: Corry (62), Vickery (75). Att: 37,460.

We went straight out to see the pitch because the day before it hadn't been marked out. It had still been an Aussie Rules pitch. We then had the warm-up inside and it all went really well. I was in charge of the defensive drill and I tried to make it really snappy and really noisy. Not me but the rest of the team. It was really good. People were really sharp. There was a good sweat. Everyone was together. It was the best warm-up of the tour.

I went out and sat in the stand for the first ten minutes to try and get more of a bird's eye view of the game and see where the space was on the field. I was minding my own business when some jobsworth steward came up to me and said I couldn't sit on the steps. I told him I wouldn't leave until he got the police, but while he went off to find them I left rather than cause a scene. As I got to the bottom and jumped over the barrier an Australian said "You're scared Healey". We were already 5-0 up, Robbo having scored a fabulous try with his first touch. When it got to 29-3 - Daf, Brian O'Driscoll and Scotty Quinnell having followed him over - I went back to the barrier to have a little stretch and to look up that loud-mouthed Aussie. "Who's scared now?" I asked. "You ought to be scared that we don't get 50, mate." The Lions fans around him liked that.

When Daf scored in the corner just before half-time we all jumped to our feet off the bench and surged towards the side of the pitch, without going onto it. The fourth official ran over and told us to sit down and we invited him to go and get lost, or words to that effect. He countered by saying that if we spoke to him like that again he'd tell the ref. So we did and he did. It was so ridiculous for him to get het up over a little thing like that. But then again he had been our ref in the NSW Country game. One of my mates later told me there had been a fight in the stand between two Australian fellas. My mate went and warned a steward that it was about to kick-off and he just shrugged his shoulders. Yet I sit on the steps and he runs at me. We jump up when Daf scores a try and the fourth official flips. Can these people not have any perspective about what's important?

But what an amazing game. What an awesome performance from the entire team. Hardly anyone had a bad game. The boys didn't stick to the gameplan, the ball went wide a lot and we scored from first phase on three occasions. Brian Ashton will have enjoyed that. My only regret was not getting on to share in the win. Henry and the other coaches had come up to me in the changing room beforehand and primed me for what I was to do when I came off the bench so I had been pretty positive about playing a part. I kept myself warm throughout and I had my tracksuit off at one stage when Brian O'Driscoll went down. But they never saw the need to put me on and that really hacked me off. I was keen and fresh. There were players out there like Jonny who were getting stung by every tackle. Brian had hurt his leg and at 29-3 I thought they could have done with some fresh legs. We'd a one and a half hour session at Ballymore yesterday and in the last twenty the boys looked dead on their feet and really struggling to find another gear to kill them off.

But they got the win and we are one-nil up. After all the propaganda in the Press, all the complaining about how dirty we are, how we cheat, even how we play boring rugby, it was so sweet to silence all the bleating. I feel a bit weird towards the tour now. Have I been wrong about Henry all this time? Has my depression coloured my judgement? All I've done so far is slag him off. He has behaved like a bit of a dick at certain times under pressure but we've won the first Test. Maybe his planning has worked. Wait a minute, the Aussies were woeful tonight. I don't think this is over yet.

Most of the boys went out but I felt a bit strange so I arranged to have a quiet drink with Johnno. I went up to the room to get changed and Daws was in there with his agent Dave Williams. All hell had broken loose about his diary in *The Telegraph*. I thought it best to give them a bit of space so I had a couple with Johnno then went to Lou's hotel and stayed there for a quiet night. It had been one hell of a day.

chapter sixteen

Justin Time Again

Week 6, Sunday July 1 - Saturday July 7

SUNDAY

We had beaten the world champions in their own backyard yet we spent the morning after the day before in recrimination mode. I came back from Lou's hotel after breakfast to hear that Daws' diary has caused a stink. The Press at home had gone big on it in today's papers and Donal was spewing. Daws was dragged over the coals by the management and made to apologise to the squad in the team room before we checked out to catch the flight down to Canberra.

We sat in a semi-circle with Daws in the middle. He stood up and said he was not apologising for what he had wrote, which at the time he said he believed to be true, but for the timing of the article which was all wrong. His intention was not to send the tour off the rails. I know because I was rooming with him. His diary was just that. A series of personal observations. "I was just trying to give a true perspective of what was going on," he told us all. "I'm sorry to everyone of you." He said he'd spoken to Johnno and the rest of the coaches and had assured them that he'd be fully committed for the rest of the tour and that he was looking forward to the opportunity to put things right against the Brumbies on Tuesday.

Donal had told the television crew making the fly-on-the-wall documentary about the tour to switch their cameras off and you don't mess with him when he's angry. He speaks very aggressively.

He's not a quiet fella, he's a top lip quiverer, a very emotional talker. That's probably why I like him. Daws, too, had his serious face on. Luckily for him I was sat in the corner out of his eye shot because I'd left mine in my room. I sat there desperately trying to keep a straight face. You know when you're trying so hard not to let laughter out that snot comes down your nose? I was like that. I couldn't see what need there was for him to apologise. After all, everyone thought he was right. None of the players I'd spoken to had a problem with him or what he'd said. The only people who had were Donal and Graham.

Daws' diary had appeared under the headline 'Harsh regime tears us apart'. Not too much exaggeration there. He spoke of 'mindless coaching', of players being 'flogged' and of the players being 'treated like children'. All true. The only problem, as he readily accepted, was the timing of the article. Other than that I think a lot of the players respected him for sticking his head above the parapet and saying what they were thinking. When he had finished he sat down and Donal said "Right, has anyone got anything to say?" Everyone went dead quiet but I put my hand up. "Yes Austin,".

"Does that mean the public stoning is cancelled for tomorrow then?" I asked.

"Yes Austin I think so," Donal replied.

"Oh shit," I said. "Because I've already bought a bag of gravel and two flat rocks!"

If the mood was a bit frosty in the team room in Brisbane, it was nothing like as cold as the temperature awaiting us in Canberra. It was only a couple of degrees above zero today. It didn't help that I have a heavy cold, a barking cough and my body is in bits. Nor that our hotel had been flooded and there are hot air blowers underneath every carpet in the foyer and restaurant area. You can't hear yourself think for the sound of those bloody things.

Canberra is an unreal place, a huge city with no-one in it. It's like everyone in the town has been locked in their cellars. Shame it's not like that in every Australian town. Only joking! But I have to say that some of the males I have come across on this trip have been complete idiots. They can't walk past you without having a go, although they were quieter today. Funny that.

Canberra means 'meeting place' in Aboriginal and 90-odd years ago it didn't even exist. Apparently, after the Australian colonies were federated in 1901 the constitution demanded a national capital and the rivalry between Sydney and Melbourne was so intense that neither would accept the other. So they decided on a spot in between and built a new city from scratch. And here we are. Backy and I rooming together again. Two guys with one goal. To get in the Test team this coming Saturday.

The coaches are now making a big deal of our match against the ACT Brumbies on Tuesday in order that we keep the momentum going. Confidence is high for the second Test and I think I've been picked on the wing. If I'm right I'll at last get the chance to play in my main international position and to start a Test for the Lions for the first time. But first things first. The Brumbies are Super 12 champions and Tuesday's game is the one the midweek side has been waiting for all tour. Balsh, Ben and I are playing together for the first time and I think that will be decisive. I'm really looking forward to the game. It's a chance to show that I should be in the Test team and I'm going to enjoy it. My knee feels a bit better, the pain in my bum has nearly gone so I'll be as close to full fitness as I can be, considering it will be my 50th time this season I've been in a matchday 22.

MONDAY

Woke up full of determination to make a good impression. The team run at Bruce Stadium went well for me. I was straight into the groove again of wing play, though I reckon we'll need a bit more width tomorrow night. I think Robbo and Larder detected a difference in my approach. I even kicked quite well. Without my knee strapped I'm a lot freer. We are up for this game in a big way. The team meeting was good, Alun's video lifted us all and Dai spoke well. I didn't even laugh at him this time. After watching the lads win in Brisbane we all want a bit of glory for ourselves. We deserve at least that, don't we? Call it selfishness but we want some of that praise. We have been on the outskirts watching a lot of great stuff from the Saturday team, a team a number of us believe we should be in. We want to go out and make a statement to that effect.

I spent the evening gambling against local card sharks at the poker table. Some fella tried to abuse me. "We do it to put you off your game," he said. Oh well, if those are the house rules! I called him a few choice names, he was duly put off and I won the next few hands. Thanks for the tip, mate. Then to really annoy him I left the table. He told me to carry on playing because he wanted to win his money back. I waved as I left the joint.

TUESDAY

Matchday and we were a lot more geared up for the game than we had been against the likes of NSW Country and the Queensland President's XV because they were seen to be games we couldn't lose. The Australia 'A' game came at a bad time because we had spanked the President's men, so to speak, and confidence was probably too high. We knew it would be a hard game but we weren't as up for it as we were for this one.

I'd had quite a bad night's kip so I got up early and went on the nebulisor. I then spent the rest of the day until the run-through chilling out, hydrating and gambling in the casino, losing more and more money. Some of the England boys have a theory that the more money you lose before a game the better you play. So I consoled myself that my weightless wallet was a good omen for the game.

The team's preparation was alright, though it still wasn't great. Obviously we hadn't had seven days to prepare like the Test squad gets. We'd had a couple of days. But the lineout was looking better because Dorian West, who is obsessed with lineouts, had really started getting things going. Mind you, after the stunt he'd pulled on his wife Claire and their children he needed to play well. They had only been in Spain for ten minutes on their annual holiday when Nobby informed them that the Lions needed him in Australia. His missus wasn't best pleased!

Match eight details

ACT Brumbies 28, British and Irish Lions 30

(Bruce Stadium, Canberra, July 3)

LIONS: Balshaw; Cohen, Taylor, Gibbs, Healey; O'Gara, Dawson; Morris (Leonard 78), West, Young (capt), Davidson, Murray, Wallace, Williams (James 27), Corry.

SCORERS - Tries: Healey 2, Wallace. Cons: Dawson 3. Pens: Dawson 3.

The game itself was full of little bits of niggle especially from Justin Harrison, my mate from the Australia 'A' game, who was constantly tapping our players on the head if they lost the ball in the tackle or gave away a penalty. He could dish it out but he didn't like it back. We started doing it to him and he snapped and started to throw punches. He seems to be a nightmare of a fella, certainly on the pitch. When I intercepted a pass from Pat Howard just before half-time he ran 50 yards to bump into me with his chest. What a waste of energy, what a complete fool. All because I'd turned round and waved at Pat Howard. That was between me and Pat. It had nothing to do with him.

We made a shocking start. God knows how many first-up tackles were missed down the middle. We conceded two tries inside the first 12 minutes, the second of which was a complete joke. Their winger was a good six inches in touch before he grounded the ball. The touch judge must have seen it and completely ignored it. It was just symptomatic of the problems we have had with referees and touchjudges in midweek games. Surely there are enough officials in the world to get a neutral ref when you come on tour with the Lions.

Having these Australian refs has been a complete nonsense. When they scored a third try in the 25th minute we were 19-3 down and things weren't looking too clever. But Pat threw us a lifeline. They broke on the left and I just knew Paddy would throw a little loop because he loves his loops. He did and said something like "take it up" which is normally a signal for the defence to tighten up so as to hit the ball carrier. But knowing Paddy as I do I took a gamble on the fact that he'd be coming round and throwing a pass. When he got the ball back I saw him look out wide to me. I think I was probably too wide for him to throw the over-the-top pass so I just went flat, managed to get an outstretched hand to the ball, held onto it and ran in.

I had half the field to cover and turned round initially because everyone had stopped and I thought the ref had blown up for offside, which wouldn't have come as any great surprise on this tour. But he hadn't and I trotted in before turning to look first at the ref and then at Paddy. I just pointed at him, as if to say thanks. Then that idiot Harrison was in my face. "That's only one try you prick. You're still losing."

I had previously made a try-saving tackle on their centre so things had started well for me. But we still went into half-time trailing 22-10 and got a fair old bollocking from Henry, who said we'd no pride in the shirt. He then questioned whether all the words that we'd spoken before the game had been bullshit. When he had finished speaking there was silence. It had been like being back at school, being told off for not doing your homework. It was a pretty shitty feeling and a pretty shitty way to be spoken to. We didn't go down on purpose. So I got up and started shouting, trying to get the rest of the lads up on their feet and motivated to go back out.

We knew we had to get out there and start with a bang and that's exactly what we did. They kicked off, we won the ball and took it up the field for David Wallace to go over. Daws converted and added a penalty and the deficit was down to two points. There was then a bit of scrapping with their openside, who had a quality Afro on him. Nugget caught him with a good punch after he'd thrown a few. Then Balsh high-tackled their fullback and Harrison went after him. He seems to pick on the small guys but never has a go at the big guys. He wants to pick on someone his own size. Anyway, Balsh was sin-binned and ACT pulled five points clear again.

They still led by that margin when the hooter went after eight minutes of stoppage time. But the rule states that the ball has to go dead before the game ends. We knew we had to keep the ball alive or we were beaten but I swear I never doubted that we would score because there was such a strong determination among the lads not to go down. I had been knee-dropped in the back of my shoulder at the start of the first half and every tackle I made from them on had been a stinger. By this time I was breathing out of my backside. But when the ball came out to me from Balsh no-one was going to stop me. I sidestepped inside a couple of defenders and went over.

I knew how important the conversion kick was as the scores were level, so I tried to get as close to the posts as possible to improve the angle for Daws. As I dived to touch down the ball I was knee-dropped and given a dead leg. I got up almost oblivious to the pain as adrenaline was flooding my body. Predictably Harrison was in my face, again bumping into me with his chest - goodness, what a chest he's got - and hurling his scrumcap at me. i assumed he'd injured me (in fact it was Peter Ryan, the bloke who had stamped on Will Greenwood in the Australia 'A' game). It was my turn to give him a mouthful: "That's two tries mate...and you've lost."

That was not quite true as Daws still had to kick the extra points. The Press saw it as his chance to redeem himself but I don't think the lads thought like that. I just knew he wouldn't miss that kick. He didn't and everyone went mad. It was just a great feeling, a great way to win a game, especially against so many guys who'd beaten us playing for Australia 'A'. Pat Howard wasn't one of them but, from a personal perspective, it was good to get one over on him just the same. He is a very good player at club rugby where defences aren't as tight and where opportunities are more frequent. I just think at Test level he perhaps lacks a yard or two of speed.

Back in the changing room the Test boys were pretty overjoyed that the momentum had been maintained. Henry came up to me and said I'd had an awesome game. My first instinct was to say, "Thanks very much but why did you wait until now to give me a chance on the wing?" I didn't because I didn't want to rock the boat at this stage and anyway there was no point turning a compliment into an argument. But it does astound me that I've got 38 caps for England and I haven't had a run in the position in which I've played most of those games until the final midweek mission.

I arrived back at the hotel very content with my performance and the victory. It's a great feeling to win a game like that but it's even better to score the winner. Daws must also feel very happy with his game and his final kick. Quite a few of the Stiffs went out to celebrate but I had pins and needles in my leg which had really started to bother me so I spent an hour and a half icing it, keeping my foot above my head. I wonder if I've done enough to make the Test team? I've got a hunch that I might have. Johnno said to me when I left the lift that I should make sure I'm fit. I took that to mean he was giving me the nod without actually giving me the nod. The problem is I don't think I've got much chance of being fit. So I just feel more depressed. I'm full of confused emotions. I'm really pissed off that I've had to wait until now to play in my most experienced international position but in the same breath I'm happy that I was able to make a statement in the game. Perhaps my overriding sentiment, though, is one of bitterness at that prick Harrison who kneed me on purpose then threw his hat at me. What a plank - his hat really hurt!

WEDNESDAY

Woke at 5.30 unable to sleep because my leg was too sore, in fact dead. Hobbled into the physio room for icing and oxygen to help the healing process. Also had a go with the nebuliser to help me breathe. Then the door opened and it was a drunken supporter wanting to talk to me about the game. You can imagine my reaction. I don't mind fans who come up and talk to you like a normal human being at a normal hour of the day. It's those people who, for want of a better word, are in awe of you and come up and say things that no-one in their right mind would say to their best friend. I've got no problems with autographs, what bothers me is the sort of people who come up to you after you've just lost a Test match and say, "So what went wrong today then?" You feel like strangling them. A tip from me and the players to all supporters: be yourself and talk to us like we're normal people. You don't have to talk about rugby because that's our job. Imagine someone going up to a bank manager and asking about the cash machine. He'd be pretty uninspired to answer. Say something like "Wasn't that number four an idiot?" not "How fast can you run the 100 metres?" Those are the sort of questions you answer when you visit kids in schools, not when you're among adults on a Lions tour.

I got even more angry when I picked up a copy of *The Australian* newspaper and saw a photo of a glowering Graham Henry beneath the headline, 'Lions remain divided: Healey'. In actual fact my *Observer* column hadn't said any such thing. I had commented on how happy we were that we had won on Saturday night and said that the midweek boys would just have to grin and bear it. Once again the Aussie Press had taken this out of context and hung me out to dry. I explained all this to Donal and showed him a copy of the original article and he agreed. In fact he thought the column was quite funny.

The Aussie propaganda machine has picked up on what Daws and I have said and tried to snowball it to give the Wallabies an advantage. But in actual fact it's probably worked in our favour because the feeling that they're trying to splinter our morale has just made us more united. What their papers say won't silence me because I'd never forgive myself if I kept quiet and things went pear shaped. But it's not a question of taking on Donal and Graham. I want this tour to be successful. I want us to win the Test series and to live up to our tour vision of being the best there's ever been. Which is why I do sometimes open my mouth if I think something could be done in a different way. Not to show dissent but to try to prompt debate and provoke ideas.

I've been consistent in my opposition to the way things have been done and the atmosphere that has been created. I admit that. What else am I supposed to think when I hadn't seen Henry smile until we won the first Test? But all along I have conceded that I could be proved wrong in the Tests. And here we are one-nil up. I still think Henry's techniques are wrong and his opinions on the game are wrong but I can't be sure of that until the end of the series.

Now is not the time for post-mortems. I've got to get fit. Henry reinforced what Johnno had said to me by emphasising that I must do everything to make myself available. So I had two iced baths before my leg was packed in a compression bandage for the flight to Melbourne. I still feel time is against me and that is such a depressing thought. I limped down to the casino on the ground floor to try and take my mind off it. I lost a packet, but strangely I did feel slightly better because I forgot about not being fit for a few minutes and fretted about the money instead.

Arrived in Melbourne and straight away plunged my leg into another iced bath. By the time I climbed out I felt as though I had hyperthermia. I had to sing 'One man went to mow' to keep myself in the bath as long as possible. I managed nine and a half minutes, which is a lot of men going to mow. The bad news is that I am rooming with Dorian (only joking Nobby!), the good news is that our hotel is across the road from the biggest casino in the southern hemisphere. The boys could lose money here.

THURSDAY

Woke early for another icy plunge and managed ten minutes this time, even if by the end I was singing "one m-m-man went to m-m-mow". Nobby couldn't stop laughing at my misfortune but I still managed to get him in a good stranglehold, one that he couldn't break. He's got a broken finger, I've got a dead leg so we're basically playing off the same handicap. The morning ended in a bit of a shock for me, literally, when Carcass put an electrode on my groin to try to stimulate the muscle and my leg jumped off the bed involuntarily.

Henry tried to delay his team announcement until tomorrow evening to give me the maximum chance to be fit but he was told that there is a 48-hour rule. So he named a 22 with me on the bench, whilst I was privately led to believe that I would play on the right wing if I could run. I decided to try to take my mind off my fitness fight by going with some of the lads on a visit to the studios were *Neighbours* is filmed. We sung the theme tune all the way there, talked about the girls we wanted to meet and arrived just as Harold and Lou were shooting a scene. I couldn't believe how small the set was. Every indoor scene of *Neighbours* is filmed in this one room no bigger than half the area of a rugby 22. Harold had to redo a couple of his lines but Lou was very good. When they had finished I went outside and bumped into Flick, the only remotely fit girl in the show. She was a very nice, normal person and I had a photo taken with her. Well, it's not every day she gets to meet an international rugby star! She told me she was working a 15-hour day and that appearing in *Neighbours* wasn't all glamour. A couple of Press lads were with us and I embarrassed one of them who suggested I give Flick a kiss for the cameras. "Don't be stupid," I said. "I'm married to a very hormonal, pregnant woman. How would she feel seeing me kiss one of *FHM* Magazine's top ten beauties on *Channel 9* tonight. Anyway, I'd be tempted to stick my tongue in."

A few more of the cast came out. I didn't really recognise any of them which is a sign of the times. Ten years ago I probably could have named them all. While some of the lads went inside to visit make-up I stayed outside icing my leg.

On the way back to the hotel we turned on Alex Broun, our media liason officer, who had arranged the trip by virtue of the fact he played Brad the Butcher in the show 15 years earlier. He tells the story of how he, and not Jason Donovan, was Kylie Mynogue's first boyfriend in Neighbours. That was worth a good quarter of an hour of piss taking. But my mood changed when we got back to the hotel, as I had missed the doc due to a misunderstanding. I thought he had said treatment would start at 3.30. In fact that was the time he had to assess my fitness at Donal's request. So I headed back to the ice bath to chill out.

FRIDAY

The Test is tomorrow and it's looking bleak for me. I seriously doubt I'm going to be fit. I've come back overnight before for big games when I thought I'd no chance, so I've not given up hope. But today I couldn't cross the road let alone jog. I have a defence mechanism when I'm injured. I constantly tell myself that I'm not going to make it whilst telling others that I've got a chance. I do this to minimise my own personal disappointment if I don't actually make the game.

This week, though, the dead leg has been so bad that I've had to admit to some of the lads that I'm not positive about playing. Shaggy still thinks I'll make it and has started to call me Lazarus but, in all honesty, I've got no chance. I've asked about jabs but there's nothing they can do. I went to training today but could do nothing. Colonial Stadium is cool, with its retractable roof, and the atmosphere tomorrow night will be awesome. But I fear I'll be a spectator.

Came back to the hotel from Colonial feeling mega depressed. I've done everything I can to be fit. I've got a fitness test in the morning but I still can't walk up stairs without pain. What makes it worse is that I would have been starting had I been fully fit. Went to the casino with Daws to try to lift my spirits but we couldn't relax; there were too many pissed supporters telling us to get to bed. Moved to a quieter part of the casino and won heavily on pontoon. Bad sign. Winning at cards, losing at rugby.

SATURDAY

Woke at 7.30 and broke my record in the ice bath by lasting 11 minutes. I then changed into kit and met the doc at breakfast before going outside to a local park. My leg was still numb from the bath and I managed to jog without pain. For a couple of seconds I thought my prayers had been answered. But when I tried to accelerate I couldn't even get out of first gear. My leg muscles wouldn't respond properly. My leg is moving through an unnatural plane. I can't kill the pain if the bastard leg won't move properly. The doc had no option but to pull me out of the match and draft Jenks in on the bench.

Totally gutted, I limped back to the hotel and refilled my wallet in the casino. I will have to stop winning if I'm going to play again! By the way, I don't have a gambling problem. I never gamble at home in casinos. I only do it on trips like this to kill time and relieve the tedium. What's more, I always set myself a leaving time whether I'm up or down. On this occasion my deadline was half an hour.

Kick-off was 7 o'clock and I changed into a tie and blazer for the short bus ride to the stadium. What an unbelievable atmosphere under the roof! There had been quite a debate about whether the roof should be left open or closed but you couldn't fault the buzz in the enclosed arena. There were 57,000 fans and the place was bouncing. It was so noisy I couldn't hear myself think. The only atmospheres I would rank higher would be Parc des Princes on the day Leicester won the Heineken Cup and Twickenham when

England drew 26-26 with New Zealand in 1997. But that is partly because they were big days for me personally.

Match nine details

Australia 35, British and Irish Lions 14

(second Test: Colonial Stadium, Melbourne, July 7)

AUSTRALIA: Burke; Walker (Latham 48), Herbert, Grey, Roff; Larkham (Flatley 84), Gregan; Stiles, Foley (Cannon 89), Moore, Giffin (Cockbain 72), Eales (capt), Finegan, Smith, Kefu.

SCORERS - Tries: Roff 2, Burke. Con: Burke. Pens: Burke 6.

LIONS: Perry (Balshaw 54); James, O'Driscoll, Henderson, Robinson; Wilkinson (Jenkins 77), Howley (Dawson 86); Smith, Wood, Vickery (Leonard 67), Johnson (capt), Grewcock, Hill (Corry 37), Back, Quinnell.

SCORERS - Try: Back. Pens: Wilkinson 3.

Ref: J Kaplan (SA). Att: 56,605.

There certainly seemed to be more Aussies than had been in Brisbane, not least because the Australian Rugby Union had splashed out £30,000 to kit them out in orange to try and make it look as though it was not another home game for us. The Lions fans chanted 'Freebies' at the Wallaby supporters in their ARU scarves which I thought was quality, and for virtually the whole of the first half it seemed the lads had picked up from where they left off in Brisbane. Daf broke up the middle and narrowly failed to get the scoring pass out to Robbo. Scott time and again punched holes in their midfield defence and Woody, Johnno and Hilly all got to stretch their legs. When Backy went over for a try to put us 11-3 ahead I thought the series was over. But then it all started to go wrong.

Hilly was caught in the face by Nathan Grey's elbow and left concussed. Then, less than a minute after half-time Jonny threw a pass which Joe Roff intercepted and ran back. Matt Burke's kick tied up the scores. Had we finished off a couple more chances, had

Roff not been so alert, things would have been different, I'm sure. Without that try they had nothing. They weren't going anywhere up until that point. As it was they saw a way out and took it. Roff and Burke added further tries and we were beaten.

What killed us off more than anything was fatigue. We weren't in any way complacent, even if we had been so much better than them at The Gabba that I honestly couldn't see any way back for them. But we were tired. The chances that went begging I've no doubt we would have finished a week earlier when the lads still had an ounce of life left in their legs. But the regime we'd worked under caught up with us at the crucial time. There was nothing left.

There were bodies lying all over the changing room afterwards and all the physio beds were full. Hilly was out of the tour, so too Rob Howley with bust ribs and Jonny's leg looked really bad. He had been stretchered off and I thought it was broken. There was more ice in that room than you would find in a polar bear's nostril. But the mood remained defiant. We had not blown the series. There was still next week.

chapter seventeen

Aussie Spies and the Heartbreak Hotel

Week 7, Sunday July 8 - Friday July 13

The adrenaline is pumping and I'm motivated to play for the Lions. For almost the first time on the tour I feel needed. I've argued in my mind that I should be in the Test team, that I'm better than others who have been given a chance. Now am I about to get the chance? The management led me to believe that I would have played in Melbourne had I been fit. Still, I'm back in their thoughts. That's important to me. My chin is up. I no longer feel I'm just making up the numbers, wasting precious holiday time before the new season comes around.

SUNDAY

Our team treatment room was busier than a backpackers hostel this morning. According to the doc we now have 16 players on the injured list. Last night's game took a serious toll. The mood is quiet and subdued. The boys are truly shagged. There was no word on Jonny as we prepared to fly to Sydney on the final leg of this adventure, only that he would not be travelling with us. The doc decided it would be best for him, Jonny, Hilly and Rob to travel independently. What likely effect that will have on team selection is anyone's guess but it certainly means that their understudies will have to take the lead this week. Daws, Cozza and maybe me.

One way or another I feel I am going to be in the team. Whether instead of Jonny or in place of Dafydd, I don't know. Perhaps even at scrum-half if they decide not to go with Daws. You never know with Henry. A lot of players came up to me after the game and wished me luck. One said: "The script has been written for you to come in and save us." I think he was taking the piss but nevertheless the prospect of me coming into the side is a very real one and I know I have to be fit and relaxed and ready to go.

Returned to my room after breakfast. Louise was still in bed. Dorian gave me a bit of chat about how he and Lou were 'busy' and could I come back in 20 minutes? I told him he was a fat ginger waster, then got on top of him and put him in a choker hold. He knows he's my bitch! Lou asked me not to hurt him, but she was too late. When he regained consciousness he apologised and I told him to get us all a coffee and get my bags down to the concierge by 11 o'clock. He blew it by putting half a teaspoon of sugar too much in my coffee. I'll get the gimp mask out for him. He'll have to wear it now.

Lou and I went for a spot of lunch only to run into more abuse, this time from a Lions fan, or rather some idiot masquerading as one in a Lions jersey. He yelled "loser" at me, which I thought strange. For one thing I hadn't played, for another if he thinks like that perhaps he shouldn't have come to Australia. And for another, could he do any better for Britain and Ireland? No of course he couldn't. It was pouring with rain as we left the restaurant and I said goodbye to Lou. Things will look better at breakie on the beachfront in Manly, I told myself.

But first there was the bus ride from Sydney airport to Manly to negotiate and it was during the journey that I had my second bust-up of the day - with one of my team mates. Keith Wood was being his usual annoying self and hitting me on the head. After one blow I bit my lip and cut it. So I walked down the bus, picked up a newspaper, opened it and pretended to show a particular article to Jason Leonard who was sat in front of Woody. As I passed it to him I punched my fist through the paper into Woody's face. He jumped up and started to chase me down the bus but before he could lay a hand on me Ronan started chanting "can't take it" at him. Then everyone joined in. He was now in a no-win situation. If he hit me the lads would have won. If he didn't I'd win. The 'can't take it' or CTI song had become a major part of tour life and had proved an excellent tool for small lads to use to get away with all sorts of stuff against the big boys - that's why Rog invented it. Genius! Woody stopped, turned round and walked back to his seat with his head bowed.

It was a particularly sweet moment for me after what had happened in South Africa four years ago when I made the heinous error of asking to be the tour judge. Woody, who was the tour judge, told me to get stuffed. He then decided I'd pay for my cheek by becoming the tour gimp. They couldn't find the leather suit out of Pulp Fiction for me so they strapped an apple into my mouth. I had to sit through the tour court in my underpants behind a plant, with this apple tied in my mouth (though I managed to eat it half way through the session).

It was good to be back in Manly after a fortnight away from the coast. Canberra was cold, Melbourne wet. The thought of Manly and its ocean view had sustained us for a while now. But whereas two weeks earlier I had been down in the dumps, easily distracted by the beach, sun and surf, now I was focused. The series was balanced on a knife edge and with it the legacy of the entire tour. Where once it didn't matter a stuff to me, now it did. Badly. Even Blackie's words struck a chord.

Johnno and Woody had spoken in the changing room after the game at Colonial about the need to quickly erase the memory. The second half had been woeful, nobody needed to be told that, but the fact remained that the Lions had had the better of three-quarters of the series to date. John Eales had told the Press that whichever side recovered the best from the physical battering of the first two battles would probably win. Johnno disagreed, insisting that, despite all our injury problems, the key to victory lay in the mind. We had failed the second test. He would not allow us to repeat that.

From the moment our bus pulled away from the stadium there was no slagging, no recrimination. Criticism was constructive. There was no doubt we would win in Sydney. It was only a matter of how best to achieve it. Blackie made an early start by posting a sheet under our doors entitled 'Why we will win', with a sub-heading of 'Believe it...No doubts'. He listed three 'facts'.

(1) We are better than Australia - when we are both fresh and at our best. (2) We are stronger, more powerful, faster and have better gamebreakers than Australia - when we are both fresh and at our best. (3) We are better defenders than Australia - when we are both fresh and at our best.

The conclusion he drew was that when both Australia and ourselves are on top form "we are without question the better and more dynamic team". And that when fatigue kicks in there is nothing to choose between us. "But by that stage it should be all over'," he argued. And if it's not, "our determination has a slightly better than even chance of overscoring their experience".

As I have said before, when all else is equal in top-level sport victory is achieved in the battle of the mind. Blackie knows this better than anyone because he has been preaching on the subject for more than 20 years. But he also knows it's about bringing mental toughness to the surface at the right time. It's fair to say that time is fast approaching so he got us to start looking within ourselves, to work on our mental strength.

"Tylney Hall (when we had the bonding sessions with Impact and drew up our tour goals) either meant something to us all or we are hypocrites," Blackie continued. "I don't believe for one moment that we are hypocrites. So we must all re-subscribe to our chosen team values this week. Remember the three categories: Pride in the Lions, Team spirit and Winning. Remember some of the key words: Courage, hunger, desire, belief, work ethic, common goal. Take time to appreciate what these words mean to you. Have the courage to do this.

"The ten-game tour has come down to this one game. The way it's transpired, all other games have been sparring sessions...but next Saturday is fight night - winner takes all. We all must do everything we possibly can to prepare our chosen team to beat Australia. We mustn't go home and REGRET. Regret is to be frowned upon - care about the situation so much that your contribution is significant this week. After seven weeks we shouldn't be ill-at-ease with each other; we shouldn't be self-conscious about what we perceive to be a meaningful point of view. We all want the same thing and we will all support you (each other)."

For the first time on tour the management, through the words of Blackie, offered us the chance to follow the course of action we considered best for us individually. "Early week," he wrote. "Do you need a session or two of your chosen in-season weight training regime? It will definitely make you feel good...and increase your confidence. Do you need a few hours not thinking at all about rugby? Can your love for the team lead your behaviour this week to help you to prepare to become a better person in life because of your unselfishness? Winning and trying everything you can in order to do that is the only thing we can expect of each other. This week will reveal our characters, not develop them."

My leg felt a bit better as the bus drew to a halt outside the Manly Pacific Park Royal Hotel so I went out for a quick nightcap with Daws at 10 o'clock. The rest of the lads were going out later but I wanted a relatively early night. It was going to be a big week ahead.

MONDAY

Breakfast on the beachfront in Manly is the perfect way to start any day, but particularly this one when our bodies and minds needed to chill out. Several dozen surfers were out catching the early morning waves. They'd no doubt been there for hours, their heads bobbing up and down in the swell as they waited patiently for the one wave which would make it all worthwhile. We had the day off so a few of the lads decided to give it a go. My leg was still too sore for such physical exertion so I watched from the hotel. They clearly found it a struggle getting out to the big waves, though Darren Morris looked like he was used to being in the water.

Appearances can be deceptive. Take Jonny for example. A day after his tour appeared doomed, news reached us that his leg was nowhere near as bad as first thought. Never mind, I'll just have to try and get into another position! I kept my focus and spent the rest of the day alternating between Carcass and the doc. I also had a massage from Richard Wegrzyk, whose career has taken him from the Vatican, where he was once an alter boy, to masseur for England and the Lions, highly respected by all the lads. He put these suction glasses on my leg to help get the bruising out. The pain was considerable and I repaid him with a sly dig on the way out. He's a top boy Rich. Just keep those suction glasses away from me in future!

Later we had our first squad meal out together at a restaurant called Ribs and Rump. Yes, our first squad night out with five days left of the tour. It's good to get a chance to start bonding like this. It's a great place with awesome food and we put away loads of it. Daws spilt a full glass of water on me, then said I'd nudged him and did it again. He left with a spare rib sticking out of each of his huge ears. I made him pay further when we played 'Guess who's coming to dinner', a game which basically involves people taking the mick out of one another. It's a simple game which turns quite vicious with banter. Everyone got it in the neck, and I mean everyone. The best line of the night went as follows:

Phil does defence, Dave likes to punt.
But what have we learned off that Kiwi runt?!

The night was undoubtedly one of the highlights of the tour.

Steak, ribs, chips, 7UP and a great laugh. Returned to camp via the arcade where Shaggy, Daws, Balsh, Charvis and I battled it out on the Daytona 2000 driving game. I bought some chips on the walk back along the oceanfront purely to throw at Rog and Brian O'Driscoll so that they would be bombarded by hundreds of hungry seagulls. It was hilarious. Hitchcock would have approved.

TUESDAY

The day began with confirmation that I will play on the right wing on Saturday. Well that only took six weeks! My leg was still sore from Ryan's knee drop on me in Canberra but I decided to give training a go. I couldn't finish the session because my leg and hamstring cramped up and I returned to the hotel worried that one knock on my quad and my tour could be finished. Another worry for me is the amount of people with video cameras I saw watching our workout this morning.

It had lashed with rain since early doors and our normal training pitch was waterlogged. We were forced to use a public pitch and one which we arrived to find surrounded by people. There must have been 250 of them, some with cameras, many wearing hats with corks dangling from the brim. Maybe, just maybe, we should have had this session behind closed doors. Yet rather than ask them to leave Henry made us rehearse all our lineout moves and back plays in full view of them. For all we know the Australians could now be familiar with every one of our lineout calls and back options.

Alun Carter, our video analyst, had previously told me that he had tried to go and watch the Australians train whilst in Coffs Harbour but been unable to get anywhere near the pitch. All access roads to the stadium they were using had been closed with security guards on every barrier. He told me it was done with 'military precision', as it is with England. Henry, it seems, prefers the precision of an abstract painter.

Don't get me wrong, I'm delighted to be in the Test team. But surely our preparation could be better. More precise. I'm convinced this has been a major reason for the tour not going so well. The standards set by Henry off the pitch have not contained any attention to detail whatsoever. He has been consistently late for meetings, he's busy writing his own book and more than once he's shown signs of strain. How can a group of quality players, not to mention the rest of the management, follow that? I believe that any of the English management team would have made a better leader. Higher standards set by coaches off the pitch lead to higher standards on it.

I got back to the hotel in time for lunch and couldn't help but notice that the surf was huge. So a load of us decided to give it a go. We met at 3 o'clock. The waves were massive. The boys had wetsuits and bodyboards, I had my binoculars. I can't imagine what it must have been like to take them on. You have to respect the guys who surf those monster waves. They must have balls of steel!

As I walked up the beach I saw the Sky boys, Mark Durden-Smith and Myles Harrison, carrying surf boards. It must be a real drag working for Sky what with the surfing, the shopping and the sightseeing during the day, rounded off with a nice bottle of something vintage at night! Took the mickey out of Durders for a bit then he started to get feisty and said he wanted to wrestle. Three seconds later I was on top of him, pressing his face into the sand whilst talking to Johnno. Stick to presenting, Durders, or get on a serious weights programme!

Dinner was with the usual group - Daws, Balsh, Hendo, Rog and Ben Cohen - and was again out in town as all of us are disillusioned with the food. I reckon we've either eaten out or had room service 50% of the time on this tour. The food has been terrible. Another attention to detail which the fitness guys should have picked up on. Apparently we've been allocated only $35 a day per man (about 15 quid). On the way home a truck pulled up next to us full of Aussie males. Out of the blue they yelled "You're going to get wupped on

Saturday you Pommie losers". That was nice of them. I returned the sentiment with some reference to tyre marks ending at a cliff edge.

WEDNESDAY

Just when I thought my luck had changed for the better I slightly pulled a muscle in my back during training. A night of incessant rain had forced us to drive for an hour to find a pitch that wasn't waterlogged. I wish now we hadn't bothered, or have I just become paranoid. It doesn't feel like anything more than a stitch now and it should be fine. As long as my leg doesn't regress I'll be there in the Olympic Stadium to start my first ever Test match as a Lion.

All the same I took things easy as I changed and headed into Sydney on the Manly Jetcat to pass on tickets to my family for the game. We get two complimentaries and can buy a further six. It's amazing that a player has to buy at least one ticket if his Mum, Dad and Wife all decide to come to the game. Do you think Elton John buys tickets for his own concerts? I'd be very surprised if he did. Yet several blazers get free tickets. Come the next big game maybe I'll sit on the pitch and watch them tackle a bag of sweets. Fortunately for all of us Joan has been a legend on this trip. She has had plenty of problems to deal with but has kept smiling through it all. When it comes to tickets, she has been our saviour.

Walked around the shops for a bit but my mind was spinning with thoughts about Saturday's game so I caught the Cat back to Manly, arriving at the hotel to find 500 shirts set out on tables waiting to be signed, 200 of which were for the Australian Rugby Union. I asked the liason guy specifically who they were for and he said an injured players' fund. No problems then, other than the timing of it all. Three days before a major international we shouldn't have these distractions. It should have been done on Monday. I personally think the commercial access to the players on this trip has been too great and has detracted from the rugby.

THURSDAY

Disaster. I think my back has gone. We went to the Olympic

Stadium today, a place I hoped would forever have a place in my heart after Saturday's game. I stood there thinking about all the sporting legends that had performed there in the 2000 Games, like Maurice Greene, Haile Gabrasalasee, Jan Zelezney and Cathy Freeman and I conjured a vision of adding my name to the roll of honour with the series-winning try for the Lions. I thought about how far our supporters had come and I told myself that no matter how hard and how unhappy the tour had been, we could win on Saturday.

I was really motivated and looking forward to the game. I did some mental rehearsal on my own. Running: quickly, balanced, elusive. Passing: accurate, dummying, off-loading. Tackling: hit Joe Roff low, squeeze, drive. Trigger words, key thoughts. But most of all I was picturing the game, looking for space, feeling the space, attacking with the ball the space. What I didn't foresee was my dream evaporating.

I thought about little things I'd learnt from top coaches like Brian Ashton, Joel Stransky, Clive Woodward, Dave Reddin and my old schoolmaster Joe Green and tried to put them all together. I knew this could be the biggest game ever for me. I was relishing the prospect of doing something to be remembered by.

Training started and I was bubbling around, trying to get involved in everything. Hendo told me to get back on my wing. I'd never played outside him before so I forgave his cheek. My back seemed fine but for what still felt like a stitch. I thought it would run off.

Henry's plan is for us to kick every piece of possession inside our own 40 deep into their half; a tactic designed to utilise my right foot and Jonny's sliderule accuracy off his left boot. It will also rely upon complete dominance in the set piece but I know we have the players to achieve that.

The session went well, except that the pain in my back wasn't going. I was kicking a lot and with one of my last kicks I felt my back wrench a bit. I stopped, iced it and thought no more of it. But by the time we stopped at a roadside restaurant for lunch on the way back, my back was completely knackered. I was suffering one spasm after another. I hoped and prayed it was just a pulled muscle and after treatment at the hotel it did feel slightly better and I felt a whole lot more positive again.

I wasn't invited to the press conference but I didn't care. I had intended to say nothing anyway. I walked out of the team room into a barrage of waiting journalists and just said how proud I was to be picked, how I would do my best and how I would dearly love to beat the Aussies in their own backyard. Another barrage of questions followed. I was asked how I felt physically. I said that my tongue was okay so I'd try and talk Joe Roff to the floor. All meant in jest.

I then got dragged off by Alex Broun who told me that Donal and Henry didn't want me talking to the Press. How stupid can you get? At least if I'd been invited to the press conference it would have been controlled. But by gagging me I was now being pursued by a pack of hungry dingos.

I walked back out, told the Press lads I had nothing else to say, and found Eddie Butler to do my *Guardian* column. We disappeared into a quiet corner, or so I thought. As I started to talk I noticed two Australian journalists out of the corner of my eye. They were within earshot and slyly taking notes. I turned to them and asked if I could help them. They said they were taking notes. I replied that it was a private interview and I'd speak to them later. Eddie then asked them to give us some space.

I did my normal thing with Eddie. He still doesn't take any notes, he just gets a feel for what I'm thinking. I told him how keen I was that we won the game because of all the anti-Lions propaganda, all the abuse I'd been subjected to, and because I would have the last laugh on that 'plank' Justin Harrison - not that he had any involvement in Saturday's game at that stage.

I finished with him, then the two Aussie journos came back over to me. I politely said I didn't have time. They snapped back at me, saying I'd made time for Eddie and I should make time for them. Why should I? What right over my time do they have? They've spun my words to their advantage for the entire trip. They really hacked me off. My back was sore and they were pissing me around. Let's get this straight: We as players don't owe our lives to outside influences. I'm quite laid back but it bugs the life out of me!

FRIDAY

Such a horror day as this could only be Friday the 13th. Every waking hour I spent in pain. Last night Carcass had given me a hot vibration massage pad to sleep on. When I woke up at 8 o'clock it felt like someone had superglued my two shoulder blades half way up my vertebrae. My muscles were fighting to separate them. I called the doc and after extensive treatment stayed in bed until 2.30, when I eased myself onto my feet and went to see Rich for a massage. Unbeknown to me my *Guardian* column was stirring up a hornet's nest back home. Harrison had also been drafted into the Wallaby side after David Giffin did his hamstring.

I was getting desperate now. I'd never had needles off Rich but I said I'd try anything. He said he'd just try to relax my back and I did feel slightly better after a rub. I decided to go out and get some fresh air into my lungs. I crossed the road outside the hotel and walked slowly down to the beach wall, stopping a few times for photos and autographs.

I was just trying to relax and get my muscles moving when BANG, I was hit by a massive spasm. I collapsed to my knees in severe pain and broke into a cold sweat. A passer-by helped me to my feet and I turned back towards the hotel, walking like an ironing board on legs, in desperate need of some form of painkiller. I just reached the entrance when another supporter asked for an autograph. I knew if I stopped they would have to carry me in, so I said to the lady, "Sorry, I'm absolutely desperate to get some medical attention. If I'm better later I'll come out and do it". I kept walking in a strange manner and some fella, who'd seen me refuse her, shouted: "Healey, you wanker." In excruciating pain, fucked off that I probably wouldn't be able to realise my goal of starting a Lion's Test match, I turned and barked back, "shut the fuck up".

This was without any shadow of a doubt my lowest point of the tour so far. Having hated being here, then hearing Willie John and feeling a sense of urgency to come back on board and get in the team, then getting picked, then injured and now being insulted whilst fighting unbelievable discomfort to get to some pain killers. Had I been physically able, I would have snapped and something bad would have happened to that chap.

The rest of the day was spent with the doc looking after me. He dosed me up with painkillers and gave me treatment during a four-hour period in which I lay on my back unable to move. I would need a miracle now to make the game. Yet my only thought was to get fit. Nothing else mattered to me - nothing. I managed to get to the captain's meeting where Johnno simply told us all to come prepared. "Make sure you're as ready as you've ever been". The chance would be a fine thing, I muttered under my breath.

There was still time for me to take another gobful of abuse, this time from the taxi driver taking me to the cinema to pick up my lucky popcorn. My crime was to be English. Even if I don't play tomorrow I desperately want the lads to win to make a point.

chapter eighteen

The Final Reckoning

Week 7, Saturday July 14 - Sunday July 15

SATURDAY

It hit me when my defences were down, when I'd just lost my fight to play for the British and Irish Lions in the deciding Test match. I was in a car with the doc on the way back from a failed fitness test, trying to come to terms with the fact that a second Lions tour would pass me by without me starting a Test match. That was when I saw the newspaper billboard. 'Rogue Lion - Up Yours Aussies'.

I'd never regarded myself as a 'rogue Lion', but the alarm bells started to ring. After all only two Lions had spoken out in anything like critical terms throughout the tour and I was one of them. I asked the driver if he had a copy of *The Australian*, my favourite paper! He passed it through to the back seat. The headline read, 'Healey finishes tour in low gear'. How did they know I was injured, I wondered? I'd not been ruled out until almost 11 o'clock this morning.

But they weren't talking about my fitness, they were talking about my column. Or rather they weren't. As usual they had cherry picked certain words and phrases, but none of them I recognised. "Up yours", "Ape", "Back-end of the world". I hadn't said anything like that. Quoted again for something I hadn't said, just like the sledging episode three weeks earlier. I was furious.

The car pulled up outside the hotel and I walked through reception. There was a copy of the *Sydney Morning Herald* on the paper stand. The story was the same. ''Up yours': Healey lets rip at Aussies', ran the headline. The story branded me Lippy the Lion (And they call me puerile!). I took the stairs up to our team room on the first floor where I found Alex Broun. I thrust the paper at him and raged: "What the fuck is this? Once again I've been misquoted." Alex said nothing. I felt a cold sweat come over me. "Oh Shit. Eddie." I turned and headed across to the ntl internet room and called up my *Guardian* column. Oh my God! I couldn't believe what Eddie had written. He'd really given it both barrels this time. Up to that point he'd been good but the timing of this was all wrong.

(Guardian column, Friday July 13)

They call me one of the trouble-makers. Matt Dawson and me, the lip machines. Matt says this, I say that; what's going on? Anything we say comes back to this back-end of the world with a whole lot of spin. Well, spin this, you Aussies: up yours.

Is that enough to get into the Sydney Morning Sun Telegraph Herald Load of Shite? If ever I wanted to do something, it was beat you lot. There, that's better. Now calm down, Ozzer.

Two weeks ago I sat on a table reserved for the replacements and watched the press go by. It was a bit different yesterday. There must have been 20 journalists around me. What were they on about? Would I swap my Leicester European Cup medal for this? Was this better than England at Twickenham for the grand slam? How would I know? Is that part of the deal, anyway?

I answered the questions as best I could. But, to be honest, what do I really know? This is the big unknown, the great rugby mystery. Blah, blah, blah. And then I saw there were a couple of Aussie journalists hovering, writing down, "Blah, blah, blah". No comment, I said. Spin that, babes. No comment.

To be honestly honest - and, look, I've given you everything bar the mutiny scoop - I said it was just great to be here in the team at last. It is. But I can't help feeling for Dafydd James. He's out and I'm in. It's not as if he's done anything wrong, really. You know this hasn't been a bundle of laughs, this tour. Just imagine what it must be like if you get to the final match and find yourself dropped.

Still, I think I might have been in with a shout of a place for the second Test. But then I was injured in the ACT game. Something else I have to thank my mate Justin Harrison for. I thought it was that flanker Peter Ryan who clouted me, but, no, there it is on video, my old pal, the plod from the second row. And what do you know, he's in the team to face us. Me and the plank. Do you think one of us will have the final say? I'll say so.

The leg's fine now. I've been trying to relax this week. A few of us got some belly-boards and went out surfing. The weather's been lousy here in Sydney, so the surf was really big. I went out among the big waves and got thrown all over the shop. Thank you very much, I said, and went straight back to dry land. I'll take on the ape Harrison but not Mother Nature.

Did I say the weather has been crap? Just another Australian thing to get up your nose. What is it with this country? The females and children are fine, and seem to be perfectly normal human beings, but what are we going to do with this thing called the Aussie male?

Look, it got so bad I found myself agreeing with Graham Henry the other day. He said he didn't mind them being the best in the world at this or that, but why did they have to rub our faces in it the whole time? It doesn't half make you want to beat them.

I tell you, I don't even know where Croatia is exactly, but did I cheer for old Goran Ivanwhatsit in the Wimbledon final, or what? Come on, you Balkans. And then the Aussies built Pat Rafter into this super-hero loser. What is this place like?

I'm trying to concentrate on the game now. But there may still be a twist or two. I'm down to play wing, so I'm thinking wing play, wing play . . . and marking Joe Roff.

The journos asked me if it meant anything that he'd been round me a couple of times in the past. I said the only thing that isn't completely knackered at the end of this tour is my tongue, so maybe I can talk him to a standstill. "Come back, Joe, I haven't finished with you yet . . . "

No, of course, it means something. It means I'm going to have to play out of my skin to stop another Aussie bloke rubbing my nose in it. I can't wait.

But, then, if Jonny Wilkinson hadn't been fit, I'd have had to go to fly-half. So I might have had to think fly-half, fly-half. And knowing Matt Dawson, he'll probably have had to go and write a special final Test supplement to his woops diary and get sent home, and I'd end up at scrum-half. That's where I was chosen in the first place.

> Funny, isn't it? Here I am on the wing. Maybe it's my turn to say something and be sent home. Like, here's to stuffing it up your so-called macho jacksie. What? I'm out of here.

Eddie was downstairs in reception when I caught up with him and told him that what he'd written seemed to me to be a bit close to the bone. "No. It's all meant to be tongue in cheek," he replied. I thought the phrase 'foot in mouth' would probably have been more appropriate. They were my words but they hadn't come out of my mouth. Yet the column was my responsibility. Ultimately, whatever the mitigating circumstances, it was my name on it, my picture above it, my responsibility.

I knew there would be repercussions. It wasn't as serious as Matt Dawson's diary, because my criticisms were directed outside of the squad, but it was still bad. However, because I was still in pain I couldn't dwell on it. I headed off to get some valium from the doc telling myself that it was done and there was nothing to be done about it now. I just hoped that none of the lads had read it. They hadn't, but Emperor Ming had. Apparently he was downstairs at reception in pretty chipper mood when he bumped into a couple of journos and asked if there was anything in the Australian papers. "Oh, haven't you seen them yet?" replied *The Independent's* Chris Hewett. "No", said Henry. "Why?" Two minutes later he went off like a bag of fireworks at Trent Bridge.

Three hours earlier he'd refused to give up on my fitness fight when everyone else had. Now he wanted to kill me. My early morning scan had showed I had a bulging disc, which had probably caused the spasm in my back. This meant I was obviously out of the game, but not in Ming's eyes. The doc, who has been a legend throughout the tour, phoned him to give him the news. But Ming said he knew a chiropractor who could help me. A meeting was arranged for 10.30 which meant I had to lay off the valium for more than two hours. The chiropractor clicked and prodded and adjusted and, hey presto, my back felt as good as new. I stood up without any pain at all, half expecting to see a vision of the Virgin Mary appear before me to complete the miracle. But it wasn't to be. By the time I'd got outside to the car the pain had returned. It was over - the 48-hour attempt by Robbo, Carcass, Rich and me had come up short. We'd tried everything but we'd failed. I would have to watch another Test match. I was gutted.

An hour later I was spaced out and very depressed. With no game to prepare for there was nothing for me to do but pack and feel sorry for myself. I decided to try a course of retail therapy so I walked slowly into Manly and spent as much money as possible to release some of my pent-up emotions. I bought some presents for Joan and the medical team who'd all been good to me on the tour and a bottle of wine for myself. I then returned to the hotel to pack and change into my number ones. Everything else was sent home in a box.

Did I feel I'd let the lads down with that column? No, the game had enough psychological edge to it as it was. Our forwards and our team were so psyched up that it didn't matter what was said in the papers. Bombs could have been going off outside the stadium and the team would still have been completely focused on their jobs. I'm sure it was the same for the Aussies. They knew they'd never won a series against the Lions. If anything, I thought it might have a beneficial effect in taking their minds slightly off the job in hand.

I saw the lads before they left and they looked fantastic. I was convinced we would win but now I could only watch and hope. I made a point of going up to Dafydd and wishing him luck. It should have been my jersey not his but that was hardly his fault so I shook his hand (something he hadn't done to me). Then I sat down with the other Stiffs and drank my wine. I don't recommend mixing alcohol with valium. I tried it and almost didn't wake up! I slept the whole way on the coach to the game.

The stadium and the highly charged atmosphere was everything I thought it would be and more. They obviously had a few fireworks left from the Olympics and put on a fantastic show but my thoughts were down in the changing rooms with the lads. Johnno had spoken really well on the eve of the battle and I was sure his words would have a big bearing on how things went. It was only a short talk but he struck just the right chord, as Willie John had in Brisbane. The lads were ready, I was sure of that. They were unbelievably motivated. No external factors counted any more.

Match ten details

Australia 29, British and Irish Lions 23

(third Test: Olympic Stadium, Sydney, July 14)

AUSTRALIA: Burke; Walker, Herbert, Grey, (Holbeck 74), Roff; Flatley, Gregan; Stiles, Foley, Moore, Harrison, Eales (capt), Finegan (Cockbain 70), Smith, Kefu.

SCORERS - Tries: Herbert 2. Cons: Burke 2. Pens: Burke 5.

LIONS: Perry; James (Balshaw 70), O'Driscoll, Henderson, Robinson; Wilkinson, Dawson; Smith (Morris 70), Wood, Vickery, Johnson (capt), Grewcock, Corry, Back, Quinnell (Charvis 40).

SCORERS - Tries: Robinson, Wilkinson. Cons: Wilkinson 2. Pens: Wilkinson 3.

Ref: P O'Brien (NZ). Sin bin: Herbert 52. Att: 84,188.

(Wallabies win series 2-1)

As the two sides ran out I saw Justin Harrison in his horrible orange scrumcap and it made me angry that he was playing and I wasn't. And yet because of a column I'd not even written I was painted as the bad guy and not him. I could have dealt with that had I been on the pitch with him, in fact I'd have looked forward to the opportunity. There's no doubt there would have been retribution of some kind coming my way. Harrison would certainly have been out for some but I'd have worked that to my advantage. While he tried to have a go at me I'd either have been able to run round him or the referee would have pinged him for foul play and the Lions would benefit. That sort of attention would have suited me down to the ground. It would have motivated me more to play better, to work harder and try harder. I knew it would be a high pressure game for me so any advantage I could have got beforehand would have been gratefully received. But as I sat in the second row of the stand it only added to my frustration. I was on a hiding to nothing.

We led twice and moments after Jonny went over the Wallabies line to add to Jason Robinson's early try, three minutes into the second half, I thought we'd got it in the bag. We led 20-16 and they opted for a lineout when awarded a penalty inside our 22. They wanted to make a statement that they could deal with our pack. Only they couldn't. They tried to roll a maul over our line and we stopped them in their tracks. There was a massive cheer from the Lions fans at either end of the stadium.

The Aussies, humiliated by the 'red sea' of Lions fans in Brisbane a fortnight ago, had worked overtime to shut out the Barmy Army. Our 20,000 fan club were posted into the Gods, high above the posts at either end. At ground level, where work was being carried out on a section of the grandstand to my left, they had wrapped the seats in orange plastic to make it look like it was packed with Aussie fans. But the seats had nothing to shout about with 37 minutes left on the clock.

Then it all began to go wrong for us. Daniel Herbert went over for his second try and our lineout ball dried up. That was bad enough, but what made it worse for me was that Harrison was becoming increasingly influential. Jonny levelled the scores again at 23-23 from the penalty spot after Herbert had been sin-binned for a high tackle on Brian, but he then missed a chance to put us back in the lead and Matt Burke made us pay with two late goals. The final indignity was when Harrison nicked a lineout ball off Johnno at the front on our own put-in. The whistle went and it was over. Seven weeks of effort and we'd fallen six points short.

The disappointment was overwhelming for the lads but I had

been on valium all day so I was pretty much out of it by the time the game kicked off. As the valium started to wear off and I got one of our support staff to go and fill up one of those Lucozade bottles full of beer. Three litres of the golden throat charmer and the pain was under control again. I was wandering around the emptying stadium when Harrison came in to our changing room and asked for Johnno's shirt. Johnno apologised and explained that he'd already agreed with John Eales that he'd swap with him but he said he was sure that Grewy would swap. Harrison continued, telling Johnno he was legend, it was his first game and would he please do him the honour. Johnno again explained that he couldn't because he'd promised Ealesy. Then somebody yelled "look, fuck off."

The post-match function was my idea of hell. Australians patting themselves on the back whichever way you turned. They are very good winners aren't they? (call me a bad loser if you like. I am). So I headed for the team bus on which a number of players' parents, wives and girlfriends were already sitting. Daws' dad, 'big bald' Ron was trying to get my Dad to sing over the mike. Just when I thought the day couldn't get any worse! Fortunately he couldn't turn it on. I sat near the back with Louise and her identical twin sister. Hang on a minute, she hasn't got an identical twin sister. It must have been the cocktail of beer, wine and valium.

The bus drove us into Sydney and I escorted Lou back to her hotel before heading into town with the lads to drown our sorrows in The Establishment. I was well away on Dr Peppers and Champagne when I decided to turn my tour blazer inside out. Daws and Cozza then ripped off a sleeve each to create a rather trendy tank top. The action moved to another bar called Jacksons, where I started arm wrestling for zambuka. Some big Aussie came over and challenged me. I'd drunk enough so Daws said I'd do it for a $500 bet instead (Daws was on 50% commission). He agreed and I put him in a body bag in less than a second. He paid up and walked off, by which time I was too pissed to speak. Luckily I had written the name of Lou's hotel on my hand, because I couldn't even remember my name. Eventually I found her at 6.30, just in time to change out of my tank top and leave with her for the airport to meet Johnno and his wife Kay. The four of us were off to Hawaii for a holiday.

They were there when we arrived and the mood between us was normal, no different. Obviously he was a bit pissed off. But we had an agreement that we wouldn't talk about rugby while we were in Hawaii. Neither of us wanted to. We were going there to relax, not to reflect. Dodging the newspapers piled up in the departure lounge, we boarded the plane and I slept all the way to paradise.

SUNDAY

"Healey the real monkey," screamed the *Australian Sunday Telegraph*. "Hey Austin, shut up and slink home," wrote *The Sun-Herald*, adding, "Rack off Austin Healey, pack up your snotty attitude, whining opinions and don't come back. Ever." There was more but I won't bore you with it. I'm sick and tired of one nation being allowed to say what they think and the other just having to take it. Almost since the day we arrived Australians have said whatever they want about us. We were cheats, we played dirty and we had asked for the 11-punch assault on Ronan. They didn't mention the honey traps, the sly knee-drops, the sledging on the field and the insults off it. But it's a two-way street. You can't give somebody stick and then complain when you get a bit back.

Why was it alright for them to stay stuff about us and not vice versa? It did my head in. Whenever we went out and tried to relax we were subjected to some barb from some complete stranger. We couldn't walk down the street without someone leaning out of his car window and shouting "Go the Wallabies" or "You're going to get your heads kicked in tomorrow night". We couldn't have a normal night just relaxing and switching off from rugby. There will be people reading this who will you say 'you should expect this, you're a professional sportsman and you should deal with it'. Why should I? If someone at your office told you that your work had been useless today and it will be useless again tomorrow, how would you react? I have to say something back.

That's why I'd been prepared to speak my mind across Oz. I disagree that I was a liability. All I did was tell things as they were. And most of the time I did it tongue-in-cheek because even when I'm upset I don't take life too seriously. I think that came across in all bar one of my *Guardian* and *Observer* columns but the Aussie Press took out certain words and used them out of context. They were very good spin doctors.

I'd had enough of the whole thing by the time I fell into a drunken stupour high over the Pacific. I suppose, in some ways you have to admire them for the way they support their teams, whereas as soon as we lost the knives came out straight away - and unfortunately most went into my back. There are some people you can rely upon in the British Press and there are others who are just there to get paid and basically sensationalise anything that goes on. I think if that was in Australia those people would lose their jobs. If our football and rugby Press built up our players a bit more then perhaps we would have the sort of success Australian sport has. After they lost the first Test they didn't lay into their players. They didn't congratulate us on playing well, they just said Australia couldn't play as badly again...and they came looking for me.

This was a tour like none I'd experienced, though I'm still glad I came on it. I was talking to the doc on the way back from the hospital and he said that although there had been some low moments and he'd worked his arse off he still would have preferred to be here than to have been watching it on the TV at home. When he put it like that I had to agree with him.

I should have had two Tests starts, but my body let me down. I can only think that I wasn't meant to play Test rugby for the Lions. I won't let it get me down, though. I'm pissed off, don't get me wrong. At one stage I really didn't care whether I played or not, I would quite happily have just left the tour and gone home. But as the tour got on, after Willie John spoke, as the Test series developed, I increasingly wanted to play my part. It wasn't too be.

Instead I will be remembered for my mouth, though I don't think ACT will forget my rugby overnight. I accept that I was outspoken at times but never against anyone in our squad. I had a great time with every player and a lot of the management. Generally speaking I got on well with them all. I didn't see eye-to-eye with Henry, that's obvious. I didn't agree with his tactics or his management style. He probably didn't agree with the way I handled myself. But we got on with it. I'd like to think that whatever has been said between the two of us he would pick me again for my rugby. I don't expect him to pick me for my personality.

chapter nineteen

Living with the Consequences

There are many beautiful things about Hawaii, and not the least of them is that my mobile phone cannot pick up a signal there. So while my character was being assassinated in the Press at home as well as in Australia, I lay in blissful ignorance on a beach under a palm tree.

It was a bit hard to settle down and relax straight away because I was dogged by this feeling of guilt. Whichever way I lay I couldn't get comfortable for worrying about it. Should I have gone straight to Factor 4 or started off with Factor 15?

After the furore caused by the Lions, people will doubtless find it hard to believe that we didn't sit and sulk for a fortnight. It wasn't hard to do. The series was over, we had lost. There was nothing more anyone could do about it. Johnno and I, Kay and Louise chilled and had some good meals out. Then we went on to Canada where we stayed in a little log cabin on Lake Windemere, found for us by our former Leicester teammate Dave Lougheed. Meanwhile, unbeknown to me, the messages were piling up on my mobile answerphone.

I actually didn't know anything about all the fuss until I called home with three or four days of the holiday to go and spoke to my Mum, who told me there had been loads written about me in the Press in the UK for being a traitor and that sort of stuff. "What for?" I asked. I didn't actually have an inkling until then. I told Johnno and the two of us went onto the Internet at Dave's house and read all the articles. Neither of us could believe the reaction.

If Johnno held anything against me he didn't show it. He disguised it well. What people have got to remember is that it's only a game. For it to have made the impact that it did in the papers, in comparison with some of the other news events that are going on in the world really was quite remarkable.

Johnno didn't make me feel that I'd let the Lions down. And I don't think I had. I think it's ridiculous to think that a newspaper article could have a bearing on the outcome of a game between 44 people. It's ludicrous. It can motivate one person, like Finlay Calder's 'Mel Gibson' jibe at Iain Balshaw did when Balsh took apart Scotland last season, but I don't think Matt Burke, say, went into that game thinking I'm so upset that Justin Harrison has been abused I'm going to stick it to them. And anyway when I did the interview, Harrison wasn't playing. He wasn't even in their squad.

For Vernon Pugh, Chairman of the International Rugby Football Board, to be quoted ,talking about banning me from club rugby struck me as completely ridiculous. People laid into me without giving me the chance to put my side of the story. Had I been at home I'd have felt the full force of the media backlash but I'd have been able to nip it in the bud by putting my side of the story.

As it was I got it with both barrels while my back was turned. It was almost as if people, including Graham Henry, were looking for an excuse for the Lions' failing to win the series. I was a convenient scapegoat. It wasn't great losing the Test series but there were other more decisive factors. Henry needs to be honest with himself as to why we lost. It wasn't down to a newspaper article was it? That's rubbish.

Henry claimed "knowing the Australian animal as I do, that was the ideal ammunition that they needed." Yet even Rod Macqueen, the Wallabies coach, when invited to hammer me, put it no more strongly than it was "just another reason why we had to be successful."

I had an agreement with Eddie that we'd do an interview. I'd tell him how things were going and I'd be honest. I just wanted to make it amusing. I didn't want to be portrayed as one of these sportsmen who say nothing in columns. But neither did I want anything to rebound on the squad and I don't think anything did until that last one. Everything else was said tongue in cheek. Yet the Australians took it literally.

I read all my other columns and while I thought some of them were quite close to the bone I also thought they were funny so I let them go. I took one paragraph out of one where Eddie had had a go at someone. I removed the word 'mutiny' from another even though I knew it to be true that the players were massively unhappy with the way the tour was being run.

Then there was that last article. My fault, I didn't check it. Why? because I couldn't move. Good enough excuse? Probably not. I normally proof read the articles on the Thursday night before Eddie filed them. But on this occasion I was laid up in bed. I literally couldn't move. I physically couldn't get out of my pit on Thursday or Friday. Anyway, at the time I'd spoken to Eddie, Harrison wasn't even in the squad. He wasn't a factor in Saturday's game. How the picture changed.

We didn't train on Friday and I spent all day in the hotel having treatment, oblivious to the storm brewing. I spent half the day on the treatment bed then I was helped back up to my room to lie on this hot, vibrating bed pad and that was it. To be honest the column was the furthest thing from my mind. I could feel the chance to start my first Test match for the Lions slipping away and I was desperately trying to rescue it.

Even if I had seen the column I would definitely have left in the stuff about Justin Harrison because he cost me one, probably two Test starts. He was a nause throughout the entire tour and I don't think anyone of the Lions' supporters, players or management would disagree with me. I think I was fully justified to have a go at him, whether people like it or not. Take a look at a tape of the ACT game. Forward wind it to the point where I score the winning try with the last move of the game, then watch Harrison follow me over the line and knee-drop me. He then had the nerve to lecture me, after winning one cap, about an unwritten rule that what happens on the pitch stays on the pitch. Not when you're trying to injure me it doesn't, mate. I missed a chance of playing in the second Test because of him. I had played bloody well against ACT. I was bound to feel aggrieved that someone could get away with doing that at the end of the game. He took me out in a malicious manner, I called him a plank. What is worse?

The fact it came out without me actually playing was what really knackered me. I think if I'd played there wouldn't have been any comeback because I would have been out there facing them anyway. That really ate into me at the time and it still does now. I was desperate to play, but we did everything possible to get me fit. We covered every base, injections, everything. None of them would work.

Deep down I bet few, if any, of the 20,000 British and Irish fans who made the trip would say, "Those Aussies were really gracious". It's not the English way to come out and say what's on your mind. Just mine. But I would have taken out the anti-Australian stuff from that article. The 'Up Yours, Aussies' line and the stuff about Pat Rafter. I can't blame Eddie. The bottom line is it was my column and my fault for not reading it. But, hell, nobody died.

Look, Australian is a great country and it would have been a great place to go on holiday until that article. But there was so much propaganda surrounding the tour, that I grew to hate the place. I'm not concerned about their press building up the Aussies, I'd like to see ours doing more of that with us. It was when they were twisting things I'd supposedly said earlier on in the tour that I'd not even spoken about.

To those people who accuse me of telling tales out of school let me say this: The Lions beat me to it. They opened the changing room door to the fly-on-the-wall documentary team; they allowed sponsors ntl to film behind the scenes. Oh, and Graham Henry wrote a book. Times have changed since the days when tours were shrouded in secrecy, and not always for rugby-playing reasons. In 1997 hardly anyone wrote a newspaper column. On this tour I think there were only three or four of the squad who didn't. I have no doubt that columns will be banned on the next Lions' tour in 2005 and I'll have no problem with that if the ban is implemented across the board.

I'll doubtless forever be condemned by many as the Lions villain and I suppose there's a possibility I'll get booed at various grounds this season, but so be it. I'm sure the Leicester fans will still cheer when I lift the trophies aloft. Those who watched the rugby closely will, I would hope, concede that I had a reasonable trip. And given half an opportunity to play on the wing earlier in the tour maybe things would have panned out differently. But I had to wait until 10 days from the end of the tour to get a shot in my main international position, so you can imagine how frustrated I was. I had to wait four games to get a start.

From an early stage Henry gave the impression that he saw me as his secret weapon. I now know what he meant. A secret weapon is something you keep in your locker until the last minute and then you bring it out and hopefully it does something. And if it doesn't you just say 'oh well it never worked anyway'. He made a point of saying I was a scrum-half when he named the squad and then all of a sudden I became the perfect bench candidate, because I was seen as v********; no, I still can't say it! It was so annoying. I'd rather have been a weapon that wasn't a secret, so I could just get out there and play. Like I did against ACT.

We've got to change this attitude about v*******ity because the game has changed. Once you get past first phase everyone just becomes a rugby player. No-one's got a position any more. People have got this misconception that I'm a utility player because I alternate between wearing number nine, 10, 11 and 14 on my back. People see that and think I'm good in three or four positions when in actual fact beyond first phase I'm just a rugby player who's not fazed popping up somewhere different in broken play. It's like playing touch, where you just move around the pitch.

Before I came away on tour I said to Brian Ashton that I hoped it wouldn't be long before England just name seven backs without stipulating positions. He felt the same. That day can't come soon enough for me because then people will stop calling me v********. Oh, how that word haunted me in Australia. I felt I was one of the best players on tour in the back division yet it took me until the final fortnight to nail down a starting place...on the wing. I was picked to tour at scrum-half, moved to fly-half and look where I ended up.

My problem was that in selection everyone was picked to do a certain job. I always got my chance when something hadn't worked. For instance, after the first Test the management weren't happy with our phase play and our continuity so they looked to me. I seemed to only come in when there was a problem. Otherwise the coaches plumped for those players they saw as specialists. Those guys got the first bite of the cherry. Only when things didn't go particularly well did I get the call. I was like a firefighter, waiting for someone to dial 999. And no matter how hard I tried it was a perception I couldn't change.

Before we left to go on tour Henry was quoted as saying, "It's my job to create an environment in which people can express themselves and perform to the optimum." Well he didn't achieve that. He wanted us to express himself. He wanted players to express themselves through his framework, not through their own. My first impressions were largely right. He's a decent enough fella, I wouldn't say he's a bad bloke, but the way he conducted the whole tour and led it lacked precision and it lacked fun.

I think the 2001 tour will prove to be a watershed for Lions tours. I don't think we'll see midweek games again, or at least I don't think we should. I think the Lions should consider a couple of warm-up games at home before setting off, perhaps one against the Barbarians like the fixture England had in May. And I would like to see players who are selected by the Lions wrapped in cotton wool from the day the final squad is named to the day they assemble. But most importantly of all the Lions have got to get it right off the field. Everyone in the party must be British or Irish to give us a sense of history and passion. We are professionals and rugby is our day job but the Lions experience has got to feel special to us all, otherwise what's the point?

British Lions Limited

Second Floor • Huguenot House
35/38 St. Stephen's Green • Dublin 2
Telephone: (00 353 1) 669 0950
Facsimile: (00 353 1) 669 0957

Roger Pickering mobile: (00 353) 872 471 286
email: rdap@britishlions2001.com

Christine Connolly mobile (00 353) 87 979 5667
email. christine.connolly@britishlions2001.com

Roger Pickering B.A. FIPD
Chief Executive

DECISION OF THE BRITISH LIONS DISCIPLINARY COMMITTEE

The Disciplinary Committee convened by the British Lions met in Dublin today to hear the charges against Austin Healey arising out of the press article that appeared under his name in the 13 July 2001 edition of The Guardian. The Committee – Donal Lenihan (Chair), Graham Henry and Martin Johnson – unanimously decided as follows:

1. The content of the article was totally unacceptable. It embarrassed the Tour Party, the Lions and those who had travelled to Australia to support the tour. It clearly brought the Lions into disrepute.

2. Mr Healey stated, and the Disciplinary Committee accepted, that he did not write the article, nor did he have the opportunity to check the article, and that if he had had that opportunity, he would certainly have found it unacceptable and would have required it to be changed prior to publication.

3. The Disciplinary Committee accepted these submissions but ruled that players have to take responsibility for the personal arrangements they make with the media, and for any statements published under the player's name.

4 Mr Healey was found to be in breach of clause 6.1.3 of his contract with the Lions in that he brought himself, the Tour Party and the Lions into disrepute and ridicule.

5. With respect to what sanctions to impose for those breaches, the Disciplinary Committee found that there existed considerable extenuating circumstances. In particular, the Committee believes that Mr Healey is the victim of a breach of trust by his ghost journalist. The Committee accepts Mr Healey's submission that he regrets the incident and intended no disrespect to the Lions or the Tour Management. Ultimately, however, the incident was a serious one that did harm to the tour and the Lions, and therefore a fine has been imposed.

6. With respect to costs, the Disciplinary Committee has ruled that the Lions shall bear its costs and Mr Healey shall bear his own costs.

Dublin

6 September 2001

A:\DECISION OF THE BRITISH LIONS DISCIPLINARY COMMITTEE.doc
Incorporated in Ireland · Company No. 318999

chapter twenty

Disrepute? I Dispute.

I didn't want to be there and I might as well not have been. Called to Dublin to explain myself, the Lions management didn't even listen. It was like being back on tour.

Graham Henry and Donal Lenihan wanted me to explain why I had said what I hadn't in *The Guardian* on the eve of the third and final Test two months before. The appointed hour was high noon. How appropriate.

I told them that the words in the offending article weren't mine but those of my ghost writer. I put my hands up and admitted that I hadn't checked the article before publication and that if I had then the more explosive lines would have been diffused. They heard me say all that. Then, in Dublin's fair city, they pronounced me guilty.

It was like being done for speeding by a camera when I hadn't been driving. Or being found not guilty in court, the judge accepting my innocent plea but hanging me just the same. They concluded that there existed 'considerable extenuating circumstances'. The Lions even agreed to bear the costs of the disciplinary committee. Then I was found guilty of bringing the game into disrepute and fined £2,000. Talk about a kangaroo court.

The final unhappy chapter of an unhappy Lions experience was a waste of everybody's time. It was as if the Lions management had to be seen to be doing the right thing through the eyes of all those offended Australians; all those people who didn't bat an eyelid for the ten years or more that David Campese ritually abused English rugby, slagging off Will Carling and basically rubbishing anything embossed with the Red Rose. Was he ever charged with bringing the game into disrepute? Was he hell.

"The content of the article was totally unacceptable," read a statement released by the disciplinary committee. "It embarrassed the tour party, the Lions and those who had travelled to Australia to support the tour. It clearly brought the Lions into disrepute." I could imagine them salivating at the prospect of making me pay, one way or another.

Three hours earlier I had arrived at Dublin Airport with Dean Richards, my team manager at Leicester, and Jonathan Barnett, my agent. For the first time in the history of the 2001 Lions we started on time. In fact we were a few minutes early, so eager I suspect were they to get into me.

I looked Donal in the eye but I didn't even bother acknowledging Henry. I didn't shake his hand at the end as he made no effort to come over and shake mine. To Donal's credit he did and he said "Good luck for the season". I have respect for Donal, I've now got none for Henry. Henry tried to look at me, I looked at him, but their was no acknowledgement. He appeared to me to be the aggressor. I think Donal just wanted to get it over and done with.

Martin Johnson was the third member of the panel. Johnno, my captain at Leicester, England and the Lions. The guy with whom I had spent the summer on holiday in Hawaii and Canada. I felt more sorry for him than I did even myself. He didn't want to be there sitting in judgement on one of his team mates. When it was all over and we sat back in our seats above the Irish Sea, I went all quiet on him, pretending to be offended. Then I called him a traitorous bastard. He is now known simply as Rumpole.

But if I felt bad for Johnno being put in such an awkward position, I felt nothing but admiration for Dean. Throughout it all he was very, very good. He proved that he was so much more organised as a person than either Donal or Graham and it highlighted to me how different the tour might have been had we had someone like him in charge. He and Jonathan were utterly professional, Jonathan holding together the legal side, Dean paying detailed attention to everything else. Nothing escaped the pair of them. Dean prepared for me three sheets of type-written A4 with an answer for any potential question and 16 points we wanted to bring up during the hearing. The only point he failed to mention was the final one. Is Austin being made a scapegoat for what was on the whole a failed tour?

We sat down and Donal said he didn't want it to be a legal hearing, he just wanted to get it done. Dean had three questions. Was I contractually obliged to attend the hearing? Was the panel impartial? What about the confession of my ghost-writer Eddie Butler that he had made it all up?

On question one, the Lions' lawyer said anything that happened on tour, as long as it was notified whilst still on tour, could be resolved after the tour. Donal said he sent me a letter on 17 July calling me to the hearing. Dean opened up the contract and pointed out that it said the tour ended on 16 July, suggested there was therefore no legal obligation for me to be there, then said "We'll stay here in good faith, anyway".

On the matter of impartiality both Donal and Graham said they had no problem. Henry said he held no pre-conceived views about me personally, only about the article. I later read that he had left the hearing and told journalists "It had to be done, didn't it?" If that's not a pre-conceived statement, what is? As for Eddie's confession, they said I had been the "victim of a breach of trust". And yet...

I've got no problem with Eddie. I respect him because he came out and put his neck on the line for me. I took with me into the hearing a sworn affidavit from him, in which he wrote: "In the week before the third Test, in Sydney, he told me about his disenchantment with Australia. This was a reaction to the system of 'quotebacks' in the Australian newspapers, whereby material in the

British Press was reproduced with spin to suit a more Australian view. I gave this disenchantment some hyperbole of my own and added some extra spice concerning the personal duel between Austin and Justin Harrison. I thought it would all make for a colourful preview to the deciding Test."

Eddie confirmed that at no stage did I have a bad word to say about any of my fellow players and he signed off, "Ever yours and joining you in raising a glass to freedom of speech". Only once did I change anything he wrote. It was early in the tour when I told him that the lads were hacked off and that a few of them were pretty keen to leave. I said he could work it into a column but don't make it look like it's a mutiny. The first sentence of the column read 'There's a mutiny in the camp'.

I pointed out to the hearing that after Matt Dawson's Tour Diary had appeared in *The Daily Telegraph*, Donal had told the playing squad that every ghosted column from there on would be checked. That he had instructed Alex Broun, our media liaison officer, to collect the contact phone numbers of each 'ghost', what papers the various columns appeared in and on what days they appeared. From that point on, I said, we assumed that Alex would be checking all of them and that he would go and get them, not that we would have to get the article and present it to him.

Donal interjected that it was the responsibility of the players, not the management. Then Johnno piped up. "To be honest, Donal, I never got asked to present any of my articles." Dean added: "If that is the only thing Austin has done wrong the entire tour party who had ghost-written articles have also breached their contracts."

As I left the Galway Room on the ground floor of the Great Southern Hotel I thought to myself that it had gone pretty well. Forty-five minutes later I was asked to go back in. They wanted to know about another article, which had appeared in *The Sunday Telegraph* on 19 July, for which Paul Ackford had phoned me up and asked if we could talk about the hearing. I said I couldn't do that. He asked if I was going to apologise. I said 'what for?'. He took my reply out of context and reported that I "remained unrepentant". The panel said they were concerned that after the tour I was still bringing the name of the Lions into disrepute. How the hell had I done that? He phoned me up, I basically told him to get lost, and Ackford made a story out of it.

They then said they were concerned that I saw England as a different entity to the Lions. I replied that because of the way I'd been widely vilified since the tour I had to think about my future career, which is with England not the Lions. I said that if I've got an opportunity to play for England I want to make sure that they know that something like this would never happen to them. I added that I didn't see what bearing it had on the Lions that I was trying to resurrect an image of myself which had been damaged since the tour.

I was again sent out for another 45 minutes, during which time Dean and I played pitch and toss next door (nearest coin to the wall wins the coin) and I lost all my money. Dean asked me how I thought I'd done. I told him that I thought they would do me whatever my defence. I estimated a £2,000 fine, Dean took a gamble on £3,000 while Jonathan predicted there would be no fine. He argued that legally they didn't have a leg to stand on. Yet when we were recalled I was handed a statement and told that they had decided to fine me £2,000. They didn't at any stage mention that I'd brought the Lions into disrepute, an indelible stain on my character which I reject but I will have to live with. I only found that out when I read the statement.

I asked them to change the second point on the statement which said I had not written the article. Everyone already knew that. What I wanted them to say was that I hadn't even thought it. They kept us waiting until thirty minutes before our plane left so we had to leg it out, get straight on the bus and rush into the airport. The gate had already closed. Johnno shouted to the fella at check-in and he gave us some runner cards and we bolted through and got on the plane. It was a fitting book-end to a shambolic tour.

I sat on the plane thinking I had wasted a day. I might have well not bothered coming. I might just as well have phoned them and said "I'll tell you what, fine me whatever you want" because that's effectively what they did. They didn't listen to my side of the story, or rather they did, then ignored it. So now it's official. The reason the Lions lost the Test series was a newspaper column. It was not down to Graham Henry at all. Yeah, right. They wanted a scapegoat and I was munching mountain grass all the way home.

Just how much I must have got under the management's skin was apparent from their treatment of the fly-on-the-wall tour video, 'Up Close and Personal with the Lions'. The producers of the video couldn't believe how much of me they wanted taken out. It seems they almost wanted to hide the fact that I went on the 2001 Lions tour. They even prevented the video makers from using me to advertise the documentary. I find that strange bearing in mind that they often turned to me to brighten things up on dark days in Australia. For example, one day they asked me to take the mickey out of Steve Black during a pre-training warm-up. That wasn't my idea. They came over and asked me to do that. Yet months later I am the villain and it is utterly unfair.

We lost because the boys were absolutely shagged in the last two games. We lost because of the structure and the gameplan imposed by Henry which ignored our strengths and played into theirs. We had great natural ability out wide in Iain Balshaw, Jason Robinson and even me but we didn't seem to want to use it. We lacked flexibility in our play. Our gamplan for the third Test was just to kick. The team calls for the last game were the same as for the first.

We should have put more in the bank and just drawn on things we needed when and where. The little things were done very poorly. Attention to detail was absolutely shocking. The closed sessions weren't closed. One was across the road from the

Wallabies team hotel, another in full view of a posse of strangers wielding video cameras. People wonder why Australia knew our line-out calls.

Before we left Tylney Hall we set standards that we all agreed to abide by and then when the fur hit the fan a lot of us, myself included, just forgot about them. That was bad on our part but it stemmed from standards set by the management.

As I travelled back from Dublin, Peter Wheeler spoke out in the Press in my defence. He said the disrepute charge was an "horrendous blot" on my name and that the verdict "smacks of overkill" for what I actually did. I appreciate his support, and maybe I should have appealed. I just couldn't be bothered with another show trial, not least because they'd probably decide I'd done something else wrong.

When I got home Dad phoned. He was angry. He said all they'd done was drag me to Dublin to show Australia and the rest of the world through the Press that the 2001 Lions do have discipline in their squad and they can be seen to be showing a stiff upper lip. What worries me is that it sends a message to the Australians that the next time they want to abuse us verbally about anything, we'll just have to say 'thank-you very much' and move on.

So Eddie went a bit overboard in one article. I look back on the rest of the columns and feel happy that I told the truth while trying to put a smile on the face of the reader. Some players don't write anything in their columns, they just take the money. That is not me. Everyone on the outside sees the Lions as this massive thing, a source of unbelievable pride. But unless you're actually sat there right in the middle of it, being pestered 24 hours a day, you can't know what it's like. I just tried to put that across.

WHAT THREE EX-WALLABIES SAID ABOUT ME

Nick Farr Jones: "He's just a child, so immature. What he needs is a good Aussie remedy - a clip around the chops."

Andrew Blades: "Never come back. He's not welcome here at all. He is highly unpopular with his team mates. He is one of the softest players to ever lace on a boot for his country and the only impact he makes is when he comes out and bags people."

Simon Poidevin: "Australian Customs have a lot to answer for letting this bloke into the country. If ever there has been a case of a person having foot-and-mouth disease it's this bloke."

I wonder whether the Australian public has been told that Public Enemy Number One actually didn't write the words I was so widely condemned for. Will the Aussie Press now make a big song and dance of acknowledging that it was a case of mistaken identity. Just like it was when they put my name to Neil Back's words about Queensland sledging. I didn't hear a word of contrition then, and I bet I don't now. You see, it's alright for them to say stuff about us but turn the tables and the Australian Embassy is onto you before your ghost-writer can say "Up Yo..."

Will Nick Farr-Jones phone me up and apologise for his remarks? Will he write in his next piece that he was so wrong? What about Andrew Blades, whoever he is? Will he accept that maybe, just maybe, he had no grounds to say that I'm highly unpopular with my team mates. Bet he won't, because if an Aussie says something about us they seemingly become a national hero. Isn't that right, Campo? No doubt when I go back there for the World Cup in two years time the fact that I didn't write the offending article will have been conveniently forgotten. No doubt it will all kick off again.

I look back on the summer of 2001 and I don't think I let down the tour party. I don't think I betrayed the reputation of the British and Irish Lions. That was the responsibility of the management and to my mind they didn't discharge it. My crime was to not check an article that was written in my name. Theirs was to allow the Lions experience to feel less important than playing for your country. If they want a fall-guy they should look to themselves - or Lee Majors

How I Rated The 2001 Lions

NEIL BACK

Good tour as expected. Very professional in his attitude. Would have played in first Test had he been fit. Found that hard to take as that game was a massive goal for him. Doesn't like people talking about his age but this was his last Lions opportunity. Credit to himself.

IAIN BALSHAW

Not given the opportunity to show his natural abilities. The gameplan and the structure imposed by Graham Henry didn't utilise his skills and his speed which depressed him somewhat. Not surprising really bearing in mind everyone thought he'd be the Test fullback. Good tourist, good friend and good laugh.

GORDON BULLOCH

Late starter, came out and played his part in some of the big games. Good tourist, nice bloke. Pleasure to have him out with us.

MIKE CATT

Came on tour with a bad back and went home with a torn calf. Didn't have much luck. Balsh missed his midfield distribution. Suspect he enjoyed tour more once he'd left party.

BEN COHEN

Of everyone on tour I felt most sorry for Ben. Seemed to be written out of script after failing to finish off chance in first game. Theme of whole trip. You got one chance and if you blew it you didn't get another. I thought he had a great tour on and off the pitch. Enjoyed many a night eating out in his company.

COLIN CHARVIS

Played well throughout tour and very unlucky to miss out on Test spot. Great guy. Mr Chilled. The most relaxed man you'll ever meet until the game starts, then very physical. Felt in Six Nations that he was one of best back rows in British Isles. My opinion of him hasn't changed.

MARTIN CORRY

Late on tour but how he made up for it. Gutted for him when he missed initial selection but he missed the hard training, enhanced his England reputation in North America, then joined us and was nothing short of awesome. Struggled with shoulder injuries through entire tour but you'd never have known it.

LAWRENCE DALLAGLIO

Have to admire his never-say-die spirit. Went on tour with really bad knee injury, yet desire to play and desire to try was admirable. I trained with him on numerous occasions. He wasn't in great shape, he was struggling. But even a 50% Lol is pretty good. I admire him as a player and as a person.

JEREMY DAVIDSON

Came with big reputation having been voted best forward on 1997 tour. Probably expected a bit more of himself but still played well and gave his all. Only problem for him was the nickname he picked up for causing more than his fair share of accidents in training.

MATTHEW DAWSON

Widely condemned for his Tour Diary but most of midweek boys admired him for what he said. First player to stick head above parapet and reveal truth about what was going on. Apologised and got on with it. Went on tour as probably third choice scrum-half and got picked for last Test. Good tourist and a good mate.

SCOTT GIBBS

Late, late starter but brought bite and much needed boost to midweek team. Should have been on tour from start. Great fella and good laugh.

PHIL GREENING

At least Lol and Luges got to play. Phil didn't even get to pull on a Lions shirt. Lively, funny, bubbly and witty as per usual. But fluke accident in training ended his tour before it had really began. Love way he plays rugby. He's a centre embedded in a hooker's body. Top fella. Even if he didn't get to play for Lions was still one of us.

WILL GREENWOOD

As in 1997 was on fire in early games before injury conspired against him. So unlucky. Destiny probably states he will never play in a Lions series. Great tourist, great arcade competitor.

DANNY GREWCOCK

For me one of the players of the series. Very professional, very physical, a player in serious shape. Knew when to relax and when to train. Great tourist. Gold star.

ROB HENDERSON

Legend of 2001 tour, a real funny man, Sarcastic is his middle name. Could turn any sentence into a jail term. My first roomy and we immediately hit it off. Well loved throughout squad. Angie Henderson must be the deepest sleeper in entire world as Hendo snores like a dying rhinocerous. Awesome series. Silver star.

RICHARD HILL

Simply fantastic, the way he played in first Test was admirable. Utterly dependable. Always know he'll go for entire game and make right decision every time. Up there with best of tour. Claims to be an unsung hero but in players' eyes he's a massive hero. But boy does he know how to complain.

ROB HOWLEY

Blatantly pre-selected for Test team before tour but didn't let anyone down. Great physical shape and highly motivated to go one better than in South Africa where he was cursed by injury. At least he got to play this time. Played some great rugby and was a good laugh. Valued member of our card school, as he seemed to like giving his money away.

TYRONE HOWE

Latest starter of all but still had time to win award for comedy moment of tour. First touch in first game vs NSW Country. So keen to do well with first run that didn't realise he was 15 yards off side of pitch. As always, came back with smile on face. Good fella.

DAFYDD JAMES

Surprise packet in wing department. Got selected in all three Tests, played really well and was credit to tour. Didn't see much of him away from pitch as lot of Welsh boys stuck together but not a problem. Good lad.

NEIL JENKINS

One of nicest blokes you'll ever meet. Could stop him in street and he'd talk to you all day long, if you could spare the time. Struggled with bad knee throughout, had to have it drained a couple of times, but ask him to kick ball over an H and he never fails. One of my favourite tourists and a good friend.

MARTIN JOHNSON

Living legend, having skippered second Lions tour in succession. In America they described him as world's best rugby player. Unusually for US, that's no exaggeration. Showed sense of humour on this tour probably unseen in '97. He's still a *goofy mongo.*

JASON LEONARD

Crafty Cockney geezer and quality fella. People who meet Jase don't forget him. Old style rugby player, likes a drink and a chat, except he's full of professionalism, very fit and well rehearsed in his training techniques. Not given chance to show himself in Lions shirt. Underused and in my opinion undervalued. That was all wrong. Should have been right up there. Truly one of rugby's greats.

DAN LUGER

Possibly unluckiest man ever to play rugby. On fire, looking really sharp, strong and motivated when picked up freak injury. Devastating blow to squad. Could have made a big difference.

ROBIN McBRYDE

Sarcastic, down to earth, quality fella. Someone you knew you could count on in times of adversity. At same time possessed sense of humour and softer side. Just needs to work on his dancing. He cuts some weird old shapes.

DARREN MORRIS

What a laugh! Always had smile on his face. Set up my match winning try vs ACT with some great skills. Top fella and someone I hope to call a friend for rest of my life.

SCOTT MURRAY

So laid back he was almost horizontal. Wary about how I'd get on with him but shouldn't have worried. Very funny and good company. Well valued member of Stiffs.

BRIAN O'DRISCOLL

For me probably 'back of the series'. Went through gaps in first Test which defied belief. Awesome. Very rare you see a performance of that magnitude in so big a game. But my best memory of him was when he was divebombed by seagulls as I threw chips at him in Manly High Street.

RONAN O'GARA

Funniest man on tour. His sayings became squad sayings. How you feeling today Rog? "Oh, I'm unnaturally good today". Could see how popular he was with squad after McRae episode when everyone wanted to go and sort out Duncan Disorderly. Rog's tour highlight was creating "can't take it" song - great mental device to prevent smaller guys from getting beaten up by big boys in squad. He had to use it on several occasions. Threatened to retire if I got picked at 10 for Lions ahead of him. I was, against Australia 'A'. Hope he enjoys life after rugby.

MALCOLM O'KELLY

Formed other half of 'terrible duo' along with Jeremy Davidson. Another top Irish fella. Great skills, massive guy yet very skillful.

MATT PERRY

Strange tour. Told he had no chance of making Test team and played all three Tests. Can't ask much more than that. Will be very proud of himself and deservedly so. Good mate. I'll get on with Pezza for rest of my days.

SCOTT QUINNELL

Big old Welsh boy and one of our major ball carriers in structure invented by Henry. Awesome tour despite struggling a bit with arthritis in his knees. Played league, played union, done it all. Great family man. Good friend.

JASON ROBINSON

Well, who'd have thought it? No time in union yet played in Lions team, scored awesome try and was generally life and soul of party. Doesn't drink, doesn't go to bars, yet a really good laugh. Always rely on Jase to come out with a funny story. As cool as ice and one hell of a rugby player. Will be hard to dislodge from one of England wing slots.

TOM SMITH

One of the cornerstones of scrum. Fantastic talent. Didn't have his mentor Jim Telfer this time but still made Test team. Great athlete, great prop.

MARK TAYLOR

Recipient of one of Henry's worst lines on tour. Had come off bench and played us right back into contention against Australia 'A'. After game Henry congratulated him "but it's not going to effect selection". Always fighting an uphill battle for recognition but a really valued member of Stiffs.

SIMON TAYLOR

Tour ending injury in first game but had already shown great promise. Bound to be big force to be reckoned with in future. All very tired in first week so don't think anyone really got to know him. Great shame.

PHIL VICKERY

One hell of a rugby player, a big old unit. So much natural strength it's frightening. Likes relaxing and chilling out. But also a very dedicated rugby player, one I admire and respect immensely.

DAVID WALLACE

Like his brothers a great athlete. Loves the craic. Great to have on tour, even though was a late starter.

DORIAN WEST

Called up late but immediately started hanging out with big fish like Woody and Johnno. We called him Pilot as he always stayed close to the big fish. Always a good laugh and should have been on tour from start. Did really well.

MARTYN WILLIAMS

A true tourist. Great fella. Everyone got on with him. Put his body on the line week-in week-out for Stiffs and managed to get on bench for couple of Tests. Another valued member of card school. In same bracket as Rog. Top fella. Shame so many other back rows on tour.

KEITH WOOD

Good old Uncle Fester. Everpresent figure. Always baiting me, always slapping me on the head. Everyone knows he's a top fella. Nothing more for me to add. Just wish he'd stop hitting me.

DAI YOUNG

Midweek captain, consumate pro and top tourist. Kept his dignity and his humour in times of deep adversity for Tuesday team. Kept us all together and kept us all going. Without Dai there I think there'd have been a lot more problems. I admire him as a man and as a leader. Can't say enough about Dai. One of my all time favourite fellas.

AND THE MANAGEMENT...

GRAHAM HENRY *(Head coach)*

Good bloke, pretty funny. But took everything on his own shoulders. His attitude seemed to be 'My way or the highway'. Wasn't far away from pulling off series win but ultimately failed. That's the way it goes in sport. I felt he was just too engrossed in the whole thing and closed himself off to other ideas. His man management techniques were poor and, if the truth be known, I wish we'd had a British coach. That's the whole ethos of the Lions. Getting together as a bunch of British and Irish fellas and trying to do a job. I've nothing against Kiwis, I admire them as people. I just think we should have had a British coach and some of his speeches only reinforced my view.

DONAL LENIHAN *(Team manager)*

Great fella, very passionate about the whole Lions ethos, which is why I couldn't understand why he selected a Kiwi coach. Ultimately responsible for every single detail; not just hotel and flights but absolutely everything and I think the way the management handled the Press, Donal in particular, was poor. I'd like to have seen the management turn up on time for things and setting better standards off the field. Perhaps if Donal had his time again he'd think about every fine detail more closely. But I got on with him, admired his passion for the job and, if I see him around,

I'll buy him a drink.

ANDY ROBINSON *(Assistant coach)*

Very positive all the time. Always driving the whole squad forward, Andy has so much energy it's frightening. Very professional, very thorough. Probably just 20% away from being the perfect coach. He likes to bark at times to get a reaction which I find quite good. Have to take him for what he is: a very intense rugby coach. He was also a pleasure to tour with.

PHIL LARDER *(Defensive coach)*

Hard job trying to get everyone up to speed defensively. We have a system with England which we are well rehearsed in. But trying to implement our defensive plan onto other nations understandably took time, a lot of training sessions and a lot of contact, which probably some of the celtic boys held against him. But he kept his humour and was always someone to whom you could ask advice.

DAVE ALRED *(Kicking coach)*

Like Phil, knew he had his work cut out. Didn't have enough time to get players up to world class standards of kicking. Dave is possibly the most professional man I've ever met in terms of his preparation and his consideration towards what he's going to do. A fantastic coach. We under used him outside his kicking. I suspect the tour got on top of him in the end and I'm not sure he enjoyed it.

STEVE BLACK *(Conditioning coach)*

One of the most genuine men you'll ever meet. But he's a motivator, not a fitness coach. Blackie's ideas on fitness were closer to happiness than pain. He didn't motivate me but others found him very useful. A top fella and a good laugh. Always had a smile on his face, even when he was tired. Had to respect him for that. Tour highlight: Telling us "Right lads, I want you to go back to the hotel and stretch off, but don't actually stretch, just think about it and you'll be fine."

JAMES ROBSON *(Doctor)*

The medical team, led by Robbo, were the real heroes of the tour party. Put under unbelievable stress throughout entire trip. One of the most professional, helpful, friendly men you could meet, as well as a connoisseur of fine red wines. He was one of the players without touching the ball. A really top fella.

MARK DAVIES *(Physio)*

Another legend. Worked his already manky hands to the bone. Had so much Ibuprofen gel on his hands that his skin came off, but we had great fun with him all the time and I consider him a friend for life, someone I really admire and find exceptionally funny.

RICHARD WEGRZYK *(Masseur)*

You can always judge how hard a tour is by the way Rich looks at the end. He was shagged. He worked non-stop for the lads. Always a great tourist and a great mate to everyone. His room became a cinema throughout the tour. Need to know anything about films? Ask Rich.

ALUN CARTER *(Video analyst)*

Hard worker whose videos got better as the tour went on.

JOAN MOORE *(Admin assistant)*

Dealt with numerous jobs, handled all the problems put her way, and kept a smile on her face throughout.

PAT O'KEEFE *(Baggage Master)*

Very funny fella who started with a bang, but the magnitude of the job tired him out. Couldn't do anything towards the end of the tour.

ALEX BROUN *(Media liaison officer)*

How hard was his job? Coaches regularly turned up late or cancelled press conferences. Caught between a rock and a hard place. The man between 110 members of the media and a 50-strong squad. It was a bad situation to be in and one which the Lions' management should have foreseen. England have a press team, so should the Lions.

ANTON TOIA *(ARU liaison officer)*

Passed away on tour. Given to us by the ARU, Anton was one of those fellas who you instantly like. A quiet fella who just went about his business and kept smiling. I remember seeing him sifting through the laundry, putting people's kit back together, totally chilled out. He will be very sadly missed by his rugby family as well as his immediate family.